A
HEAVEN
in the
EYE

A
HEAVEN
in the
EYE

Clyde Rice

BREITENBUSH BOOKS
Portland, Oregon

First Printing August 1984

Library of Congress Cataloging in Publication Data
Rice, Clyde H., 1903-
    A heaven in the eye.

    1. Rice, Clyde H., 1903-   . 2. California— Biography. 3. Oregon—
Biography. I. Title.
CT275.R532A35   1984   979.4'05'0924   [B]   84-6238
ISBN (cloth) 0-932576-22-2

The epigraph is from *The Lady's Not For Burning* by Christopher Fry. Copyright 1949, 1950; renewed 1976, 1977 by Christopher Fry. Reprinted by permission of Oxford University Press, Inc., New York, New York.

Breitenbush Books are published for James Anderson by Breitenbush Publications, Post Office Box 02137, Portland, Oregon 97202.

A Heaven in the Eye is distributed to the trade by Kampmann & Company, 9 East 40th Street, New York, New York 10016.

Cover and illustrations by Laurie Levich. Book design by Susan Applegate of Publishers Book Works, Inc., Portland, Oregon.

Manufactured in the U.S.A. Additional production information contained in the colophon which appears on the last page.

The author and publisher are grateful to the National Endowment for the Arts, a Federal Agency, for a grant which aided in the publication of this book, and to Marylhurst College of Marylhurst, Oregon, for offering a course in Literary Book Publishing, sponsored by Breitenbush.

for Virginia

◇   ◇   ◇

The author and publisher wish to express their gratitude to the small army of the faithful, many of them volunteers, without whose assistance and moral support A Heaven In The Eye *might not have been published. These include, but are not limited to: typists Virginia Rice, Sam Yahn, and Barbara Garrett; friends James and Diane Waggoner, Patrick Ames, Jean Ann Randolf, Susan Applegate, James Mooney, James A. Lawson, Patricia Cassidy, Alicia Griffin, Cathy Beck, and Mr. and Mrs. Donald Cushing.*

Our very special thanks to Gary Miranda, Executive Editor, for his exceptional devotion of time and energy over the three long years it took to bring A Heaven In The Eye *into print.*

The night's a pale pastureland of peace,
And something condones the world, incorrigibly.
But what, in fact, is this vaporous charm?
We're softened by a nice conglomeration
Of the earth's uneven surface, refraction of light,
Obstruction of light, condensation, distance,
And that sappy upshot of self-centered vegetablism
The trees of the garden. How is it we come
To see this as a heaven in the eye?
Why should we hawk and spit out ecstasy
As though we were nightingales, and call these quite
Casual degrees and differences
Beauty? What guile recommends the world
And gives our eyes the special sense to be
Deluded, above all animals?

Christopher Fry
From *The Lady's Not For Burning*

CONTENTS

PROLOGUE

In this introduction I want to point out that both the editor and the publisher of these reminiscences asked me to delete the first fifty pages. Those pages, which concerned my childhood, meant more to me than most of the tales of my so-called maturity, but they said you'd not be interested in why my mother was certain I was going to be a genius because she didn't see the popcorn wagon and I did; nor in the eagle that I thought I did battle with at five-and-a-half; nor in how the Army fed two thirteen-year-old boys for four days because we handled a problem they were not equipped to take on, and how we gained access to the area they were guarding by tumbling their armed sentry on his head; nor in how or why I stole the Reed College swimming pool; nor in my surprise at discovering the elegance and uproar of masturbation; nor in my lone camping trips in the high Cascades; nor in the great cave and log cabin and boats we made. All this, I am told, you will be pleased not to read about. Nevertheless, in the front of this book imagine three virgin pages that hold these untold tales.

Had I invented a razor blade with an aperture in it for warts and named it the Pass Over and established the POCO Corporation, or were I an archaeologist who had dug up a bronze axe seemingly smelted from Gesundheit Ore instead of the usual copper and tin, I would be justified in writing my autobiography and telling about my hemorrhoids, about my wife's needlework, or about her selfish desire to emulate the Madonna. I'm without such splendid reasons for telling of my life. Still, I've told of it—or a small portion of it— in the following pages as honestly as I can, looking back from the distance of half a century. With this strange memory of mine, I see things exactly as they happened back there (more exactly, if the truth be told, than I remember last Saturday), and I continue to find second and more important meanings to events which, when they occurred, I couldn't seem to understand. I guess the center of this effort, this autobiography of mine, is to find out if my life has really been worthwhile; to find, by extension, if we as a people are worth our salt, if life was as rich as it seemed or if romanticism fit me with invisible glasses that, prism-like, caught a hundred half-hidden colors in the prosaic garments of those who passed me by,

1

colors that only I perceived long ago as an art student in Portland or as a deckhand on a ferryboat carrying the wonderful, ordinary people to their daily rendezvous with San Francisco.

The story begins in the year 1918. The World War is over; we have won it for democracy. Things have settled down in the world and I, along with many others, have gone back to reading the funny papers instead of the headlines. I would have you see me as I was at that time: medium sized—five-feet-eight, to be exact—my arms a bit short, my hands a shade small, and my shoulders a tiny bit narrower than I would have liked them to be. You would have had to study these shortcomings to be aware of them, but I was acutely aware of them, and exercised and strained until I acquired an enlarged heart and big lungs in a husky chest that tapered and angled into a bull neck, where rode my near-empty head—which, at that time of life, was as it should have been. I was, in a word, sixteen.

The story continues through a period of explosive politics, recurrent earthquakes, and ever-rising technology, all of which I have purposely left out. Why should I talk about President Hoover or the San Andreas fault when I can talk about myself and my own faults? If I regret anything, it is that I couldn't give more space to the San Francisco Bay itself. In the twenties, the use of both planes and trucks was limited, with the result that the Bay was a scene of endless activity. The beautiful white passenger steamers—the *Yale* and the *Harvard*—shuttled continuously between San Francisco, Los Angeles and San Diego. At least twice a week lumber schooners came through the Gate from the north, and the steamship lines, Coastwise and Deepsea, were always entering or leaving port. The McCormack Line, the States Line, the Matson, President, and Luckenbach lines were keeping the Red Stack Tugs busy pushing their ships into the docks or out into the channel. Fishboats, hay barges, river steamers, rum runners, Coast Guard clippers and hijackers thronged the Bay. And through all this, the ferries maintained their schedules. Because of the ferries the people about the Bay knew it intimately. Spray from paddlewheels bedewed the faces of those who strode the sterns. Commuters were involved with the weather and the Bay's moods of tide and wind. The traffic that creased the water was always going somewhere, was vital, but flotsam and jetsam, great rafts of boards, dead horses, barrels, boxes and long timbers also rode down the tide.

This story ends in 1935, when, at the age of thirty-two, I return to Oregon, the place of my birth. Why it ends where it ends I prefer to leave to the professional critic or the amateur psychologist, but I would not have my reader believe that I have spent the intervening half-century—for I am approaching my eighty-first birthday as I write this—rehashing, in nostalgic idleness, my early manhood. Far from it. But that is another story.

I

In Which
I Decide Against A Prosperous Waddling,
Become A Lookout,
and
Encounter Young Mrs. Courtland

◇   1918   ◇

When I was sixteen there was talk in the family about what I should study and train myself to be. My mother felt I should be a professional man, but because of her religion, Christian Science, she had to rule out doctors, scientists and teachers who taught children about their muscles, spines and things—as well as lawyers, who defended criminals and were therefore without proper rectitude. Her vision of me as a professional man was gradually whittled down to a Christian Science practitioner, sort of a guru or faith healer, who, if he didn't heal you, at least knew the truth about you—or for you. My father wanted me to enter business, be a merchant, sell something—apples, steel calipers, steam calliopes, or a brand of canned goods. He would take me downtown on Sunday afternoons and teach me how to walk as a young businessman should—with a kind of prosperous waddle. He felt a businessman should be stout: if it looked like somebody bought the stuff, perhaps more would. To start a trend like that you had to look, well, prosperous: a big belly would help, even flatulence if controlled, and a double chin.

I wanted to be a woodsman, trapper, guide, a stalwart friend of the noble Indian, a quiet, knowing fellow who affected a disenchanted air when speaking of fellow humans, and who kept two full-grown grizzly bears—first as pets, but finally as companions. Still, I was dutiful and considered other possibilities. I studied the men teachers at high school and the farmers I met, the grocers, the small businessmen and the people hanging on to too much money. At the time a lot of conventions were coming to our town— royal orders of this and that, herds of eye doctors or real estate agents or people with their collars on backwards—and one of the traditions of such gatherings was the group photo taken in front of the convention hall and dutifully printed in the *Oregonian*. The groups were usually arranged in three rows: a back row of people standing; a middle row of those seated on hastily obtained chairs from the hall; and a front, rather broken, row of the less rheumatic who sat or squatted or lay in poses of arch and effortless ease that had been too long maintained. I would study each face with a magnifying glass for hours, trying to get at the essence of the men somehow. Always I came to the same conclusion, that if there were a God, he certainly had slipped up in not giving these men a cud to chew. I was supremely unaware of how quickly fate can erect a labyrinth around you from which you can be rescued only by death. The lack of cud rather supported my growing agnosticism, and my studying of the photos made me sure I would look for other lines of work. "Nope," I finally said out loud, "not for me."

I eventually decided that the place for me was the U.S. Forest Service. There I would deal with tall timber and mountains and, once in a while, a fellow human or a river. I had been a partner in building a log cabin, was fair with an axe, was an above-average woodsman, and I loved the wilderness. Because of those qualities, combined with a certain dullness that has been my constant companion, I was sure I was suited to be a ranger of the Forest Service.

Having made this momentous decision, I read everything I could find on subjects pertaining to the green world and what it grew on. I learned the diseases that beset the black willow, how to care for a pack animal with the gleet, and that you can't chip away white pine rust.

Then, a little before school let out for summer vacation, I would skip classes each morning and arrive at the offices of the U.S. Forest Service before they opened, greeting everyone as they came in. I'd wait until Mr. Girard, the top man, came in and ask him for a job. If he'd stop for a moment, I'd tell him of all the government pamphlets on forestry I knew by heart. He seemed to be impressed, though whether by my persistence or my knowledge I can't say. Still, he told me, I would have to wait two years to be old enough. But I came every morning for two weeks, and, sensing my determination to keep it up for two years if necessary, he gave in. He sent me to the Wind River Forest Experiment Station, one of the first of its kind in the United States. We Americans knew nothing about growing timber trees, only how to cut them down, so the station was run by a forester from Austria, a Mr. Hoffmann, a small, alert man who could do his forty miles a day in the up and down mountains.

In retrospect, I think Mr. Hoffmann decided to give me my chance and get rid of me at the same time, for he gave me a list of fifteen plantings, each planting twelve inches square, of one-year-old seedlings that were scarcely two inches high. They were separated by uneven distances in rods and on compass courses, and my job was to locate and diagram them.

I set out in the morning, going ninety-seven rods this way, three hundred and eighty rods that way, on compass course in degrees—this in a brushy old burn on a steep mountainside looking for little reservations scarcely bigger than a grizzly's footprint. I loved it, though I had the devil's own time finding the first one. It was in a deep gully with fallen snags all around and over it. I had to burrow down and found that two of the tiny seedlings were dead. I made a diagram of what I found and went on to the next. Don't ask me how many strides equal a rod, or how you keep the strides of equal length over logs and brush, around cliffs, and deep in ravines. Somehow or other, I found the second one. By three-thirty, I had found them all. When I presented my diagrams to Mr. Hoffmann, he was very pleased. I heard afterwards that he and his assistant had tried to find them the week before and had gotten only the first one.

For my next trick I was sent out—along with my housemate, Warren, and a ranger—to measure the growth and casualties in ten acres of various-sized second growth. Warren, a quiet and industrious ex-doughboy, used a measuring pole to measure the heights, which varied from four to fifteen feet. I measured the diameter at ground level, using a caliper. Before long, we were using our tools five minutes each hour, the rest of the time estimating by eye. We grew to be incredibly fast and accurate, and so attuned to one another that, lying down among blackberries and ferns, I could tell which trees he was naming the height of as the ranger recorded our calls—all this in a burn of towering snags, the residence of hordes of biting ants. The ants were at least as busy as we were, but I just slapped them silly under my clothes while I shouted out diameters.

Now, none of my feats as a fledgling forester amounted to

much, but for some reason I very quickly became the fair-haired boy at Wind River and back at Portland headquarters too. Maybe they sensed I was mad about the deep timber they were custodians of. In any case, after I'd been there several weeks the U.S. Secretary of Agriculture visited the Experiment Station, and, being told of my prowess, asked to see me. Imagine my state of mind when, after shaking my hand, he told me that he wanted me to stay in the Forest Service and that he would pay my way through college if I would agree to make a career of the Service. Agree, mind you. I felt the Forest Service was Olympus and that all those connected with it were not people, but Gods. As soon as I could talk, I agreed.

As if in confirmation of my meteoric rise in the ranks of the Forest Service, I was assigned to a fire lookout—not on Olympus, but on Mount Dana, fifty-three miles up the Clackamas River from Estacada, the jumping off place. The trek to the ranger station was twenty-eight miles, which I figured I could walk by noon.

The twinges didn't come until several miles up the trail. By now the sun was up, and soon the sharper pains in my stomach made me realize I shouldn't have eaten that stale potato salad as part of my breakfast. Soon the cramps were so fierce I could hardly walk, but managed to stagger on for several hours, bent almost double, before I was forced to stop and lie down on the trail. It's a wild country up the Clackamas—or was—just this one trail that ran along the river skirting the cliffs of the gorge. I was still lying there, bent double, when the chorus girls arrived. At first, of course, they were just two pretty young women— perhaps even apparitions—but they told me they were chorus girls. The story of why they were way up there, though interesting, would take too long to tell. When I explained my plight, they gave me a large chunk of uncooked bacon fat, saying that it would grease my stomach and stop the cramps. Then they left, saying that they had to get back to civilization by the next afternoon or they would lose their jobs.

I managed somehow to down the bacon fat, and in a short time could resume my stumbling trek. Hours later, as late dusk crept through the timber, I saw perpendicular bars of faint light, and as I approached these openings between the tall trunks, I looked down on lighted cabins in a great meadow full of late evening light. I had made it.

Floundering down, I was met by the crew, and told them what was wrong. They gave me a heart stimulant and one of the strongest physics known to man. They let me sit for a while and then, timing it more by lore and intuition than by the instructions on the bottle, two of them took me out and told me to take my pants down. When I obliged, they aimed me at the forest. I want you to see it: the deep dusk, the utter stillness, the tall pillared forest around the meadow, and these two fellows, one on each side of me, solemnly aiming my pale hind end at a nearby stump, standing well back like bombadiers by a piece of ordnance. At the right moment, one of them forced my head down a little lower, and I vaguely realized he was trying for distance.

Although it was four or five days before I recovered from the food poisoning and the cure, I got along well with the crew after that peculiar hazing. They seemed to feel I was an athlete of sorts, but—always a modest fellow—I give most of the credit to the croton oil. My standing with the ranger, Ed Williamson, was another matter, however. He was an ex-logger who didn't go for newfangled things, and he thought the Wind River Experiment Station with a "furriner" to run it was un-American—and, as he put it, "a lot of crap." My coming with excellent recommendations from the District Office and that alien up at Wind River didn't help. He disliked me before he saw me.

Still, if it hadn't been for the delicate matter of the ranger and Mrs. Courtland, my career in the Forest Service might have turned out quite differently. Mrs. Courtland was one of three travelers who appeared in the evening before my last day at the Ranger Station. The three were mounted on fine horses and led a piebald packhorse and a mule. Two of them, an elderly husband and wife team, were Eastern writers of wildlife stories. The third, Mrs. Courtland, was the young wife of an elderly California senator. She was riding sidesaddle, and leaped to the ground in a long, full, split riding skirt of soft brown leather. The older couple, too, was beautifully outfitted— even the packhorse was resplendent in carved breaststrap and halter—but, next to Mrs. Courtland, they looked downright frumpy. We, the crew, stood around them in the twilight, a motley assortment of loggers and woodsmen of one sort or another, and all starved for a woman in the solitary maleness of the camp. As the young woman stood within our circle, she raised her arms to refasten the cascades of dark hair that the ride had loosened. The full, supple riding skirt came up from the ground like a pedestal, and out of the top of it she seemed to bloom— willowy, deep breasted, with back arched and arms raised and fingers tucking in strands while she spoke to her horse. I stood on a slight knoll and saw the scene over the heads of the circle of men. I can't conceive of her knowing how we fed upon her beauty.

Next day our guests went fishing with the ranger a mile or so down from the station. In late afternoon the elderly couple came back and reported that they'd become separated from Mrs. Courtland and the ranger. When, well after dark, the two had not yet returned, I volunteered at once to search for them. Taking a smoking lantern, I hurried down the trail toward the river. I hadn't gone two hundred yards before I stumbled and fell on them where they lay in the trail, oblivious to most everything. A soft hand touched my face. There wasn't much to say, so we said nothing, got up, and went back to the station.

Next morning, the wildlife writers, Mrs. Courtland, the ranger and I set out for Bagby Hot Springs, where, on the following day, I would take off from the party for my lookout peak, which lay twelve miles to the north of the Springs. Mrs. Courtland acted as if nothing had happened the night before, and was so gracious toward me that I fell helplessly in love with her by the time we arrived at the Springs in the early evening.

Bagby Hot Springs were very popular with old time prospectors, who believed that any hot, evil-smelling spring would do you a great deal of good if, after drinking all of it you could hold, you would soak in what was left. This I was advised to do—my walk was ludicrous by now, my legs intent on straddling the absent horse— so I decided to heed the advice and headed down to the bathhouse. It was built of shakes and had a hall admitting to five or six small rooms, each with a big cedar tub. I entered to find—at the opposite end of the hall—the ranger pressing Mrs. Courtland against the wall, minus the leather riding skirt and so forth. She murmured something to the ranger, who turned and saw me before I had time to slip into a tubroom, where I proceeded to soak away my weariness and absorb the fact that I would never become a friend of Ranger Williamson.

Next day, the assistant ranger, Cary, and his lineman, Ralph, rode up with me and my packhorse of supplies to Mount Dana and, there, set up the sighting equipment. It was late in the afternoon when they left. I watched them a long way, and then I was alone with my cabin, which sat in a slight saddle with the lookout on a high ridge above it. The trees around the cabin were of several kinds of fir and hemlock, but all were twisted from the wind and heavy snows of winter, so the cabin made from them was a fort of misshapen logs through which the wind could blow—at times with a shriek.

My weeks on Mount Dana were among the most sublime in my life, though I have to confess that, on that first night, I had my doubts. I had made my first lone campfire when I was thirteen, and had spent the night beside it pretty scared, but now I was sixteen and practically a veteran in the woods, so I began arranging my belongings in the cabin, though I didn't start a fire. I went out and looked down the trail. It was quiet. I strolled over to the spring. I went back to the cabin. Mosquitos were humming. I went out and walked back down the trail a half a mile and came back. I started along the trail the other way, but it dipped down in a series of switchbacks into an awesome canyon. I came back and looked at the cabin. Finally, as twilight edged toward night, I stole to the spring, scooped up a pot of water, and scuttled back to the cabin, where, after barring the door, I lit the lantern and made a fire in the stove. Later, eating a meager meal of bacon and hardtack by the warmth of the fire, I tried to laugh off the intense sense of solitude that all but controlled my breathing, but the laugh died in my throat.

The next morning, though, as I looked out from the top of the knife-like summit, I was greeted by the endless green ridges of the Cascades. Mount Jefferson was near at hand in all its angularity. Mount Hood and Three-Fingered Jack in opposite directions also held snow well down their sides. I stared out at the great wash of the world. I stared for hours at all points of the compass, ridge after ridge of dark forest, with snow-capped peaks at intervals marking the backbone of the Cascades. I stared because it was my job to look for the faintest vestige of smoke and I stared because there was nothing else to do and I stared because the world was beautiful. It dropped away from me on all sides. I could sit, but there was no place flat enough to lie down, so I stared and my mind became empty, became part of space. I was above things. A fire lookout is an exalted place. I became somehow cleansed by it and the tempo of living slowed magnificently. True, the mosquitos, no-seeums, and deer flies that welcomed me at the cabin and traveled with me to my lookout made for hours of endless annoyance, but for the rest, my mountain was indeed Olympus and I Zeus looking down in majesty upon my world.

One day—a day so foggy that the lookout was useless—I was out trying to cut firewood for next year's occupant. The axe had been so blunted by a former lookout chopping a rock that it bounced off the trees. I was banging away at a tree—knocking away the bark and slightly bruising the sapwood—when I heard a conversation. I spun around and was startled to see the assistant ranger, Cary, and his pal Ralph sitting behind me, taking inventory of my efforts.

"When he bangs that tree it don't sound like chopping, but it's real purty," Cary said.

"He ain't chopping," Ralph replied. "He's gone cabin crazy and is playing tag with the trees."

The assistant ranger said: "Gimme that axe, fella, and I'll show you how it's done."

I did and he took it and was about to start chopping when he decided to look the axe over. After a moment, he handed it back and turned to his partner. "Good thing you brought yours. This kid's got an axe what's a hammer at both ends. Well, we'll eat now. Come along, kid. We want coffee with our lunch."

At the cabin I took their hazing in high good spirits, for I admired them greatly. They had come up to my territory, after profuse rains had reduced fire danger, to find a way to make a trail through the split-up cliff country just south of my cabin. If they were successful, the new trail would save many miles in the trip to the outside. The job would be difficult—at times, treacherous—

and they would use me as their flunky. They took my bunk for theirs, and I made a bough bed on the dirt floor. They roused me at daybreak to haul water and wood and warm the cabin and cook their breakfast. They tripped me, wrestled with me, and tricked me out of some of my meals with games of chance, but all in such good fellowship that, to tell the truth, I was delighted. Also, I was going to gain their respect or die trying.

I came close to accomplishing the latter feat several times during the week or so Cary and Ralph stayed with me, what with the hundred life-or-death chances we took each day trying to worm our way through those cliffs, but one close call especially sticks with me. It happened on what turned out to be the last day of their stay on Mount Dana. We were several miles from the cabin, working amongst some extremely dangerous going. We should never have been asked to do what we were doing without lifelines, pitons and such. It was sheer all around us, but across a very nasty bit of maneuverings was a slight knoll where one could sit and rest. In the middle of that dangerous place was a little, near-perpendicular, gully. It contained a slight seepage, and there in the seepage was a pad of roots and grasses and minute huckleberry brush— about twice as big as your foot. Cary and Ralph went first and made the knoll, but when I stepped on the little pad, without which the place would have been impassable, it moved. At once I sat down on it and tried to cling some of my weight to the surrounding walls, but the roots that anchored it were tearing loose, bush and all. Slowly, or so it seemed to me, I slid over the brink.

"Here I go!" I called out, as if watching myself in a mirror, and hid my face with my arms, ashamed to show fear in that dire moment. Hundreds of feet below me at the cliff's base the rocky debris awaited me, but, to my amazement, I was stopped in another little alcove about thirty feet below, where several bushes, hidden from above, had collected a pad of roots, mud and grasses that held at my impact and stopped me. I was severely jarred, but alive. From this spot there was a fairly easy way to ascend the knoll. I came up behind my friends, who were motionless as they listened to hear me strike down below. When I said "safe and sound," they turned their pale, stricken faces to me, got their Bull Durham sacks out, but were too shaken to roll a cigarette. We sat there about half an hour and then it started to rain heavily, a cloudburst, and Cary, looking around, said, "Look here, we're in a bad way. We gotta get back. Some of these steep draws is gonna have waterfalls in 'em if this rain keeps up."

He was right. Threading through the mazes of cliffs and skirting the rocky abutments was tough—there was no up or down to avoid bad places—but moving through the waterfalls we had to be especially deliberate and precise with the fall of water pounding on our heads and any wrong step a possible passport into eternity. It began to sleet and hail and snow mixed with the rain and, soaking wet, we shivered and shuddered and took our chances. I don't know how we made it, but after another hour of narrow escapes we arrived at the cabin shivering in great shakes and pretty well spent. Ralph started cutting up the table and bedslats and the supply of wood I'd cut for the next year's lookout. They made a bonfire right next to the porch while I struggled with the stove. They stood naked under the porch and toasted themselves with a fire that threatened the porch and cabin, and would have burned it down except for the tremendous downpour that went on until dark.

Next morning we found that one corner of the cabin was quietly smoldering, and we bailed my drinking spring dry to put it out. Ralph and Cary sat around glumly after breakfast, rolling and smoking their cigarettes. "You think we're through here?" Ralph asked his partner.

Cary rolled another cigarette thoughtfully, lit it, inhaled, spit bits of tobacco from his lip, got up and started putting their gear together. "I wouldn't go out on that chute to hell for all the money in the mint," he said.

Soon they were gone. But Ralph came back after they got about fifty yards down the trail. He came back and looked me over appraisingly for a moment, then said, "You'll do, kid," and turned to catch up with Cary's disappearing back. I stood on my mountain, absolutely glowing with pride.

Several days later Cary came back with an extra horse to haul back the rest of their gear, and when he left I didn't feel the aloneness. I simply went back into a poem that was happening on the mountain. All but food, work and sleep—yes, and wonder—was erased from my mind. I was engaged in a very slow rhythm, the aggressiveness of our culture gone. Until the phone call, that is.

I was still trying to whack out a new bedstead and slats when the call came. It was Ranger Williamson, telling me to leave at once as a storm was brewing and anyway the season was over. "I want you out of there in a half an hour," he said. I told him of the bedstead and table and wanting to wash the dishes, but it was no use. So with seventy-five pounds of duffle and the gun, I headed back to Bagby Hot Springs. Ranger Williamson was away from headquarters when I got there the next evening. I slept in the bunkhouse and next morning, stuffed with food, started the last twenty-eight miles to Estacada.

It wasn't until I was back in Portland that I figured out what the hurry was all about. I went down to the Forest Service office to pick up my check. Mr. Girard, the regional head of the Forest Service, my friend and backer, looked up at me rather skeptically.

"What happened, Clyde?" he asked. "We thought you had the makings of a very good man. There was a career here for you. Secretary Anderson was willing to pay the bill for your education and help you any way he could. But this! Insubordination, destroying all the equipment, the cabin a shambles, and no wood left for the next lookout, the axe made totally useless. Ranger Williamson also gives you a very poor character report and says you hindered the survey across the cliffs near your lookout. Can you explain the sudden change in yourself?"

Suddenly I knew the score. Williamson was getting even for my accidental discovery of him and Mrs. Courtland. He had learned from Cary about the condition of the cabin and had arranged things so that I wouldn't have time to repair it. That was the only explanation for this, but I wasn't going to inform on Mrs. Courtland at any cost. I loved her, she had been so kind to me in spite of the unfortunate contacts. Besides, my upbringing had been very strict about blaming others. I stood there, stricken. I loved the Forest Service with all my heart. I felt I was made for it. I stood very straight in front of my accuser.

"Will you give me my check, please?" I asked, and when he did, added, "I am through with the Forest Service. Thank you for all the help you have given me."

Then I whirled round, ran out of the office and went bawling down the hall, for I had lost my first love.

II

*In Which
I Discover Art And Nordi,
Lose My Mother,
and
Am Invited To Spend A Few Years
In The Penitentiary*

◇   1919   ◇

For a month or so after leaving the Forest Service I dreamed of young Mrs. Courtland. She stood in the circle of men, as I had first seen her, with upraised arms reaching to create order in the disarray of cascading dark hair. And then the men disappeared, and there were only the two of us, framed in the twilight. She turned and looked at me, and in her eyes there was great kindness and eagerness. She came to me, unbuttoned and rolled up the sleeve of her white shirtwaist almost to the armpit and held out her arm to me. I kissed her hand, then along her arm, and the upper arm under my kisses was so soft, so alive, so sensing, that desire struck me deliciously, and I was awake. Always it was just her arm, but under its tutelage and her kind, knowing smile, I became an adult and felt the need to join with a woman, to know woman's depth.

During the day, though, I was sick at heart at losing my dream of working for the Forest Service. My mother sensed this, but never alluded to it, and the rest of the family, with my prompting, decided that the Forest Service was a passing fancy of mine.

I went back to high school in the fall. Lonely, irritable, and without purpose, I got into several fights and took vicious pleasure in hurting, not winning over, my adversaries. I was also beginning to be critically aware of how narrow the culture of our teachers was. H. L. Mencken's writings in *The Smart Set* substantiated my feelings. These were prohibition times and everyone was required to write an affirmative essay on prohibition or flunk English. I felt that was too much curbing and took the opposite view in my composition. As a result, I was suspended, after fierce denunciation by the principal in assembly. I sent the essay to a magazine, which accepted and printed it, and when I flaunted this, the teachers looked on me as on a hardened criminal. As I studied, I fought them, but always with humor. Then I made a speech before the full assembly, as other boys had done. It was something about our football team winning the game next day. I referred to us pimple-

21

faced youngsters as "men of the team," and urged, with dignity and gestures, that we back them in the game. Rah! Rah! Team! As I left the podium to clapping, I passed the coach, who was also a typing teacher. He took my reluctant hand and, shaking it fondly, said: "Clyde, I always knew you had it in you."

In the locker room, I thought I'd vomit. How had that creepy speech found residence in me? Even though I was beginning to disagree with much of the culture around me, I had absorbed it with unwanted osmosis. I was in a fury later when I met several male teachers in the hall. In response to their congratulations, I told them I was going to quit the school before it made a complete idiot of me.

I began to spend more time in the school's art department, feeling more at ease there than in the rest of the school. The room next door was the music department. One of the music students at that time was a tall, sharp-nosed, over-dressed sissy, who wore pince-nez glasses and an air of overweening self-importance, always adjusting his coat and fussing with his tie. He fancied himself much abused to have to associate with us, and told one and all that his mother had said he was the most outstanding person in the school. We tolerated him for laughs, but either his mother was right or his attitude was conducive to success, for he later became a world-renowned conductor of symphony orchestras.

One day while I was working on a large, elaborate poster, he began to play Rachmaninoff's "Prelude in C Sharp Minor," which is so popular with novice music listeners and was so detested by its composer. Through the open classroom doors the Prelude, which he played very well, caught me, shook me, completely controlled me until sometime after the last sounds of the school's great Steinway had faded. It was more powerful than life—at least the life I was living. I was wildly alert now, but completely nonplussed. Yeah, I thought, Yeah. Here was a place for discovery.

After that I felt better about painting. I decided that good painting, like the music I had heard, must be far more than mere decoration. Vaguely I was becoming aware that I might find a place for myself as a painter or sculptor. I began to think of attending art school. One Saturday I visited the Portland Art Museum, which housed the school, and some of the pictures in the galleries touched me. I became involved, trying to see how the painters did it. Finally, I broached the subject of art school at home.

"Artists and their families starve," my father said. "Do something that leads to money. I'll put you through college and law school, or I'll send you to business college. Think it over. The way I look at it, the artist is done for now we got the camera. It's like learning to make buggy whips with the automobiles driving horses off the road."

My mother was worried. "I'm inclined," she said, "to think your father is right. If most artists are paupers, I wouldn't want you to be one no matter how much you desired it. Still, if you could train for some simple job like working in the Post Office, you could paint at your leisure."

Eventually, sensing that I was not about to be swayed by reason, they allowed me to attend the night classes at art school. I suppose they figured that this new fancy of mine, like the Forest Service, would pass soon enough, but my evenings at the art school served only to make high school more intolerable. Hell, I just wanted to paint!

Then one day Lady Luck, with a little prompting, came my way. I painted a big poster to announce a wrestling meet at the high school. It was a good design: the two wrestlers strove, standing in a manner that presented both their backs to the viewers. I had not, however, put wrestling trunks on the wrestlers, for they were clearly painted to convey an ancient sculpture. Later that day, I learned that two of the women teachers had taken the poster down and torn it up. Accepting the challenge, I made a large poster and put it on the bulletin board the next day. The poster read: "CLYDE RICE WILL TEACH MODERN MORALS TO OLD MAID SCHOOL TEACHERS AFTER HOURS UNDER THE GYMNASIUM." There was no space under the gymnasium, but I liked the sound of it.

Well, three men teachers wanted to fight me, but when I tried to drag them outdoors, they clung tenaciously to furniture and door jambs. I was denounced and expelled from high school, and as I left the office, the assistant principal, a quiet, learned man (it was said he drank), brushed by me, murmuring: "Nice going Clyde! Now you can go to art school."

"Art school my ass!" my father said. "It's to work with you."
So I got a job in a furniture factory painting stripes on kitchen
furniture—a dull job, but a definite improvement over high school.

By now, in the evenings at art school, I was meeting students
with similar interests. One evening I was drawing from that famous mutilated statue, so glorifying of humanity—a great reclin-
ing figure attributed, I think, to Praxiteles. I was thoroughly involved in it when two girls came up behind me. One was older and
the other about my age. She, the younger one, was blonde and
slight, not beautiful, not even very pretty, but with the most friendly smile I'd ever seen and a quiet, but musical, voice. When the
older girl left, she stayed. We talked about a certain kind of candy
that had disappeared long ago from most stores. I told her I had
found a store back among the stump ranches that still carried it,
and that when next I could I'd hike out there and get some for her.
She was pleased and, as she left, gave me a quick smiling inspection. I responded in kind and, though I didn't know it, the die was
cast. As I went back to drawing that Promethean form I resolved
that I would court the girl and have sex with her. I didn't think of
marriage, but I meant to mate with her, as I had seen Mrs.
Courtland and the ranger do.

She came again next week and I had the candy for her. She was
delighted, and her smile was rather intimate and soft, almost like a
touch. Every time our glances met there was a shock in me, as if we
had made physical contact. Soon she went back to her class, while
I stubbornly worked my inept abilities in the cast room.

A month went by, and I had improved enough to enter the life
classes. The girl—her name was Evelyn Nordstrom—was there,
along with Mr. Wentz, the teacher. The rest seemed to be strang-
ers to me and all older, until I saw a Chinese fellow whom I had
known in high school—Wy Long Fong—who greeted me. There
were two Japanese men and a woman, Catherine McKenzie, to
whom Evelyn introduced me, and who was to become a friend of
long standing.

At first I was fearful, wondering if, at the sight of a nude
woman, I would have an erection. If I did, I decided, I would
simply do my times tables until it subsided. But when the model
disrobed, another thing happened. I fell headlong in love with the

beauty of a young woman's body. I marveled as I drew, and I have marveled ever since. Men, too, are splendidly constructed. Rodin's St. John makes us realize what paragons of symmetry some of us can be. Still, we lack the felicitous, half-concealing natural plumpness that makes women a delight to behold. I drew and stared and and absorbed with all my late-adolescent being. The model was very slightly knock-kneed. Her pelvic region was well-developed, the upper legs wonderfully plump, and her slighter torso and narrow shoulders emphasized her hips. Her breasts were full and pointed their rose-colored nipples not straight ahead but out at an angle, as if to survey a larger segment of the world with their blind, staring need to soothe and succor. But her face above that delicately strident fecundity was the pretty face I had seen everywhere—faces riding atop great swathes and layers of clothing, stumbling along on pinching high-heeled shoes, crowned with enormous hats, beneath which they appeared like piquant fairies peering from under giant toadstools.

So this was woman. Oh, I'd seen pictures and statues, but what a tremendous gap between those artists' concepts of woman and the young comely woman standing without coyness or coquetry before us. I made a fair drawing, chatting once at the model's rest with Miss Nordstrom, who helped me a bit with a knee. I am a senser in that I don't absorb things linearly but *en bloc*, and tiny explosions of *en bloc* thinking resounded in me all evening.

Very quickly my circle of acquaintances grew. I met Kinzu Furiya, Mizino, Charles Heaney and other students who were in the advanced day-class under Harry Wentz, the teacher. Kinzu Furiya was a red-cheeked Japanese of about forty—a well-read Oriental philosopher whose paintings were tied much more to Oriental concepts than our own. Mizino, also Japanese, was a tiny, mouse-like man who painted landscapes in the western tradition. Charles Heaney, a slender fellow of about twenty-four, was very eager to push on with his studies. And then there was Wy Long Fong, my high school acquaintance, who was already a superb draftsman and a fine painter.

It wasn't long before some of these male students and myself joined in a loose group. Looking back, I can see I hadn't much to offer. I was only a fair draftsman, though I tried by diligence to improve. Not only did I lack in skill, I lacked in perception. My drawings were strong and vivid, but inaccurate. They appealed to the teachers and some of the students, but not to me. They were very modern for 1920, but that wasn't what I wanted. I wanted photographic realism as a start and then much more. All the half-felt inchoate disturbances in me needed art as a way to express these most tenuous feelings. Study and improvement and constant drive, I felt, would in time give me the wherewithal to express myself lucidly, perhaps strongly. Somehow I would communicate with people.

Our loose group began to coalesce. We met for coffee regularly after class and soon expressed a common feeling: we had to work harder if we were going to reach our objective. We decided to band together and get a room where we could continue our studies. As I had more free time than the others, I agreed to search for a room where we would share the costs of rent, models and second-hand easels. I soon centered in on a room in the Worcester Block next to the City Jail—an old office building in which there were several studios, including Mr. Wentz' and that of a poet whose work I admired, and others in penthouses on the roof. Our small room had poor light, and in our toilet the screams resounded from the jail's drunk tank.

I made a model stand and wheeled it to town in a wheelbarrow. I dyed old sheets to hang behind the stand and made a screen for the model's dressing room. I made some drawing boards, and the building manager supplied some chairs and stools and a long narrow table. With some rickety easels we'd found we were ready to go. We hired my good friend from my high school class, Ralph Holmes, a muscular black, and began drawing and painting. We also hired one of the girl models from the school and sketched and painted her until she was too tired to pose any longer. When models left, we sketched each other, or chairs, or easels, or our own feet. There were eleven of us all told, and we were inexhaustible in our efforts to become good painters. What we needed, however, was a critic, someone who knew quite a bit about art, and, as luck would have it, we acquired one.

One evening as we left the school life-class a man appeared in the foyer. He was slender, of average height, with flowing white

hair. His features—short nose, broad brow and chin and lips—
were chiseled, as they say, faultlessly. He wore an expression that
gave him an extremely comprehending stare, as if he was even
more aware of what you were thinking than you were.

Who was he? We inquired around, and a few days later learned
that he was a famous art critic named Pushells, a guest of one of
the homes on the hill. Some of the daughters of rich families, who
were dabbling in art before marriage, told us he was staying here
and there with different people. Very brilliant, everyone agreed, a
former French army officer in intelligence who had been severely
wounded on the Marne in the groin.

In the weeks following this incident, I had lunch several times
with Evelyn Nordstrom, whom I now called Nordi, and went for
several walks with her during the noon hour. But my main focus,
for the moment, was the studio in the old Worcester Block, which
had gathered several more members and acquired three finely
proportioned girl models through ads in the paper. Also, our
mighty muscled model, Holmes, brought us a young man, all
tendons and bones, who eventually made the Olympics as a mid-
dle-weight wrestler.

Then one evening, as we were engrossed as usual in our drawing, there was a knock at the door and the white-haired art critic
entered. He told us to go on with our work, but soon was helping
Heaney with his drawing. He looked at mine as well, after which
he gave me that incisive, knowledgeable wisp of a smile and turned
to Fong. At length the model left, and we gathered around to talk.
He talked marvelously well about artists, about materials. He
dripped names. He was a friend of Trotsky's, knew this and that
about prominent radicals, and gave fleeting glimpses of himself as
an intelligence officer in the French military. It was a splendid
performance. We asked him to come often, telling him that we
needed a critic. Smiling with suave irony, he said he'd help for the
price of a Chinese dinner after the meetings. We were happy with
the terms.

We knew even then—in our bones perhaps—that he was in some
manner a fraud, but we were charmed, and would continue to be
for some time. He was homosexual and talked openly and endlessly about it. Later, in the larger studio we eventually moved to, he

would parade around imitating the more flamboyant queers. He had a friend whom he often brought along—a humorous fellow who seemed to have very little volition. When I brought an ancient Victrola and a sheaf of records to the studio, Pushells and his friend would dance to the music, Pushells acting the super queer. In no time it became annoyingly distracting, but we allowed it, for we were learning much more from him than at the school.

There were far too many sides to Pushells. There were great blocks of integrity, at least as concerned art, and a hundred strands of duplicity wound into everything. Once, I'm sure, he had been a brilliant scholar, though I don't know where he got his schooling. He had apparently been highly esteemed by wealthy parents, and he could imitate his past glory of integrity with the most secret irony and, at times, with a shuddering sadness, but he never let remnants of the past conquer what deviltry he was up to. Not that I believe in gods and devils, but in terms of those who do, he had given up his soul and his abilities as a scholar and artist to some leering demon-god. But whatever else he had been or was, he was what we needed.

Three nights a week we would start the evening by drawing or working with pastels to reproduce some dimpled dolly whom we treated respectfully—always Miss Peterson this or Miss Olson that. As Pushells moved from easel to easel with his almost whispered instructions, it was always in the tradition, I learned in time, of the great teachers. It was under his tutelage, too, that I read prodigiously of the literature of Russia, Spain, France and the Scandinavian countries; comparative religion; Marx, Haeckel, Hegel; but no study of music. Inexplicably, he hated music, except to dance to. Other friends introduced me to the then moderns— Debussy, Richard Strauss and Sibelius. I painted and drew and read until dawn, and still kept up as a ridge runner on the hills back of the city. I also made a so-so garden that year, but nature was kind to me, and my family had more than enough corn, tomatoes, root crops and fruit. Indeed, my whole life at the time seemed enormously abundant and fertile.

Then, not without warning, my mother became very ill. She'd always been quite frail and had gradually been getting worse of late, but she had an unbelievably strong will, so I never thought she was in danger. Now, though, I had to quit work, stop my studies and care for her. I carried her everywhere—upstairs, to the bathroom, into the kitchen to see that the food was properly prepared, and sometimes, when the weather was clement, out to the porch for a bit of fresh air. She would not have a doctor; that was a dirty word in her religion. Each week she seemed paler, and each week the Christian Science gurus came, said or thought their mumbo jumbo, and left, sure that their checks would be there on the following tenth of the month. She had terrible catarrh, and the endless eggnogs we fed her seemed to support the condition, but she fervently persisted in the dogma of her particular sect. Not until it was too late did she begin to doubt her religion's particular brand of cant. One day she spoke to me from the lethargy of her sickness. "Clyde," she murmured when no one else was about, "you've spoken to me of this Darwin and others. Consider them with an open mind. Cut a broad swath, my dear." I wanted to reply, but she had fallen asleep and was never to speak of it again.

For several days previous I had stayed up with her around the clock. My father, who had been up with me in this vigil, became exhausted and slept. We had built a stockade of love around her, and over the stockade she had seen death looking at her. When my father awoke, he took my place. "Go see a show, Clyde," he said, "then maybe you can sleep a few hours," for I was unable to. I did as he suggested.

Rudolph Valentino, as an Arab sheik, was striding around in flowing robes, turban pasted to his head, when something inside me tugged. You know what it is when it happens. I got up and hurried out, knowing that my mother had just left me.

Back at home, I took over calming everybody. I was in a strange place, serene even at the funeral. My father leaned heavily on me, but we were all quite composed, as she would have wanted us to be. It wasn't until about a week later, as I was hoeing up bean bushes one evening, that, without the slightest forewarning, I was struck a terrible blow. It drove me to my knees, but I raised myself, plunged across the garden, cleared a high fence and tore down the road, unseeing, mad as a runaway horse. The withheld grief, the hammer blow that my mother, my dearest, was gone forever, had at last struck me.

Shortly thereafter, an aunt came to keep house for us. My father seemed to hate the place. He left for California on a month's trip to set up a branch of the business. I stayed, and went on with art school full time.

When I came back to class, Nordi informed me that the advanced-class students and instructor, Mr. Wentz, all wanted me to study with them, but I couldn't accept, for I didn't think I was ready for it. Catherine McKenzie, too, spent time with me. Suddenly I was buttressed on all sides with quiet warmth and friendliness.

Too, I was asked to recitals and gallery showings and—because I had become well-acquainted with the two sisters who started the school and museum, and with Catherine, who moved in their circle —I was invited to a few of the fine homes of the old first families of Portland. Scattered throughout the downtown area, these houses were very grand, but the impression I had about the people I met there was of lap dogs atop embroidered cushions, nor did their young impress me any more favorably. Life, my mother's death had recently reminded me, was rich and priceless and soon gone, but here in their fabulous boxes these people were the quiet antithesis of gusto. The sap of life was lost here. After visiting four or five of these fine houses, I said out loud, not to the mirror but with some self-consciousness: "What you seek you won't find in money or prestige." I added this motto to the things I already knew about myself—for example, that I never wanted to catch myself simpering in the acclaim of however many mutts, and that I was going to do the sexual thing with Miss Nordstrom.

Day followed day, and with Pushells as our art critic, we moved along. Now, after our model had departed, we had discussions that usually lasted until the small hours, though first we would scurry down to Chinatown and stuff ourselves on the cheap and savory, then back to our room for reviews of what we had read or what paints were really permanent.

One day, as I occasionally did, I went to Mizino's photography studio. Poor Mizino was wrought up, to say the least. Several hours earlier a big brassy blonde had come into his studio and told him she wanted to be his model. She started to disrobe, but he yelled "No, no!" and pushed her out of his door. In the hall were two beefy individuals of the plainclothesmen type, who left with the blonde.

I quieted him down, and we hurried to our own studio, sensing that something was up. It was late afternoon, and Held, who worked in a mattress factory and drew his own peculiar brand of English landscapes, was at the studio as usual. He told me there had been a man hanging around in the hall, seemingly interested in our room. I went out and found him and asked what the score was.

He grinned evilly at me: "We're on to you," he said. "You're the one that's been getting the girls for your friends. Oh, we're on to you all right. Six years in the pen for you. Mrs. Watson's got the whole pitcher."

"Who is Mrs. Watson?" I asked.

He laughed a filthy laugh. "You'll know soon enough," he said, "but I'm gonna tell you 'cuz it makes no difference now. Mrs. Watson's head of the Woman's Protective Division of the Police Department." That was all he would tell me.

Well, I decided to take the bull by the horns and went to the police station next door. Mrs. Watson was not in, but was expected, so I waited with two enormous matrons whose steely glances pierced me hither and thither. Finally the infamous Mrs. Watson arrived. She was a dumpy, narrow-eyed woman of middle age. She led me into her office and rang a bell on her desk and would say nothing until another sly man, like the one I'd talked to outside the studio, arrived. Then she launched into a diatribe about protecting "unsullied American womanhood from them Asiatics."

"Ah, we're on to you all right," she concluded. "A pimp at seventeen! Betraying not only those poor girls, but the whole white race. You're going to the pen, son. Six years will give a traitor like you time to, as we say, reconsider." Her deputy grinned his sick enjoyment of my predicament.

"Mrs. Watson," I said, "there's been no crime committed. We have life classes just as we do at art school, and with the same propriety. No one has ever addressed any of the models by first names, let alone ever touched them or dated them. We've treated them with full respect."

Mrs. Watson snarled. "You mean I'm supposed to believe you could look at a naket woman and not start something lewd?"

"Mrs. Watson," I said, "if you were to disrobe right now, I could look at you indefinitely without sexual interest."

The deputy burst out laughing and tried to stop, but the snickering kept seeping out.

"You're a damn fairy," she said from between her teeth.

"No," I said, "I'm just a guy studying to be an artist."

The deputy had another fit of throttled laughter. Mrs. Watson glared at him, but he couldn't control it, so she told him to get out.

"Well," she said when he was gone, "we'll get you and them yellow-bellied Japs and Chinks and that nigger that poses naket. Just wait until the papers hear about this. That's all," she said, "that's all. Only don't try to leave town."

I had no intention of leaving town and, luckily, my father had returned to town from San Francisco that evening. I told him of my predicament. "Are you sure that's exactly how it was?" he asked. I assured him it was, exactly. "Okay," he said. "I'll see the mayor about it in the morning."

Next evening he told me the mayor wouldn't touch it. As the mayor explained it, it was the damn papers. "They love her for the headlines," he had said. "She can always rake up something to give them. You know—naked white girls found in downtown Jap den, or 'It could have been your daughter Wednesday night on Sixth Street,' et cetera. I believe this studio is on the up and up like your son says, but if I back you on this I'd lose my shirt, and the election is coming up. I'm sorry, Jim, but I just can't help you. But you know Chamberlain. Call him into this. A congressman ought to be able to make her back down."

But when my father called on him, George Chamberlain could only speak of the terrible adverse publicity. Mrs. Watson could imply enough, he felt, to ruin a politician's career. "She's mad with the power of scandal. Headlines," he said, "—she's got the kind they want. I'd like to help you, Mr. Rice, but the way I'm sitting I just don't dare."

My father was furious. His son railroaded to the pen without cause. He went to his long-time friend, D. C. Grove—in fact, both of us went and explained the situation. Why he brought such matters to D. C. I could never understand. But we drove over to D. C.'s drugstore. My father was soon ensconced in an armchair in the back office with a glass of bootleg in his hand as we told our story. When my father brought it up to date, D. C.—who'd been leaning back in his desk chair—righted himself to the shrill rasp of the ancient chair's springs. "Shit and God's mercy," he swore, "town's got so big that right's wrong and vice versa. My mother always said them on the west side of the river would come to no good."

My father and I sat waiting for this oracle to speak further, and D. C., a short pudgy man, sat in his chair, cogitating. Finally he leaned forward and tapped my father's knee with his finger. "Jimmy," he said, "didn't you tell me once you was close to Governor Oswald West."

"Ex-Governor West," my father said.

"Ex or not, he's still the big man in this State. Didn't you tell me once that when you was kids together Oswald could shy a rock farther out into the river than you or any other boy in Salem?"

"I suppose I did," answered my father. "Oz was the top boy at the swimming hole."

"Well, you may not know it," said D. C., "but he's still top boy, but he don't hold office so he can't be smeared by Mrs. Watson's allegations. Here," he said, "use my phone."

My father did, and caught that excellent man at his office, and after five minutes of explanations and exchanges of childhood memories, received assurances that the matter would be dropped. And it was.

The one repercussion of my close scrape with the law was that we were asked to leave the Worcester Block, as Mrs. Watson had informed the manager of our utter viciousness. So we found a new place—a corner room, much bigger and with all the windows one could hope for. It was next to a great unused hall, formerly the meeting place of a royal order of something.

The new place, so light and airy, seemed to attract other art students—Sunday painters and such. There was always someone daubing away at canvas, classes or not, and room enough to have discussions on all manner of topics. We worked hard on our portraits and figure paintings, but also made forays in good weather to paint in the Columbia River bottoms.

Once, in private, I asked Pushells with the brass and silly optimism of youth what sort of painting I'd be doing at forty. He looked at me, ridicule and compassion fighting to color his next words, but as he waited to speak and drew in his breath to expel the words, his expression changed: it blanked and became one of looking back into himself with eyes unfocused on what was before him. Then he came wearily back from the scan of past experiences, back from oblique layers of old dismays.

"Christ, Clyde," he said, "I just don't know. You're not for the middle course, that's certain. Maybe you'll spend your youth perfecting a technique and arrive at the productive years with nothing to say, or you'll live richly, absorbing as much as you can of the life around you and come to maturity with a great charge to shoot through a gun barrel with inadequate rifling. Hell, I just don't know."

Though he didn't mention it then, one of the reasons he didn't know was Nordi. Before the trouble with Mrs. Watson, Nordi and Catherine had visited us several times, but now they came often, sometimes bringing their paintings for Pushell's criticism. One Saturday Nordi came up with a portrait she had done at the museum school and asked for criticism from Pushells or anyone who wanted to comment. Half a dozen fellows had their say after Pushells had given his view. Later, Nordi and I went into the hall to dance some of the Hesitation Waltzes we enjoyed. It was fun, sort of a run in one place, though we had some difficulty. I kept getting a very obvious erection, which we were both aware of, but instead of going on from there I would excuse myself and do my multiplication tables, silently, until it subsided. Then we would dance again, until once more I'd have to excuse myself and do some more counting. Understand: I had not kissed her, nor even held her hand, and certainly not told her I loved her, all of which I planned to do under a more romantic setting. Nature, in other words, was a long step ahead of my romantic soul. The dancing and counting went on for some time. I would apologize, to which Nordi would say, "It's quite all right. I understand," though I couldn't imagine that she did. After she left and I returned to the studio, a solemn circle of my friends awaited me.

"Clyde," said Pushells, "are you preparing to be an artist or a Sunday painter or just a craft artist?"

"I'm going to be an artist with a capital A," I said.

"Capital A art doesn't pay," said Pushells. "How would you feed your family?"

"What do you mean?" I asked.

In unrehearsed unison several of them said, "Nordstrom."

"Look," said Heaney, "we're your friends. It seems like you're on your way to produce a situation where the only thing you'll be able to do is commercial art."

"I'd dig ditches first," I replied.

"That won't support a family either," said Pushells. "Look, it's up to you. We're all a lot older than you and we agree you have great possibilities, but you have to decide now. Is it to be art or Nordstrom?"

"Why, art, of course," I said. "Nordi's just a friend." I was amazed at myself and what I was saying, but art had helped me forget my lost love, the Forest Service, made me forget everything except improving and experimenting, totally involved in an enterprise of mankind that's older than agriculture. "I want to spend my life painting," I insisted.

"Tell her quickly then," said Heaney, "before she begins dreaming of marriage. Don't let her get her hopes up."

I told her the next day, and, I thought, she took it very well. Still, we continued to go on walks and it wasn't long before I began holding her hand as we walked. Then one day I kissed her—on the cheek, mind you—though it wasn't very long before I was kissing her lips. Then I got the notion that I should protect her from my evil designs. If I couldn't marry her, I shouldn't seduce her. My sentimental heart turned noble and stayed that way—for awhile. And then, hardly aware of it, I fell in love, and then utterly in love, with Nordi. We were soon aware that our times apart from each other were waiting periods, but that after such intervals, from the time we first glimpsed each other and as long as we were together, we were very close to a state of ecstasy that could continue hour after hour.

While I still wasn't about to give up art for Nordi and marriage, I gradually began to feel that art school was, at the moment, no longer the place for me. For one thing, we were starting to talk about art almost as much as we painted, and though I enjoyed our late night discussions in the studio, I didn't want to become one of those artists who spouted words, wrote words, endless harangues about their paintings, and certainly not one of the critics, who, with a quick glance at that modicum of effort, the painting, outdid the artists in geysers of the strangest concoctions of words ever known to man. Anyway, I decided to quit art school and move to my grandmother's on a hill out in the country where, I told myself, I could have more time to paint.

My grandmother's house sat on a hillside and surveyed a valley that opened finally on the Willamette River and Portland, with its backdrop of hills. The house had many rooms, though my grand-mother, who had been a widow for twenty years, lived alone. Born in a blockhouse in the early days of Oregon, she was a lovely old lady, well-read, a great quoter, and a mine of misinformation about Oregon's past. Her charm, however, was balanced by her terrible cooking. Her lamb stews were bad enough, boiled to death like everything else, but her pies — and she made one for me every day —were the ruination of fruit, their lower crusts a foreshadowing of the coming of plastics. Her personal favorite was raspberry, which she pronounced as it was spelled—as though "rasp-" rhymed with "clasp," and with a softly molded *a*. Had she been gentler with the fruit and harder on the *a*, the whipped cream on the pie might have seemed less like a marshmallow on an anvil.

But I had come to paint, not eat, and paint up a storm I did. "Very strong!" people said. "Sure sense of design," people said. Poppycock! I wasn't doing what I wanted at all. I wanted to be saying something about myself and my surroundings that words couldn't say. I tried, God knows: I made two or three good-sized sketches every day, expending paint and canvas and a lot of fury, but in only three out of almost a hundred did I escape abject failure.

Nordi came out each weekend and stayed with Grandma and me, and her visits redeemed me from the despair I felt viewing those paintings and those pies. Saturday at one she would arrive at our drear little station where, years before, I'd carved my initials. We would take a lunch and hike through the surrounding hills and it would be dusk before we made our way back to Grandma's to partake of her clean, adequate, but invariably overcooked food.

After our meal, the "ladizz," as Grandma pronounced it, would do the dishes while I built a fire in the great fireplace, and then we'd spend the evening popping popcorn while Grandma played some of her childhood tunes on the organ and the flames' flickering light cast shapes and shadows on the walls of the dim-lit room. Finally, we'd all ascend to our separate bedrooms and I'd lay in my bed until sleep took me, firm in my resolve not to sully my darling, whom I couldn't marry because of my upcoming career. I never asked her if she wanted to be sullied. I was young, and took a lot for granted. I found out later that she would have enjoyed being a little sullied, but had felt that it wasn't proper for a young girl to ask, so we met again at the breakfast table.

I had other visitors too. Catherine McKenzie, who'd become a very good friend, came out several times to see what I was painting, and one of her visits triggered a series of events that have stayed with me ever since. I was walking her down to the station one night for her return home when we heard screaming. Catherine said it sounded like an epileptic having a seizure. Then she told me that her brother, who was twenty-seven years old, had had such seizures since he was a baby and that they were very violent and came about every three weeks. She said he was given medicine to bring on a seizure when one was imminent, so that he was sure to have it at home rather than at work in his father's office. Anyway— on a silly impulse, I don't know why—I said I would try to help. Though I no longer believed in a deity, Catherine thought I was still a Christian Scientist and for some damn reason she was impressed and said she would hold me to my promise.

Now, I had taken a job hoeing and taking care of a large field of corn—a boring job, but one that left my mind free to roam. Chopping at weeds in the rocky soil, I got to thinking of my promise to Catherine. I remembered that once, as a child, I had been healed of a burned hand through Christian Science, so I was convinced that such things could be done, though I didn't know how. Down the endless rows of corn I went and, needing diversion, I said to myself, "I'm strong and Catherine's brother is weak." I was ignorant of the great men—of Caesar and Alexander the Great—who were epileptic. "I'm stronger," I would say, "and my mind can stop him from having seizures. I'll press on him." So as I hoed I said aloud, "You can't have a fit." As I said it, I tried to visualize a target to aim at: him in the city twelve miles away at work in his father's office. Every time I rested on my hoe—and you rest often hoeing corn—I would stubbornly mutter my statement: "You can't have a fit!" I would say it every ten minutes or so, gradually putting more pressure in it. I would scowl in my mind—and on my face, I suppose—and make a little gesture with it, forcing against my forehead and eyes with my thoughts and swinging my body and fist in a close punch to gain emphasis. I did it a hundred times a day, always aimed at that brother of Catherine's. By God, I had an experiment going!

Well, Catherine came to see me some time later and asked if I was praying for him as I had promised, and I said I was. She was excited. Her brother, she told me, had not had a fit since I started working on him. They had given him his medicine, but no seizure resulted. They gave him more pills, and still no seizure. They were worried. He was needed at the office, but was home in bed under a doctor's care. He still had the slight *petit mal*, but none of the violent seizures that had plagued his life for so long.

With this encouragement, I worked even harder. My experiment seemed to be working. After six months, Catherine told her father about my efforts, and he came to see me. He offered me his daughter, a large block of stock, and a place in his brokerage office. I finally had to be rather rude to get him off my back. The doctor, of course, said it was a new medicine that had stopped the seizures, and sent a mighty bill when they were sure no more seizures were coming. For myself—though I am hesitant to place myself in the dubious company of doctors, chiropractors, faith healers and other shamans—I feel that I had something to do with the cessation of the violent seizures. Of course, they may have stopped for totally unrelated and inexplicable reasons, but, were I a betting man, I'd say that the odds were four out of five that I did it. In any case, I was never again to have that tremendous certainty about the compact body of knowledge that has produced technology and its machines and a neat explanation about the world we live in.

As the weeks, and weekends, went by at Grandma's, I began to falter in my solicitude for Nordi's morals. I remembered that my original intention had been to have sex with her, for her to be my Mrs. Courtland. One day I took her down by Johnson Creek to get her clothes off with the excuse of playing in the water. It was a dry year, and the creek was very low. She took off her dress and, in her chemise, started to get into the water, when we realized that the stream was half urine—a flow that even drought didn't affect, since the stream drained a country of dairies and stock farms. That ended the excursion, along with my plan, but it formed in my mind the picture of disrobing her on the banks of a clear mountain stream. Ah, romance.

I had to wait two weeks to get enough money to buy tickets to Eagle Creek, twenty miles up the line, but before this fund was amassed Nordi called to tell me her mother would not allow her to come out any more on the weekends. This she told me weeping. That broke my restraint, and as she came out anyway, I met her at the station with a blanket over my arm and took her into the hills and laid her down on it and started to remove her clothes. In a masterfully inept manner I first removed her shoes and then her stockings, but when I raised her skirts, she burst out crying. I got them off, however, and started to remove a stout pair of bloomers. At this she started to wail loudly that I had gone mad and struggled with all her might to keep them on. I found that she was strong for her size, which should not have surprised me, since both of her parents were Scandinavian and from Duluth; they say it takes a strong individual to cope back there—with the climate, I mean. I reasoned with her—"Look, dear, we've arrived at this point in life, as have countless others," etc.—while I tried to get that hated elastic waistband down over her buttocks. Firm, but not really rough, in my efforts, I was careful not to choke her or cause her undue harm.

After about a quarter of an hour of extreme activity I got her bloomers off, only to find that the wailing and the fighting had wilted my erstwhile eager staff. I considered doing my multiplication tables backwards, but decided instead that a few strokes of the hand—anyway, I turned from her to do the necessary and then turned back to find her dressed and tying the laces of her shoes, so, in similar masterful fashion, I started all over again. I had noticed, of course, the well-filled bosom of her dress when we had first met, and had assumed it was full of breasts, but now I began to believe it was all lungs. How else could such a little girl give out like a steam calliope? Toward evening, she became pretty hoarse. Still, each time she reached sixty decibels my equipment became inoperative. However, with the contest going full tilt we somehow managed to achieve a meaningful, as they say, relationship and, strange as it seems, loved each other even more when it was over.

On the following weekend I met her at the station, and I could see she was pretty near waterlogged with anticipation, so I had a feeling that she wouldn't battle so fiercely to keep herself encased in those bloomers. Acting as if she were unaware of the blanket on my arm, she came along, and when I spread it on a grassy place in Hemmerling's brushy south forty a cursory survey revealed that she had left the bloomers at home.

With bloomers, modesty and shyness cast aside, we lived a life so rich and good as to actually bewilder us. We reveled in joining our bodies. Sometimes the sunlight played wantonly upon our twined limbs as we happily dallied, suppressing shrieks and laughter, until, joined utterly, we began to mount the honeyed ladder, helping each other up each rung with touches of ecstasy, never understanding the tears and sadness that support the cosmic grief many mortals must go through to reach that moment of inexpressible sublimity. Then I would come back slowly to the world, to be greeted by smiles, to touch hands, to touch toes, to kiss sweet breasts and sleep entwined. Why do we speak of ourselves as mere mortals when condensed eternities are ours with each orgasm?

One Sunday at Grandma's, while Nordi was out sketching by herself, my father arrived unexpectedly. Hearing of my activities from his mother, he took me aside and told me how disgusted he was that I would waste four months out of art school "drawing pitchers without a teacher."

"And I hear you been sleeping with a girl out here," he went on. "Well, I'm putting you in a military academy, young man, where they have tough instructors that can handle you. I already signed you in."

I had sense enough not to battle him on that; I just changed the subject. "I want you to meet my girl," I said.

As I hurried off to get Nordi, a plan began to shape in my mind.

"Nordi," I said when I got to her, "will you marry me?"

"We're too young, Clyde," she replied, but her eyes were sparkling.

"Look, honey," I said, "if we wait something will happen. We'll be separated somehow and we'll marry other people. Does that appeal to you?"

"No, Clyde, of course not. But what about your art, your career?"

"I'll try to keep up with that too," I replied. "But if I ever have to make a choice, do you doubt how I'd choose?"

"No, I don't," she said, and, sliding off the big log where she was sketching, she rushed into my arms with such fierce surrender that it left us suddenly haggard and shaken. Somehow we realized what an uncaring world it was all around us, and we clung to each other as if a great storm wind was trying to tear us apart. I told her about my father and about the military school, and she agreed to swear that she was pregnant.

"It's the ony way," I reassured her. "Otherwise we'll lose each other."

Arm in arm we went down the long sled road, and I brought my sweetheart before my father. Though it was unlike him, he didn't rise when I introduced her: he was the judge here, and felt the moment. He kept looking at her most keenly, however, and while we talked I saw that they liked each other at once.

"Nordi's pregnant, Pop," I said, "and I aim to marry her. You've spent years trying to teach me integrity and to be a gentleman. Did you mean those teachings?"

My father looked at us steadily for a long time with a harried look and then said, most quietly, "I guess I did, son."

"I'll get a job, Pop—any kind to start with. Military school's not for me. I'd end up in jail for what I'd do to any bullying instructor who laid a hand on me."

"Maybe not," he answered.

"Let's not try to find out," I said. "It'll be costly for both of us."

"About this girl," he continued. "Are you the first?" And then, turning to her, "Excuse me for asking, young lady, but I got to know."

"First for both of us, Pop," I said. "We love each other. Besides, we're just naturally good friends."

"You say you got her pregnant?"

"That's right, but it isn't the main reason, Pop. It's just that I can't explain, even to myself. It's just so."

"Probably puppy love," he said. "Then again, maybe not." He turned to her again: "Do you really want to marry him, Miss Nordstrom?"

She was silent for a moment, staring thoughtfully at him. Then she said, "Yes, I do. I think it will be a good marriage." There was something solid and final in the way she said it. I'm sure he noticed it, for he too hesitated, and, as he did, the starting of a smile came on his face. Then he grinned. A release of tension flowed through the room.

"You seem to have a good head on your shoulders, young lady," he said. "But if you want him, he's yours."

III

In Which
I Ride The Rails To Frisco,
Become A Pariah,
and
Finally Find A Job

◇   1920   ◇

After our marriage, Nordi got a job, but I couldn't land one. At five in the morning I was out standing in line before some outfit that advertised for help, but always they'd turn me down. No experience. And my looks: for several years I had been troubled with acne, and now it burst out. I certainly didn't look wholesome, and that spoiled me for salesmen's jobs. I'd gladly have dug ditches for half pay if only I could have gotten started.

Also, I could not seem to come out with a lie. I've always been poor at it, and wonder how Pop fell for that pregnancy story. Potential employers would ask me what I'd done in the last two years, and I'd fake around, but finally tell them about art school. They could barely wipe the smiles off their faces as they told me that art school wouldn't fit me for bailing lathe, galvanizing anchor chains or skinning dead horses, or whatever the job was.

I hunted uselessly day and night for almost two months. It had been a difficult year, 1921, and long lines queued up at each job opening. Once, I saw an advertisement for a cabbage chopper in a pickle factory and decided to be first in line to get the job. I spent the night at the pickle factory door, a windy, rainy winter night. When they threw the door open at seven, I was alone there. I stepped in and was informed that the job had been filled an hour before. I had been standing at the wrong door.

I roamed the district looking for other work, then wandered uptown. I'd been looking too long, and I thought I was just about stumped. I stood under the awning of the Imperial Hotel, soaking wet from the vigil, glassy-eyed and wordless, when someone caught my arm and a concerned voice said:

"Why, Clyde—you're soaking wet! I've heard you're having a rough time." It was Catherine's father, well-tailored and robust. "Catherine keeps me posted," he said. "Well, all that's over now," he went on. "I still have that place for you in my office. I'm on my way to luncheon at the Benson. Will you join me?" With that, he stepped out into traffic to cross Broadway, but I didn't accompany him. My pride drove me, instead, to turn and walk down the street. I needed work—God, how I needed it—but I couldn't accept a handout.

I hadn't been a very good companion to Nordi. I was so intent on getting a job that I thought of nothing else, and I can't believe my uselessness drew me closer to her. Still, the five hundred dollars my father had given me to tide me over until I got work was dwindling, so I decided to take fifty dollars and leave Portland for San Francisco. Nordi and I swore to each other that we'd meet wherever I got work, and I left her.

I was going on the freights to save money. Pushells turned me over to a Wobbly organizer friend, who turned me over to a young tramp, some years my senior, and told him to show me the ropes. The tramp and I caught a ride on a truck with a great, two-wheeled trailer behind it. My mentor rode with the truck driver, I in the trailer along with boxes of canned goods and stacks of gleaming milk pails. Half way to Salem the trailer was rear-ended and broken up so badly that there was no way to get me out. "Well," the driver said philosophically, "if it will hold together long enough, they can get you out at the shops in Salem." The milk buckets didn't seem to be worried, being made of sterner stuff, but I was glad when they pried me free in the shops.

"Well," I whispered to myself, "I'm alive and in Salem and heading south," and joined my mentor as we headed for a long line of freightcars. Here he began showing me how to board fast-moving cars, how to get in on the rods under the car. It seems absurd now, us out there in the rain doing all these tricks on a line of standing freightcars. Guess he'd never had a chance to play teacher before.

Eventually the freight pulled out. We hid in some bushes beside the track, and when it was rolling along we dashed out and grabbed the boarding ladders and swung ourselves up. All this was quite unnecessary, of course, but he was teaching me. Then we ran along the wet, slippery, rolling catwalk on top of the cars and climbed down and crossed the slamming couplings between the cars. We opened little doors at the ends of boxcars and dropped inside. We both took some terrible chances on that swaying, jerking train before he left me, having carried out his orders to show me the ropes. The trouble was that it was rainy and windy, and unless I could get into a boxcar I would freeze in my soaked condition.

I found an open boxcar and joined the half a dozen bums in it. When we reached Roseburg we all got out and down into a swampy place by the river. It was pitch dark and raining heavily, and we agreed to scatter and collect some wood to make a big fire. They scattered all right, and left me creeping along the dangerously swollen river among the cottonwoods, gathering watersoaked limbs and bark.

Finally with some damp newspaper that I carried around my waist under a sweater and some dry cedar that I'd come upon, I started a fire. As the flames rose and I scrounged around for more dry fuel, a particularly heavy downpour put out the fire. Crawling around, I couldn't even find where I'd made it, so I gave up and felt my way directly away from the sound of the river until I finally found the town, which was all locked up. After much wandering through the empty streets, I came upon the courthouse and, going nearer to find a place protected from the weather, I heard talking. It was the bums I had ridden with, who were all in the jail, warm and cozy. "Hunt up the night watchman," one of them said. "He'll let you in here."

But somehow I couldn't do that. I kept looking for an open shed, anything to protect me from the wet winds. Several times I saw the night watchman's lantern as he made his rounds, but managed to avoid him. Finally, beaten by the elements, I went back to the jail. There I learned that the watchman had gone home, his shift ended, so now I couldn't get in even if I wanted to. I ate some salted peanuts—I had brought two pounds of them for the trip—and crawled into a pile of stove wood, where I shivered and shook out the night.

In the morning, I hunted up a gasoline station and asked a man heading south if he would take me over the Siskiyous in his car, offering to pay ten dollars. "Look at you," he said. I was covered with coal dust and mud and carried a wet, filth-smeared blanket under my arm. "No, I won't take you. You're a filthy bum," he said, adding as he drove off, "Look in the mirror, kid."

I stepped into the station's restroom and looked in the mirror: my face was aflame with great running sores. I don't know whether it was the cold, the flying coal dust from the locomotive, the peanuts I was living on, the stress of the last month, or a combination of all these that did it, but I was an ugly sight. I had thought of buying a big breakfast with lots of steaming coffee, but after seeing myself in that mirror, I couldn't face anyone.

I left the town and went down by the railroad tracks, where, in a little grassy place, there was a sheet of rusty metal. I lay down on it, wept a few childish tears and, light rain and all, fell asleep.

Hours later I sat up and looked about. All around me bums sat on the grass. My clothes were dry and warm; a fine sunny day—one of those rare ones of winter—had been working on me for hours as I slept. Beside me on the grass sat a great jovial black. He smiled—actually smiled—at me, the rejected.

"Thought you'd never wake up," he said. "Train starts in about fifteen minutes. Too late to go up town and get something to eat."

"I've got a lot of roasted peanuts," I said.

He cast his eyes down, as if in modesty, and murmured, "Do tell." Then, laughing happily, he said he'd be glad to partake, and, both laughing now, we partook, as he put it, of the peanuts.

When I look back over meetings like this one, where I've felt the bond of humanness most splendidly, it has usually been with someone of another race. That black, whom I talked to for maybe fifteen minutes and never saw again, a man of great drollness and great good fellowship, is never far from my consciousness when I think of all mankind and wonder if we're really worthwhile.

The train wound south through canyons in the mountains. Further on, in wet clothes again, I got caught on top of a boxcar while trying to walk back up to the open car where the rest of the bums hunkered. It was night, and we were out on a great frozen plain. Two inches of frost stood up on the tops of the cars. I slipped and fell, but managed to save myself. I looked it over. The moon was out. Under it the frost gleamed. To try to walk those planks back to the others as the cars jerked and swayed, and to jump the spaces between the cars and land on the slippery frost on the next car, was absolute suicide, and to stay up there the forty miles to the next town would freeze me solid. But to stay seemed the best gamble, so

I spread my sodden blanket on the frosty boards of the catwalk and lay down on it on my belly with my knees and elbows pressed tightly against the outer edges of the catwalk. From my pocket I drew a pair of wet socks, put them on over my hands and worked them over my coatsleeves. I nudged a bit of the blanket up over my face and was set. My feet and hands were free to beat on the boards, and this I did as the bitter cold wind swept the animal heat from my body. By ceaselessly pounding my hands and feet I kept those extremities from freezing, and an hour or so later was able to crawl down with only one heel frozen.

On and on we went over the Siskiyou Mountains and down through the endless Sacramento River Valley. One morning I crawled out of a reefer. The air was warm and lazy, and on another track was a flatcar heaped with Muscat grapes. They had been left on the vine to produce the last bit of sugar and flavor and were now being shipped to a processor to dry for raisins. There was a switchman nearby, so I asked him if it would be all right to take a bunch of grapes. "Take ten," he said, "There's at least ten tons on the car." God, those grapes were good. I was half starved, my bag of peanuts long lost in the mountains of southern Oregon. I gobbled several bunches of the rich grapes and sauntered out of the yard to look at the town. In the parking strip grew orange trees full of oranges, many of which were lying in the gutters. This now, was surely California. I'd made it.

Next evening I was walking out of the Oakland railroad yard into the lower part of the city. I had decided at the last moment to look up my father in San Francisco. I tried to tidy myself up a bit, but it was useless. Pus from my face was crusted over my collar and coat and down my shirt front. I needed a shave, but how to shave such a face I couldn't conceive. Four establishments would not let me enter, but the fifth did, and at last I got in touch with my father. He told me his address and, after crossing the Bay, I trudged my way to his apartment building. In the foyer I waited for the descending elevator. It opened with a couple in evening clothes and my father. All three looked at me with astonishment. The couple stepped out, using great care not to brush against my clothes. As soon as Pop was sure that it was really me, we got back in the lift together and went up to his apartment.

After a hot bath, a shave and food, I slept many, many hours. Later, Pop assured me I could live with him while I looked for work. Though he didn't believe in doctors, he took me to a skin specialist, who said that with such an infection it was a wonder I was alive.

Every morning I was out early answering ads. No one wanted anything to do with me — or, rather, with this mass of dripping pus. Finally the doctor gave me a mask and a letter to possible employers, stating that my condition was not contagious and was neither leprosy nor syphilis.

Most of the time I walked to job openings. Rejected at every turn, I never wept. I was far past that. The loathing I saw on people's faces struck not me, but a wooden me. The real me had retreated to some private place, maybe my back pocket, where a modicum of my former self was encapsulated with a nubbin of hope, waiting as seeds do in a hostile environment for change and a chance to grow.

And then one of those countless people I'd faced while looking for work said, "Yes, I think I can use you. Be here at seven in the morning." I couldn't absorb it. He turned away, as they all did, and, thank God, didn't see the confusion that wracked me. At length I hurried out before he could change his mind. I had a job.

Next morning when the whistle blew, I was shown how to do my job — operating a primitive glue press. I was the helper of the fellow who ran the tongue-and-groove machine. After he grooved the boards, I ran the tongue-and-groove over the glue roller, held them in place, tongue to groove, and, jumping on a huge treadle, forced them together. I leaped up in the air with my hands on the boards in the machine and came down with all my weight on the treadle. God, how I went at that machine! I did it as if the world depended upon it. My world did. I wondered if I'd be fired at noon. All day I jumped and jumped. The third day the owner came to me and told me I was doing a fine job of gluing. "So often," he said, "they don't put enough force on the treadle."

At the end of the week he put another young fellow on the treadle and I ran the tongue-and-groove machine. Across the whining blades I shoved boards that were often only four inches long — an extremely dangerous maneuver. If the board kicked back you lost your fingers. They saved everything in that shop, except fingers. Luckily, or because I was so intent, I escaped maiming.

Now there were two fellows working under me, the gluer and the offbearer man, while I was still running the tongue-and-groover, and when that was slack I ran several other machines, always going full tilt. I soon noticed that all of the machines were constructed to do their jobs with no consideration whatever to the safety of the operators. Men who worked with their hands were simply expendable, even the very skilled ones. The turnover in laborers from accidents was assumed to follow some natural law. Most of the men in the shop had one or two fingers missing. Those who lost a hand, of course, didn't come back.

One day the owner said I was not separating the perfect joints from the near perfect, so I told my helpers to be very careful to sort them in their right stacks. The owner complained again, loudly. Eventually, spying as I worked, I found the mistakes were deliberate—an attempt to mess up my output. I whirled around and caught the tricksters in the act, knocked one into a corner and had the other one by the throat when the power was shut off on all machines. They whirred to a stop as the twenty or so men in the shop closed in on me.

I picked up a piece of scrap lumber for a club. They stopped, but they were all around me. "These guys have been goofing up my work," I explained.

A fellow said, "We told them to."

"Why?" I asked.

An older man answered: "Sonny, you're doing the work of two journeymen at beginner helper's pay. We can't allow that."

"Then why didn't you tell me?"

"We like to see a fellow get in there and take holt," the old man replied, "but you don't know when to stop. The boss could use you to pace us in a speedup attempt."

"Not me," I said. "I'll talk to him." They must have believed me, for the machines started their whine and everyone went back to work. I went to the office and explained that I had to have more wages for my work. He said he'd see me in hell first.

"Okay," I said, "I quit. Write it out while I change clothes." When I came back to his office to get my pay, I had my sketchbook with me—I had planned to sketch an industrial scene that had appealed to me. The boss looked startled.

"Is that a sketchbook?" he asked. "Are you studying painting?"

"Two years in art school," I replied.

"Hell," he said, "my wife is an opera singer. We're both up to our ears in art—culture, I mean. You keep on working for me. I could use a young fellow like you."

But I was already out the door, furious at a man of even slight culture who could put kids to work unprotected on maiming machines. Incredulous, I shook with anger. Then it hit me. My God, I'd walked out of a job. I was numb. The whole looking-for-work rejection setup would have to start all over again.

My father was disgusted with me. "Don't you see anything?" he asked as I stood there contrite. "You could have become a favorite of his. It was a chance to move up."

"At the expense of all those other guys, with all those missing hands and fingers, climbing on their misery?" I looked at my father's manicured hands and revulsion boiled up in me. "There will be a day very soon when the masses rise up and make everything equal," I blustered, resorting to the revolutionary jargon I'd picked up from Pushells.

"I've heard that before," replied my father. "This is 1922. At what date do you think it will happen?"

"I can't set a date, because I don't know," I answered feebly, and left the room.

Again, I put on my mask, took up my letter, and looked for work. I ranged the city, but to no avail. After two weeks or so I saw an ad: "Wanted: a man to learn polychrome work. Good pay while you learn." I hurried across town and applied. I told them of my years with every kind of color, of pastels and oil paints, and of my week of learning the technique of making gesso masks. The boss seemed interested and said it might work out.

A Jew, he had about eight men and women doing the packing and putting in the wiring, for what he made were big, ugly floor lamps. He got the turned stands and the center column and then, with a gesso of glue and paper, fashioned the weird concoctions, which were eventually painted in many layers of colors and iridescence. I considered them hideous, but they had a long vogue. He told me that the painter who fabricated the many color effects was an alcoholic—"a good man, but he won't or can't give up drinking, and he knows the next attack will kill him, so he wants to train someone to take his place." He offered me a good wage as I learned and said, "If you're able to handle it I'll certainly make it worth your while. We're sorta like a family here," he went on. "Can you start tomorrow?" I couldn't believe my ears. I had shown him my letter, and he said he would show it to the crew.

That night the infection, which had been responding to treatment, regressed, and the next morning I arrived on the job with such a discharge from the sores that it kept me constantly holding my handkerchief under my mask to keep it from dripping on the work.

I had worked for about an hour, puttying up flaws in the bases, when the Jew, my boss, came over to me in a fury, yelling that I was doing a bad job of puttying and sanding. "You're fired," he said. "Get out!"

I left hating Jews. In fact, I hated Jews for two years or more, never letting a chance pass to denounce them, until I met one of the men who had worked in the polychrome place. I cursed our ex-boss as a typical Jew and a fool. When I finished my harangue, the man set me straight: it was they, the crew, who had refused to work with such a diseased and repulsive creature as I then was. The Jew had no choice but to fire me, and did it in such a way that I would not feel rejected because of my person, but because of my incompetence—a fine and considerate man. I was the fool.

When my father heard that I had lost the job, he made no comment. I kept on answering ads. My face took a turn for the better and rapidly healed. I was scarred, but the shame was gone. Then one day I went to see my father after the usual day of ad answering. He had rented a big loft on Battery Street and had made the many improvements required by the city for the manufacture of food additives containing alcohol. When I got there he seemed unusually happy. He left the office and fired his helper, who was also his shipping clerk and the brother-in-law of his best salesman. After the man left, Pop said, "I don't know how I put up with that loafer so long, Clyde, but I had to have someone to hold down your job while you learned about the nitty-gritty of the uncaring world. I'll tell you," he said, "I know you're a good worker. I ought to—I trained you. When you came down here, I decided to hire you, but you've had it too damn soft, boy. You needed to be kicked around by life. Frisco's done her job. Can you start tomorrow?"

"I can start right now."

"No, tomorrow will be plenty of time. Say," he added, "you're face's all healed. No more mask for you."

IV

In Which
I Avoid A Disastrous Amputation,
Am Lectured By Pushells On Fidelity
And Ignore It,
and
Discover My Wife Is Missing

◇　1921　◇

So I went to work for my father. I hunted about until I found a room, a big one, in the top of a house that looked over the Golden Gate. Then I sent for Nordi, with whom I had held correspondence to a minimum when bad news was all I had to offer.

In time she arrived in Oakland, and I escorted her across the Bay, showing her the sights from the ferry's upper deck, being very knowing about the city and its environs. Really it was a dark night and I only showed her lights and named names. We took the cable car out to our room, where, in the light of a candle, we surveyed each other and were soon joined. We were both filled with wonder and awe that two beings could be so blessed with one another's presence. That night we joined and joined again in our marriage.

Gradually, as we took streetcar rides in the evening, Nordi became acquainted with the town. On weekends we visited whatever museums and galleries were open. We'd hike through Golden Gate Park or along the bluffs on the Frisco side of the Gate and stare at the cliffs of the opposite shore. We missed Oregon, but in other ways we were pleased: here we were, married and disguised as adults and in fabulous San Francisco. Our delight was really childish glee. We didn't want to be real grownups, but, hand-in-hand, still tinged with adolescence, we set out to explore all that lay about the Bay.

In time we made a little shack down the beach from San Francisco, half burying it in the sandy cliffs high above the tide. To get the materials, we towed rafts of driftwood in the breakers with two lengths of bullwhip kelp tied together. We scavenged the beach half a mile in each direction, and eventually had enough odd, battered boards to build our refuge. Around it we planted the bushes of the cliffs, watering them until they made a bramble in which our low-ceilinged hut couldn't have been discovered even by a fox.

Each weekend we walked down four miles of lonely beach, stuffed our clothes into the hut, and played naked in the sunlight. When cold fog drifted in in the morning, we drew sweatshirts on over the upper parts of our bodies. Our legs, our feet, our sex parts, and our buttocks all were cold. But our bodies under the sweatshirts were miracles of protectedness. Nordi got her sweatshirt all out of shape by sitting on the sand and drawing her knees up under it to her chest for warmth. Sometimes rain would catch us far down the beach in our nakedness, and we would run through the showers toward the hut. We bounded along, svelte bodies in the rain, no sagging jounce of aging belly, no floundering sway of flaccid thigh. Tight-made and new, we sped gleaming through the gloom, except for the dance of Nordi's breasts and the soft, unheard jangle of my pendant testicles. We leaped up the path from the beach—no trudging for us—and burst into our hut, scrambled onto the bed and writhed our bodies dry and warm; writhed in the very joy of being alive, before we lit the fire and commenced cooking, then sought the wine bottle with laughter.

Eventually we met some of the painters, the people of Telegraph Hill. We found they talked art, art, art, but painted little. We were disappointed, to say the least. In the galleries, much of the contemporary painting we saw also seemed banal. Often it was as though photographs had been painted over in pure pigments, and the effect was loud and pointless. Good draftsmanship was evident, but all spaces outlined with drawing were filled in with color directly from the tube, an effect derived from French Impressionism. They were extremely tiring to look at, but we did look, and, like tourists, we hadn't time to consider what we saw, which was all for the best.

My own painting suffered in California. I was used to a hundred variations in atmosphere, but around San Francisco the great outdoors seemed to be stabilized into half a dozen aspects. I missed the frequent showers of western Oregon that kept the growing things green, the streets and atmosphere clean. The great vistas were more powerful, the contours of cliff and hill were not hidden under conifer forest, the green grass of early spring matured quickly and the hills with their mantles of dry grass became golden under the hot arches of the southern sky. I began to paint calla lilies filled with cigarette butts, but soon found I was not the first to observe this symbol of California.

While I had my work and my painting, Nordi showed little interest in sketching at the time. She had a few friends, but must have, at times, been quite bored, though I did my best to relieve her boredom with an occasional practical joke. One day I explained to her that whales were mammals who had once lived on land, but had taken to the sea because they had short limbs and their stomachs dragged, and they were always getting rocks and dirt in their navels. But though they lived in the sea, I elaborated, nature urged them to make love on land, which they did—on sandbars and low islands in the arctic. To her credit, she didn't believe me, so I went to the library and produced a studious paper full of quotes from bogus authorities, laughing so much at the pompous quality of my imitation sources that the librarian threatened to have me ejected. Nordi accepted the paper and allowed her friends to share her knowledge for some time, until someone put her wise. I was soundly thrashed for her embarrassment. My whale story did have some lasting effect, however—not on Nordi, but on me—for it led me to visualize a certain portion of Sibelius' Second Symphony as two sternwheel steamboats copulating on a Yukon River sandbar.

Despite my efforts, however, Nordi became fed up with the role of the little wife waiting for her young husband to come home to the furnished room. She decided to become an artist's model and set out for the studios of the professional artists. She made appointments with three: Maynard Dixon, an artist named James, and another whose name I can never remember, a painter of portraits. She also sought work at the Art School, an institution similar to ours in Portland, though on a grander scale, and was accepted.

The ancient Greeks would have liked Nordi's figure, so it was no surprise that the locals did. She posed a dozen or so times for James, who was doing some careful illustrations for a book by Marion Headly, a New Zealander who wrote about Australia. She also posed for Maynard Dixon in his great studio up Columbus Avenue. In talking to her, Dixon found she was married to an art student and was a good draftsman herself. He asked her to come one evening to pose and to bring me along with some of my drawings and sketches.

When we arrived at his studio, which was loaded with paintings, large and small, Dixon showed us a few of his more recent works. Then Nordi took a simple standing pose, and Dixon and I had at it. I started, and then turned to see what he was doing. I had never seen such facility. Using a soft lithograph crayon, he drew the outline of the shadowed side of the figure, while at the same time manipulating the crayon in his hand so that it also produced the shadows. After that, he outlined the lighted side with a soft, incisive line. Another three or four minutes and he had a speaking likeness of her face and had caught quite a bit of her quality. Nordi struck one more long pose for me and I produced a poor drawing. We repeated the same performance several times, after which Dixon served us wine.

"Let's see the drawings you brought," he said, and, after looking them over briefly, remarked, "Like most students today, you can't draw." Then he stepped up on the model stand and told Nordi to draw him. Nordi produced a good line drawing in short order. It pleased him immensely. "You're good," he said. "A model who's a firstrate draftsman. You're certainly on the wrong side of the easel." After that, the talk turned to camping, something we were all interested in, and he asked us to come again the next week. "Bring a painting," he told me.

The following week I brought a painting of Nordi that I'd been working on with glazes for more than a month. I had started with heavy, blue darks and rather yellowish highlights, then had glazed the figure with thin rose madder until it was a pink, sugary nude with the deeper shadows coming through. After that I'd begun glazing it with thick varnishes and very weak, transparent yellow ochre. It was amazing. The shadows had an almost hidden gleam, and the whole piece had a depth and stillness that I had never before achieved.

Dixon was astonished. "Nobody in San Francisco can touch this," he said. He studied it for some time. "No, not at all. We've all tried glazes. This is your medium," he went on. "You know, I want to help you, but for selfish reasons. A painting like this can't be denied. By itself, it makes gibberish of most of the talk you hear of late." Then, as we were leaving, he asked me to come and work with him the next Sunday on some light-hearted murals he was doing for a friend.

Later, lying in bed, Nordi replied to my question about him: "Well, I like him, and I know you do too. He's an honest painter and he has great facility. Still, I think he has the same problem I do." I knew what she meant: it was said of Nordi in our Portland school that on a four-day portrait session she was far ahead of the class on the first two days, but that on the third or fourth day she couldn't carry it further, but could only outline what she had done. "It's hard to explain," she went on, "but I'm sure I'm right. I talked to James about it. James said that everything Dixon takes east, he sells, and that most of the art community here is jealous. They say he comes up to a wall and can't get his painting past it. The wall says the painting is finished, but something tells Dixon that past the wall is where the great painting takes place. Of course, some of it's probably self-serving gossip."

"How about the painting I showed him tonight?" I asked.

"It's way past the wall, Clyde. At first I didn't quite get it. Still, it's unfinished, and I doubt that you could carry it to completion."

I knew I couldn't, but said, "I could feel hurt by such a statement."

She reached over and pulled my head down against her lovely bosom, "No, honey. I couldn't ever hurt you. It's just that you're way too young and so naive to be painting like that."

All this time I was getting on famously with my father. The work was simple, and I did it well. My father was in a strange and precarious position at the time. He had loved my mother very much, and the loss of her took a great deal of his force from him that he never recovered. Soon after I went to work for him, he married a woman a few years younger than himself and took a fine apartment on a hill overlooking the Gate, which they never looked at. His new wife, who was a Scot, pouted, for though it was a grand location, it was so far out from the center of the city that she had to spend a dime for streetcar fare to go window shopping. They soon established a fighting relationship and settled down to domesticity. Pop would often ask me out to dinner so that he could regale me with their most recent all-night bout, round by round, as his tears rolled down over his chops and into his chops or cutlets.

My father's product was flavoring, all kinds of flavoring. His partner ran the production and he the sales. In those days flavors were crude, barely adequate, but the best to be had, and vigorous selling of a needed product was profitable for both the flavor manufacturer and the grocer. It was about this time, too, that the bookkeeper at work quit to go back to Boston. The new book-keeper, a Canadian named Miss Crippin, was of the same sect as my father. My first impression of her was that she was a conserva-tive, rather sour individual. Still, she was very attractive in spite of it, and I was determined that, sooner or later, I'd get a smile out of her.

In the meantime, life seemed to be smiling on me as never before. My job paid well, I had a lovely wife, I was drawing every night, and I could work for Maynard Dixon on weekends. When Sunday morning came, I was down on California Street at the restaurant where Dixon was working. He had painted the walls and the ceiling with tip-tilted tables, around which sat nude ladies wearing cute hats and sipping their drinks. The light backgrounds were dappled in to give a soft vibration. My job was to put back the molding that had been removed and to finish the dappling where needed. One of the fringe benefits of the job was that the owners of the restaurant, Mr. and Mrs. Koppa, interrupted our work to serve us a lunch that would make most dinners blush: tiny potatoes, little cubes of lamb and veal, leeks, and what looked and tasted like very bland, plump mint leaves, all brought to perfection with a very delicate white wine sauce. I began to see that they loved Maynard Dixon and were saying so with the subtleties in their dinner-like luncheon. After lunch, we worked for as long as there was light for him to paint by, and then arranged to finish on the following Sunday.

The work at the restaurant got me in a decorative mood. Nordi and I painted the floor in our room shining black and the slanting sides of the ceiling pearl gray, while the flat upper part of the ceiling we painted somewhat darker. We made a low bed frame and bought four plain chairs with woven rawhide seats, which we made lower by sawing a bit off their legs. We were happy with the changes, which fit the room, but felt we needed a more exotic touch. In Chinatown we found some strange Chinese lanterns to put over our lights, and then we acquired a big snapping turtle, its undershell very colorful in reds and yellows. He was over twelve inches across and longer in the way he went.

To go with the turtle, I decided to buy a cheese—not just any cheese, but a fine old cheese like the ones my father had bought from a New York salesman when I was a boy. I went to the Italian quarter and entered a building that housed a food-importing firm. Two old men with little pig eyes and enormous, pitted, blue noses listened to my desires. One made a gutteral sound and turned from me. The other took me out back, and among barrels and crates, we came upon what looked like two or three dozen filthy gray bricks piled on the cement floor. This, he said, was what I wanted. I demurred, but in a deep bass voice that sounded like the breaking up of old boards, he told me that they were very old, very fine. As I didn't know and he was supposed to, I bought one.

At home I put it on the table where Nordi was caressing the shell of our turtle. We looked at the cheese. The turtle gave it only a glance, drew his head into his shell, then continued his unblinking perusal of it. It did look as if it had been around: you could see where rats had eaten into the decrepit rind, come nearer the inner contents, and left—or died. The head of a nail was imbedded in one end and we pulled it out. Just a bit of the shank of the nail was left. We realized later that it was only a tack, but in this moment of malignancy we could only feel that the cheese was alive, or had been, and had eaten the nail. So we cut into it with the greatest of trepidation. At once we knew that the cheese was dead, long dead. With the gaiety of an embalmer, I put some of its cream-like interior on a slice of bread, bit into it, and could not get the horror of it out of my mouth quickly enough.

We put it on the windowsill, closed that window, and opened all the others in our charnel house with the polished black floor. When all was aired out, we crept in and went to bed, only to wake up in the night with a shriek, convinced that the cheese had somehow gotten in the bed between us. It was the turtle, nesting into what would have been Nordi's lap if she sat up. On reflection— we'd heard that snapping turtles can, with one bite, cut a broomhandle in two—we realized that, though he seemed to be a thoughtful turtle, sometimes cogitating for hours, he might also be headstrong and given to snap judgments. Why, crawling around in bed while we slept, he could, with one quirky move, do our marriage irreparable harm. So we put him in a box, tied down the lid, and Nordi spent the rest of the night clinging to me, sobbing each time she thought of what we had narrowly escaped.

I was loathe to leave her in the morning, but she came up to me and gave me a little hug. "I'll be all right," she said quietly. "Don't worry." When you are young the vicissitudes that would shake a more mature person can be shed as water off a duck's back, for I soon found myself hurrying to the cable car unmindful of the fact that our Eden, though there was no snake in it, had become complicated. Two things squatted there, two things for which time was not of the essence, two things that cared not for the edelweiss or the daisy. I tried to tell my father and Miss Crippin about our problems, at coffeebreak, but I felt the significance of it was lost on them, for later I heard my father explain that he had dropped me on my head when I was a baby.

"But what about Nordi?" demanded Miss Crippin. Finally, nonplussed, they let the matter drop.

The following evening we carried our turtle down near the Bay where the fountain of the beautiful rotunda of the Fine Arts Building of the late World's Fair was situated. Here we set down our turtle. He marched solemnly down to the pool and, still marching, disappeared beneath its water. Next, we bought a screened box, brought it home, and nailed it up outside of the north side window. In the box we placed our cheese. I subsequently discovered that a minute amount of its interior, adhering to a silver knife and with it transferred to a proper cracker, produced a remarkably salubrious flavor.

Next weekend I was again working with Dixon and, as we finally finished our project, drank far too much wine. We ended up with a jug at his studio, putting away the ladders and other equipment. He had done a large canvas of Nordi in a thing loaded with Indian symbolism. I was admiring it, when he told me I could have any painting in his studio. We were both pretty drunk, but I stumbled and swayed through his canvasses, knowing full well that I should not take unfair advantage of his offer, for there were a score of really splendid ones about. At last I settled on a very small one, about sixteen inches square. He wanted me to take a better one, and our argument soon became a quarrel.

"You think you're a hell of a lot better painter than I am," he said.

"I certainly am not," I replied. "I'm not even a good student."

"You're mealy-mouthed," he grated out. "I'm on to your fake modesty."

"Here—take your picture," I said. "I don't want it."

"Won't," he yelled. "Where you gonna hang it? There isn't room enough in that dump you live in to hang a picture."

"It's just right for the bathroom," I squalled.

He turned white. "Gimme my picture," he said. "Now get out!"

I turned and staggered out, disgusted with both myself and him. Of course, I never went back, nor did he call for Nordi's services as a model after that. In fact, he left his studio soon afterwards for a lengthy stay in Taos.

Nordi was posing about this time for the portrait artist. They got along splendidly. One day, Nordi made a line drawing of his little daughter. He had it framed and hung somewhere in his house. He had done a small nude and two portraits of her when the annual showing of the member artists of the world-famous Bohemian Club was held. Graciously, he gave Nordi two invitations to the showing. It was a small showing, less than a hundred canvasses, a great deal given over to landscapes, but there was also one by Maynard Dixon in which Nordi looked out over desert buttes clad with a feather in her hair, now bluish black. There were five other canvasses very obviously of her; one a searching portrait by the giver of the invitations. It was amusing. Surely there were other models posing in San Francisco. I think her popularity stemmed partly from her knowledge of art, partly from her exquisitely constructed body, and mostly from the warmth and camaraderie that radiated from her like sunshine.

Anyway, Nordi did continue to pose, and often posed for the Art School, a rather pretentious institution. The school had brought in some big name teachers from Britain and other European countries. One evening she was posing for a large life-class.

In a rest between poses, as was her custom, she wrapped herself in her kimono and moved about, chatting sometimes with students. This particular evening one of the students asked her what she thought of his drawing, and she saw that he was having trouble drawing the lower part of an arm. She explained the rotation of the radius and ulna bones and, as he didn't seem to understand, made a quick little sketch of the arrangement in the corner of his paper. He understood then, and was thanking her when the painter-teacher, who was British, came blustering over with a "So! The model teaches anatomy to the student, does she?" Coming closer, he stared and said, "Just as I thought. You're wrong."

He was an overbearing man, and his tone was consciously offensive. It annoyed Nordi. "You're the one who's wrong," she said. "That is the way the bones lie in that arm position."

Every eye in the room was on them now. He drew himself up and back, the right stance for his forthcoming question: "Does the model feel," he demanded, "that she can teach the instructor?"

Nordi's smile became impish: "It's obvious from this," she said, "that I could give you a pointer or two." She stepped over to the cabinet where the articulated skeleton was kept, raised the forearm of the thing and placed it in the position of contention. "You can see from this that I'm right," she said. The class gathered around, murmuring full agreement. Somebody cheered and there was much laughter. The instructor plunged from the room. Nordi, now rested, again took her pose and the class resumed its drawing. When Nordi passed the office at the end of the session, the curator came out with her check.

"We will have to dismiss you, Mrs. Rice," she said, "but I can't tell you how indebted the school is to you for puncturing that vain, arrogant man. I would have loved to have been in on the fun—and, oh yes, I enjoyed seeing you so many times at the Bohemian Show. Good night, Mrs. Rice, good night."

Despite these employment setbacks on the artistic front, our lives were exceedingly carefree and happy. We ate out a lot, but not in the big fancy restaurants. We went to the small cheaper ones. There was a long place of high ceilings with an open kitchen at the back that served splendid Italian food where we went often. We also found a basement Chinese restaurant, unknown to whites, where the Chinese families ate, and for French cooking we tried La Favorete and the Hotel Entella. Life was just to laugh and enjoy. With our few new friends we consumed much bathtub gin and of course red wine that was called Dago Red, and we smoked only Egyptian tobacco.

Oh, we were happy and carefree and my studies suffered. Nordi, having posed for some illustrious artists, seemed to feel, with some validity, that her talent as a model was wasted on me. Gradually, she became bored with our life and began to talk of going home for a visit, and it wasn't long before she did go to stay a month with her family. Left alone, I cooked my own breakfast, sometimes had lunch with my father, and dined out before seeing a play or movie or dropping into the library. Then my father left for a conference in Portland, taking his new wife north for the first time, and the bottling girl left on her vacation.

Miss Crippin and I were left to hold down the fort. We realized in our separate ways that this was a famous old situation, so hackneyed that it could only result in burlesque. Still, I began looking at Miss Crippin—not that I hadn't noticed her before. Two things about her were rather outstanding. One was that she blushed deeply if addressed in any personal way. The second was that nature, far from frugal with most of her, had allowed for only a tiny waist in her construction. She was a small woman, with chestnut hair, big eyes, and a small mouth. She reminded me of the young ladies that Cruikshank drew for Dickens' novels.

The first day, with nothing else to do, we talked. She thought the Prince of Wales the epitome of manhood and, as most Canadians do, thought the English the most wonderful people ever to exist. She liked the dress shops and department stores of San Francisco. She was a Christian Scientist, and knew that "matter is mortal error." I asked her how she liked Toronto, her native city. She cast her eyes down, and the blush suffused her face with color that coursed down her neck and plunged down the deep vee of her shirtwaist. I could only wonder where it stopped. "Yes," she said, "It was pleasant there in the summer." She never smiled. Once in a while she would raise her eyes, look deeply into mine, then look down again, at which point that blush would sweep over her countenance and down the vee.

By the third day our inane conversations began to take on a wordless significance. I tried to say it, managed to get out "In a situation like this—" and stopped, my throat much too dry for speech. I affected a coughing spell and looked at her. She was very pale—looked downright sick, in fact—but I tried again and was able to croak out, "Don't you think in a situation like this, we're bound to become sexually aroused?" As I said this, she grew positively ashen, but said nothing. "Isn't it possible?" I begged in a whisper.

"Oh yes," she whispered back, "yes."

Not believing my ears, I loudly stated, "It's the proximity that does it."

Still pale, she whispered "Yes" again and reached for her typewriter and was feverishly putting a sheet of paper in it when I asked, "When?" At which, trembling visibly, she whispered, "Not in here," and began typing madly.

Suffice it to say that when my father returned, less than ten days later, he found me in a state of some exhaustion. "You've lost some weight doing your own cooking," he guessed. "Do me a favor: take a long weekend and go down to your beach shack. Three days in the sun will put some color in you." I didn't argue, either about his diagnosis or his prescription.

Two days in the sun did tan my skin, and the solitary recouping of my force was miraculously quick. I didn't get out to where the water of the Bay met the sea until Sunday afternoon, when I decided to go on a sketching jaunt. The tide ran out before I got there and the low tide rocks were black with olive green seaweed tied to everything. I braced my canvas against the rock along the toothed shore of the gate and stared at the inrushing tide, felt the wind and saw the far off creeping blot of fog. Over near the cliffs on the other shore a green-hulled fishing schooner from the Othosk Sea ran before reaching fingers of mist, gray of old sails against the bronze and magenta, the copper and brick red of the Marin shore. I was wild to catch the portent in the assault of elements upon the harbor. I saw it in many shades and colors, but felt it in blacks and leaden hues and in the dirty lemon-yellow light. The sky where it met the sea was full of an unspeakable callousness for men and land. It was brazen, not in color, but in impact.

Yes, so with the blacks, I muttered to myself, and a hard dirty blue for the tide. No whites, the crests of charging seas must be luminous—hard driven gray. Cliffs of bronze and black and the hills that topped them glum for the onslaught. I painted the sea where it curved away over the horizon under a bitter, empty sky as gray—almost black—and hard as iron. North up the coast stood a great bank of fog; reaching hands of it sought for the gate. I must hurry, catch the scene and the feeling. The unceasing wind buffeted me: I who was drunk with environment was harried by scouts of the coming gale. While through the maddening clumsiness of creating, I found myself whispering: How can I get it in—the smell of the shore, wind over decaying seaweed, the old onion, the used grapefruit halves, the carcass of a dog fish, the undulation of a piece of butcher's paper all in the wash along the shore, brushed up in the sand, sucked back, struck, raised and borne ashore again by the next wave? The abrasion and the stirrings unraveling a rich skein of shore smells down the wind.

Let it in, I begged, it will seep in, if you let it. Quick, the light lemon-yellow of the sky is changing, darkening. Here's the gale now, while the storm is still down below the horizon, whoosh! It is blowing sand and here comes the fog. Sand in the painting? What of it; it should help.

I covered the sketch and put away my paints while loose sand scudded along the beach and into the rocks where I worked. When I stood up, the fog had all but hidden the rocks and the shore immediately around me. After several tries I lit a cigarette and took the winding path up through the tall grass.

Monday morning, tanned and once more robust, I greeted Miss Crippin and my father. I had come down early, swept and dusted, and had bottled a new batch of imitation vanilla and had it ready to label. After two-thirty my father left to visit a customer or two and I was left with Miss Crippin.

She was the same—very reserved, extremely shy—but she never looked away. It was always a matter of looking down or raising her eyes to look deeply into mine. Her sexual fragrance was unbelievably exciting and, joined as it was with the perfume she wore, drove me half mad with desire. But her talk was commonplace, her interests mundane. She didn't sing, but if she had, she was the kind of woman who could only have sung contralto. She never spoke of the fierce lust of our joining. We knew it wasn't love that drove us, and I'm sure she knew as I did that lust failed to explain it. It was as if we were two magnets that this unknown force slammed together. We had a trysting place, out among the rolls, boxes, and bales, and, because of it, no one ever discovered our secret.

I found a wonderful Italian grocery up on the south side of Telegraph Hill and began buying lunches there for Miss Crippin and myself. How she loved it! We ate on the roof unless it rained: a crusty loaf, a slab of gorgonzola cheese, a small carton of olives, a section of salami, and a dozen ripe black figs. What open happy camaraderie we had over our lunches, so different from the need to give utterly of ourselves to one another. We both knew there was no middle ground, and we never groped for it. I was married, I loved my wife, and I was ten years younger than Miss Crippin.

Nordi came back from Portland early. The constricting concepts and religious absurdities to which her family clung suffocated her. Not long after her return, we had another reminder of our Portland days, for who should appear on our doorstep but Pushells and his boyfriend, Willard. They stayed with us several nights, sleeping on the floor, just long enough for Pushells to regale us with his most recent escapade in Portland. It seems he had learned that an international convention of Episcopalian clergymen would meet in town. Knowing a photographer of the Portland rich who also dabbled in the arts, Pushells borrowed a fine camera from him and, before the clergy arrived, worked it so that he was their official photographer. When the convention began, he took countless pictures of its members, always managing to get the pompous posturing of the bishops into the local papers. What Daumier did to the legal profession of France, Pushells strove to do to the clergy in Portland. Oh, he was a happy man. When the day came for the massed, three-tiered picture of them, all in front of the civic auditorium, it was an august scene, an august occasion. In the dark, somber tone of bishops' clothing, the white clerical collars of all shone out like bits of the Holy Grail. In the center of the seated bishops, however, none shone more brightly than those of Pushells and his boyfriend, for they were made of brightly glazed typewriter paper. Pushells had arranged for someone else to take this final shot, enlarged copies of which he mailed to friends far and wide.

That night, Nordi and I, lying in bed, got to talking about Pushells and Willard and then about relationships in general. Somehow the discussion came around to divorce. We agreed that we didn't mind others resorting to it, but we loathed the thought that we would ever part.

"I wish we knew more about marriage in general," Nordi said. "We've very few facts with which to protect ourselves."

"Let's ask Pushells," I offered. "Would you be embarrassed?"

"No," Nordi replied. "We don't know anyone else to ask who wouldn't wind up with cantankerous religious views and the stuff grownups say and don't exactly mean."

"Pushells," I said, when we'd gotten him alone, "you've been up on everything I've ever asked you about. Can you tell us about marriage and sex and divorce?"

"Why ask a queer about marriage?"

"Because you've never steered me wrong about other things."

"Okay," agreed Pushells, and he put on his very intense intellectual look. Still, for all his histrionics, I knew there would be no fat in what he would tell me.

"I'll bulk matrimony, sex and the home and family together," he said. "We're an animal whose offspring mature at a very much slower rate than any other animal. The young need protection, sustenance, and teaching much longer, so the perpetuation of the species is accomplished by the home. The home also offers a base from which the members operate, and a place to store surplus for a rainy day. It's also the place for sexual gratification with the least effort and trouble. Do you get the picture?"

"Yeah," I answered. "You mean it came about because it fits many needs of the animal, man. Makes a lot of sense if we think about it a bit. But divorce—hell, Pushells, we don't want our marriage to dissolve. What can we do to protect it?"

"On this I'm no authority, but looking the scene over with a detached eye—Jesus, what a concept!" Pushells shook himself and went on. "As an outsider I look at it this way. Some couples find they have nothing in common but sex. We're complex animals, Clyde; sex is not enough. If you have companionship and sex—

well, even then, money, alcohol, adultery or sheer meanness can chew up a marriage."

"How about us?"

"Well, a person training for the arts is less interested in money than are the people in the core of humanity, the Smiths and the Joneses. Lack of it ruins as many relationships as too much, but knowing you, I don't think that money will be your problem, and I've got a strong hunch that alcohol won't loom large in your lives. You, Clyde, could be mean; Nordi never. Still, I think if you became mean, you would see and curb it, for your ego would never allow it to blur your narcissistic view of yourself. Adultery, though—that could break up the union. Marriage is based on monogamy, but man's essential nature is not, so here's my advice." He put on his summing up air. "I think you'll have no problems except from some infidelity. Infidelity is poison to the mate not involved. Jealousy and loss of status with mate and society are hard to bear, but if you two want to sustain your set-up, never let a lover break up your home. A lover is a great excitement, and we need excitement, but you can't live on it, and while you're enjoying it, you're depriving your mate of full attention. Never withdraw from one another to get even for an infidelity, and you'll stay together all your life."

Thus spake Pushells. Though by now he had assumed the mien of one of his Episcopalian bishops, he made sense to us. The result of this was a solemn pact that we would never part for any reason, and that we would never have children until we could give them a real home, one that we owned.

Pushells and Willard disappeared after a few days, though we knew they were still in the neighborhood and probably up to new mischief. In the meantime, Nordi and I abandoned our weekends at the shack down the beach and wandered the hills about the Bay. We sketched in the heights back of Berkeley, but more and more often it was north of the Bay in Marin County that we hiked and wandered. After a month or so of this, we hiked down the beach to our shack to spend a weekend. Apparently, some farmer from atop the bluff had found our low, hidden abode and, with a team of horses, had torn it apart in sections and dragged it up and away, probably as material to build a woodshed or a floor of a chicken house. We left sadly and never returned.

Nordi was never aware of my relationship with Miss Crippin. I didn't like deceiving her, but convinced myself that, not knowing, she wasn't being hurt anyway.

We had just seen the movie *Scaramouche* with Ramon Navarro in the title role. We had enjoyed it immensely and, after a dish of ice cream at Hass's, had traveled home on the cable car. We had hardly gotten our coats off before Pushells and his boyfriend knocked on our door and demanded tea. They were in great spirits. Willard, Pushells' boyfriend, wore a large, dark floppy hat, the kind much affected by artists at the turn of the century, and a limp silk necktie of the same period. Pushells himself wore a look of total triumph.

"You thought that this young man was from Portland, didn't you?" said Pushells, gesturing toward Willard. "But no. You see before you young Clark Winson, a starving young artist, formerly a student at the Art Students League in New York."

With this introduction, our Willard staggered to a chair with his ragged portfolio, laid it and his great floppy hat before him on the table and, with courage weakened by starvation, bleated, "I'm a bit dizzy. Could you perhaps give me a little water?" and raised the eyes of one wronged by the world but full of forgiveness. Then they both gave way to whoops of merriment, pounding each other's and our backs too.

Finally, they told their tale. It was a design of Pushells', one that obviously pleased him. First he had painted the pictures—a dozen or so watercolors—for bait. They had to be executed so that the middle class would have to reach a bit, but not too much. Pushells was emphatic about this—no pearls before swine. The floppy hat and silk tie were easily procured, but the suit had taken some time —a splendidly tailored suit worn thin and with a small tear at one knee that Pushells sewed up with imitation ineptness. He taught Willard to hold his hand over it, as if in embarrassment—oh the poor boy! Then the fine portfolio that had seen better days, and they were through with the hock shops. Next they went to Oakland, where Pushells cased the artistic community and its patrons. Thus it came to pass that Willard, who had been forced to do without his breakfast, fainted in a room in the Oakland Art Gallery next to the one where the Ladies Auxiliary for the Arts and Drama was having a luncheon. No one came for quite a long time. In fact, Willard was thinking of getting up and fainting much nearer to the ladies, with sound effects, when he heard steps and then a mild shriek, and knew that all was well. The ladies choked him with sandwiches and cookies, sent out for roast beef and a hearty broth, and wormed from him his story. Tears came to his eyes as he let drop the essentials of his tale. He searched his pockets for a handkerchief and the ladies offered him lace ones. He said he had one in his portfolio and, reaching for it, knocked the watercolors, now beautifully mounted, out onto the table. There were gasps from the ladies—"Did you do *these*?" "Oh, how utterly marvelous!"—and the young starving artist from the east was in, really in. He lived off the fat of the land, first in one fine house and then in another. Slightly over-plump but splendidly perfumed ladies slept with him. He moved about languidly and, when Pushells was outside at night, slipped him fine cigars through a window. And then Pushells appeared on the scene, playing almost himself—the great art critic—and, after seriously pondering Willard's pictures for several days, always with audience, pronounced them the work of a master, adding that one of the big museums in the east would be eager to buy them. But, of course, the Oakland Museum bought them first.

Now, Pushells informed us when he had finished his tale, they were heading north, to make Seattle the next recipient of their roguish offices. When they were gone, Nordi and I could only shake our heads in wonder at this strange combination of energy, talent, and decadence. We would speak of Pushells often in the years to come, but we were never to see him again.

It was August now, and I was twenty years old, and things in general were looking up. I received a nice increase in salary, President Harding died in the Palace Hotel, and Miss Crippin arrived at work with nothing under her skirt and blouse but her perfumed self—the only acknowledgement she ever gave, except in my arms, that she was aware of our relationship. Then one day my father received a telegram. His partner had died of a heart attack. Pop left for Portland and was soon back. They, the partner's widow and he, had decided to give up the California branch and operate entirely out of Portland, where they had just finished building a small plant. He offered me a job as salesman there, and said if I would stay one year he would make me sales manager. He offered me a good salary, but I decided to talk it over with Nordi before replying.

Nordi sat a long time staring out the window at fishboats coming in the Gate. "What is it you really want, Clyde?" she finally asked.

"Why you, of course, and to find out. Not to prove. It isn't that –," I stopped. "I'm stumped," I said.

She didn't laugh. I'd never seen her so serious. "How about your art, your career?" she asked.

I felt like a fool. "Nordi," I said, "I don't think that's enough. Life seems to reach out in every direction. I guess you'd say, I want to scatter myself uselessly."

"I didn't say it, Clyde, and you're wrong. I think maybe you have a bit of the eternal scholar in you."

"Don't say that, darling. You're trying to clothe my wandering mind with dignity."

"Well, what is it you don't want to be? Maybe we can come on it that way."

"Well, one thing I knew by the time I was sixteen. I wrote it down. I said I didn't ever want to catch myself simpering in the acclaim of however many mutts. I found it in the diary I unearthed from one of those boxes that came from Portland last week. Only I see it now as an unwholesome loathing of approbation."

"Maybe so," she said.

"Maybe it's growing up in the teachings of democracy, maybe reading James or Marx, or Tolstoy. However you consider me, or anyone for that matter, you see the result of many influences – excuse me for spouting, Nordi, but for myself I know I am not ready, perhaps never will be ready, to be only a ditch digger, only an intellectual, only a painter or sales executive. I've got to work with my hands and my back. I've got to be a mule and I've still got to be a mule as I take on a smidgen of intellectual detachment."

"You're raving."

"I'm trying to find out. Remember! And say, remember Catherine's brother. I've got to include that in my findings too."

"How about the sales manager job, Clyde?"

"I'll sit year after year at a desk. Sit, mind you, and in a suit and with a collar tight around my neck and always be inside away from the sun and the wind and the seasons."

"Would you do it for me?"

"Yes, yes I would—I will. I'll tell him in the morning."

"Not yet, Clyde. Let's think a bit more. Shall we go out for dinner?"

"How about The Progress? I'm starved."

So we went but were thoughtful as we ate, only communicating with smiles. When we were back in our room, Nordi got ready and slipped into bed. I came and sat on the bed beside her. She reached out and grasped my belt and started fumbling with the buckle, staring at it as if it were our problem, fiddling and jerking at it.

"Clyde," she said at last. "I think you're going to waste your life, at least by most standards. It's just a hunch, dear." She paused. "Anyway," she went on, "it's a swell idea. I don't want security. I think security steals something out of living. So you do what you want and I'll help you."

I wasn't surprised so much as relieved. We embraced and laughed and wondered what the future would bring. We found in our talking that we both had been appalled by the picture of me, an office worker, coming home in the evening to mow the lawn, while she had several batches of twins, joined some women's clubs, and we both would begin to compare ourselves to the Joneses.

My father took it well when I told him I was turning down his offer. We were lunching at Koppa's.

"You're not like me at all," he said, "but I still see your point. If you need help let me know."

I thanked him and told him of my pleasure in working for him. He was pleased it could be so but said nothing. He fiddled with a crumb on his plate for a while.

"Now that Forest Service flurry, what really happened there?" he asked presently.

I told him about it and when he at last, as he would say, "got the picture," he grinned at me. "Clyde," he said, "you're a fool. I'd say you're a damn fool, only how could I be so proud of a damn fool? We brought you up to be too ethical for your own good. Mrs.

Courtland is notorious down here for her escapades. I hear it around that the Senator is queer as hell. Married her for a front. It's even in the papers."

All that next week at work we packed and eventually got everything in boxes. And then Nordi disappeared. I came home one evening and she was gone. No note, nothing.

V

In Which
I Become A Deckhand,
Attempt Murder,
and
Attend To My Poison Oak
At The Symphony

◇   1924   ◇

In the evening she phoned. She said she was in Marin County and had a job.

"But you don't need a job," I reminded her.

"It hasn't been enough, Clyde. I can't sit around in San Francisco just posing. It isn't enough."

"What are you doing?" I asked.

"I won't tell you," she said, "but it's fun. I get board and room and good wages and I feel I'm useful, at least until you find what you're going to do. I miss you, but don't worry. I'll call you every night until you can come over here. Goodnight," she said, and hung up.

I was astounded. My darling had left me and was working. I knew not at what nor for whom nor just where. And the piquancy, that impishness—I felt it, though it wasn't in her words. Damn her! She was teasing me.

My father laughed when I told him next morning. "The first time I saw her," he said, "I took to her. She's got gumption. Give her her head, she'll come to no harm." His smile turned serious, "I'm leaving day after tomorrow and I want you and Miss Crippin to stay on for a month and handle whatever orders come in here, then send up those two barrels of vanilla extract and the rest. Those moving men will come over if you'll call them."

Once more we had a meal together. We said little. In spite of his early pressures on me and allowing the humility of looking for work with dripping pus and a mask, I loved him. He was my father and the bond was strong. We ate our steaks, drank our wine and both of us obviously savored the moment.

As she said she would, Nordi called that night. Her air now was purely mischievous. She said she was working near water and on terraces and that she enjoyed her work. She did say that she hoped we could find a way to live in that area, then with a lot of kisses into the phone, she hung up.

At the office we had a splurge of orders that cleaned out most of the stock and then gradually Miss Crippin's work tapered off to just forwarding the mail. For over a week we idled the hours away in each other's company. I was full of radical ideas, wanting to discuss books and the news of the day, the theater, a thousand things. None of it interested her, as she was involved with her religion, really trying to live up to its mores. Yet in spite of our differences, it was a wonderful time. It seems impossible but there it was. We really beamed at each other each morning. True, she never wore anything under her skirt, but that was the only concession. Her sexual need was in a logic-tight compartment that made her seem to have a dual personality, but that's not what I'm talking about. I'm talking about the companionship that's possible for people with no like interests that sometimes reaches the stage of great beauty, of complete openness, of steadfast warmth, when all signs show it to be patently impossible.

All this with my will-o'-the-wisp wife teasing me on the phone each night. At last the day came to ship the vanilla barrels and a small truckload of stock and then to lock the door on that period of my life. Miss Crippin came to me and gave me a friendly kiss. "Goodbye, Clyde," she said. "I have many happy days to remember and I will remember them." She went to the door, waved and was gone.

I went with the mover's truck to see the barrels stowed right on the boxcar. They were very special barrels, each with twelve hoops around fine varnished oak full of vanilla extract. When they were getting the barrels into the boxcar one slipped and caught one of the two men loading it between the steel edge of the boxcar and the barrel's edge. His fellow jumped out of the way. The man screamed. I went to help him, but instead of lowering it together as soon as I took hold and eased it away from him, he leaped clear and I was caught. I held it for a moment but neither man came to my assistance, so it slipped from my grasp, tearing off the whole tip and pad of my middle finger, the bone revealed. It was a shock. I got into a drugstore nearby and wrapped it in gauze, then covered it with adhesive tape and returned the keys of our loft to the owner. The finger throbbed all night.

Next morning I looked at the want ads but gave up. Until that finger was well and the bone covered I could not hold down a job. Nordi had given me a number to call in an emergency, so I called her and explained what had happened. She told me to take the ferry to Sausalito and from there to take the small ferry, the *Marin*, and to get off at Belvedere Landing where she'd be waiting for me.

She met me, quite concerned with my injury, and led me up a long gravel walk from the landing and a little way on a road and then down very steep stairs to a fairly large house on the water and finally to a room with its own outside door. We closed it and embraced. Now she was radiant. "Tell me," I said, and settled back to hear.

"Well," said Nordi, "even in a big house I'd have been bored, but in our one room—don't misunderstand—I loved it, but you left me there all day. I was desperate. Modeling, Clyde, you just stand or sit. I've always got to be busy, doing something. Like before our marriage when I went to art school or when I was a window dresser for a big department store in town or when I did tiny intricate pictures of lighting fixtures for a catalog. I was busy and I loved it. Don't you see? I had to do something, Clyde. So on the spur of the moment I answered an ad to be companion to an elderly lady. I came here and I liked Mrs. Bland at once. I work on the terraces while she cooks. Her terraces are a passion with her which I share. Of course, I've missed you terribly. Look around a bit while I get you something to eat."

It was beautiful. This was a new part of Marin County for us. The Bay over here had a shoreline of coves. To the east lay a long range of hills. The highest one beckoned me. Boats of many sorts were on the water and many large sailing yachts were anchored in the cove that this house fronted. That much I saw before Nordi brought us a lunch. She was so full of smiles, so impish, so beguiling that I forgave her desertion and the taking of a servant's position. She had taken the day off, so we left Belvedere and crossed a sandy spit on a road that took us to the town of Tiburon —the terminus of a railroad that ran north to the Redwood country. Here were a grocery, butcher shop, bootleg joint, and restaurant. The town also sported three small wharves where rowboats could be rented and motorboats hired for taxi service. Behind the town were the shops and storerooms and the main office of the railroad terminus.

The Tiburon Peninsula was a range of hills three to four miles long and a mile wide that jutted out into San Francisco Bay from the north. We rented a boat and I found out I could row easily with the injured finger sticking straight out. We went skirting the shores of various coves and in amongst the anchored sailing yachts. She begged me to look for rooms and to stay here until my finger healed and I could look for work. No matter how I pleaded she would not leave the old woman and come home, for, she said, "Until you have a good job, I'll not leave mine." Then she said, "What do you want to do, Clyde?"

"Anything," I answered, "with hard work and out of doors."

"Well," said Nordi, "you know no one will hire you to work with your hands until that bandage is off. Please go home and pack up and come over here. I heard there's a studio available down in the old building we passed at the foot of Belvedere."

The upshot was we walked over, found the realtor, and rented it. It had one big room with great windows to the north, a small dark room with a fireplace, and a bathroom. Nordi's excitement over the beauty of the area was infectious, and soon I also had succumbed to its charms.

As a resident of Marin County I looked around. The Tiburon Peninsula was once part of a vast Mexican land grant and most of it was now used by three big dairies as pasture. The ravines were full of bay and oak. Springs came to the surface just under the ridge in several places. I climbed the highest hill of the Peninsula and could look out to the Golden Gate and in other directions, to San Francisco, Berkeley, Oakland and Richmond and north toward Vallejo. Angel Island, directly south of the Peninsula, was a great hilly mass.

Raccoon Straits separated the Peninsula from Angel Island. Oil tankers used it when coming in the Gate bound for Richmond refineries. A few days of wandering and rowing up and down these straits and I knew I wanted to live there, but could I get work in the area? The working class, the blue shirts, either worked for the railroad, which employed over four hundred at its shops, or worked as gardeners, carpenters, stone masons or servants for the wealthy people of Belvedere, as did Nordi. My problem was to get her away from them. She had a powerful argument in that I couldn't work until the finger was healed. We had saved over a thousand dollars from the fine wages my father paid me. Still, the horror of looking for work, as I had done in San Francisco, was not to be forgotten, in spite of the fact that my shameful masked days were over.

A trucker in Tiburon agreed to go over with me to bring our things back. This he did for a small sum and I was set. I spent several days sketching, but that was no longer enough, so I hunted up Nordi's Mrs. Bland. We thoroughly disliked each other on sight. I knew she had inherited her wealth and handled it well, and such people's swagger and certainty always seemed cheap to me. From her side of the fence, I was a silly art student, whose wife had left him to seek menial work. All religious people seem hopeless propagandists and when she sought to make a Christian Scientist of me I told her that because my mother had died of it, I myself loathed the religion. Man, how that woman could bridle!

Then I told her of my problem. I would not be able to hold down a job for another month, but that I could use my hands for certain work. I wanted to be near my wife while incapacitated, so I'd make it worth her while. Nordi would live with me, work for her eight hours a day and I would gather driftwood logs and saw them up for her winter fuel and it wouldn't cost her a damn dime. She was plenty annoyed but agreed. On her small wharf she had two flat-bottom rowboats, and on the west and uninhabited side of Belvedere I found the driftwood logs I was seeking. I towed them back with the rowboat—a tedious chore, but using the tide, I got around the point and, finally on a high tide, up in the little space walled from the cove. With the experience in getting Grandma's wood at home and with lots of elbow grease and a sharp saw I was soon at it and it wasn't long before I had all the wood she could use for several years, neatly split and stacked. The finger was still sore in its cocoon of bandage. Why I thought the tip of my finger would grow back I don't know, but I never doubted it. And, as it was still sore, I didn't take off the bandage.

I asked her what else she had to do. She told me of a plan she had had for many years. She wanted to make a wall into the water of the cove that would surround an area big enough for a swimming pool. Stone masons could make the foundation at extremely low tides and then, working at low tide, raise the wall higher and higher until it was above the surface of the cove. With gates or gate valves she could fill her pool and the water in it would be warm, taking the heat of the sun until it was much warmer than the cold water of the Bay. The problem was she had no rock to build with. She left it at that. I looked around to see what could be done about it.

Belvedere Point, the southern terminus of Belvedere, juts out into Raccoon Straits and catches the full force of the tide. There are tidal rocks off the point, and about two hundred yards out from them, a great bell buoy clangs in the tide. Between tide rips it is dangerous to small boats. There were plenty of the right-sized rocks where I had gotten the driftwood logs on the western side of the island. I saw that I could go around the point, load the two boats with rock and come back only by working carefully with the tides. But as time meant little to me then, I was able to handle it. By working early and late I could make two round trips with the two boats, which would net me over a ton of rocks a day. Loaded almost to sinking, rowing one and towing the other, I would labor along rowing hard, the boats hardly moving, battle the currents at the point and on up the other side, unload, grab a bite and head back. Why did I do it? I guess I needed something to identify with. Without steady employment, I felt sketching was loitering, but on the windy days when a big chop made garnering the rocks impossible I got out my paints and headed for the hills. And what I produced annoyed me.

California is a country to explain with posters—a big, bang-biff arrangement of values. I loved to look at it, but to paint it brought out a nameless sullen quality in me that ruined each painting. The poster concept should have worked, for I believed then that one should paint with a hammer, but I didn't, so I agonized over my paintings as the strong wind churned the grass and leaves about me. Next morning I'd be out at four, catching the right tide so I could load up and come around the point with the current carrying me on my way into the cove. Those rock-scrounging trips of leaden movement pleased me many times more than my sketching. One afternoon a rough heavy rock I was carrying snagged my bandage off as I tripped and dropped it. My finger looked like a mummy's—deadly white and wrinkled and smelling horribly of rottenness. My upbringing had been calculatedly deficient about the care of the body, which in our religion was always treated as if it weren't there. The flesh, however, had grown back covering the bone with the usual pad. Realizing from the smell (I don't know how I escaped gangrene) that the bandage was the wrong treatment, I left it off and soon the sun dried and colored it until it was normal. And after several days of using it carefully, I realized that I could now look for work.

I got the most unskilled job in the railroad yards. I worked in the bullgang. We piled ties, rolled boxcar wheels out of gondolas, dug holes, filled holes. We were the bullgang, one step below mules. How I enjoyed it! At first. Here was the bottom that I had yearned for. Here I expected to find what basic man was like. This was to give me a picture of the animal man in the lowest fringe— early twentieth century culture, USA. I wanted to be at one with the guy Marx and Rousseau talked about. I found at the bottom you were paid less, worked harder, did more dirty and dangerous jobs than those one step up. I began to get the swing of it, but there was no excellence. We dragged through our work.

When I was a small boy, a water main was laid down our street. The ditchdiggers were small, dark men from southern Italy— immigrants. Their eyes and gold earrings shone down in the depths they dug. The value they put in their work was architectural. They made a fine thing out of digging a ditch and took great pride in it. I told my mother and father I wanted to be a ditchdigger. "A son of mine wanting to be a ditchdigger, like a dago?" said my father with disgust. But I never will forget the excellence of their work.

Now, looking for that quality in the bullgang, I was shocked. We Americans have been taught that hard work is demeaning and there are always immigrants arriving to do it for us. As a result we Americans in the bullgang felt degraded and dragged around like zombies. We worked for the Stores Department and one day the head of that department, a Mr. Beavers, got all his people together, even our bullgang, and we had a rally. He made a speech. It was such a speech as I had made in high school, voicing all the inaccurate, one-sided, self-righteous sentiments, hiding the sad side of it with humbug. Pep talks, they were called. The superintendent had been taking elocution—that was obvious. I got up to leave. He stopped orating and asked me why I was leaving. I said I couldn't stand pep talks. He said, "If you leave you're fired!" I thought a moment then began moving away. "It's worth it," I told him.

Next day I applied for a deckhand job on the ferries that the railroad ran between Sausalito and San Francisco.

Mr. Wasser, the port engineer, asked me a few questions, and then said, "What's this rumpus you had over at the storerooms with Beavers?"

"When I work for somebody," I said, "I give them their money's worth and then some, but I don't like to be harangued about it."

"We'll see about that," Wasser said. "But why did you quit?"

"I don't know," I answered. "I didn't mind his talk so much, but he waved his arms around a lot. Somebody's been teaching him the gesture business and he ought to go back and take some more lessons."

Mr. Wasser, a man of essential and unobtrusive dignity, grinned and had to look away and fondle his mustache. "Yes," he said, "I don't go for pep talks much either," and he hired me. "Start tomorrow on the *Sausalito*. She'll be tied up here for repairs. Bring old clothes; it's a greasy job."

Greasy or not, it was a job, and Nordi and I were delighted. The next morning found me climbing down the steel ladder with Mr. Wasser to the dark engine room of the *Sausalito*, where several extension cords lit the gloom. Five men stood waist-deep below the floor plates working on a black piece of machinery—a fuel pump, Mr. Wasser said. They glared at me, as I was brought to help them and to be rather cuffed around. Among them were the chief engineer of the *Sausalito*, Ed Creighton, and Al Tuckey, chief engineer of the big *Eureka*. We worked along removing steam and oil lines, unbolting the pump from its bed. Chief Creighton was slowly removing the steam line in a way that seemed wrong to me.

"Here, let me have that," I said, and shouldered in and removed it in another way that I had seen would work. I had the piece in my hand now and asked Wasser where he wanted it. I laid it there and looked up. Both the chiefs were standing there glaring at me with actual astonishment in their eyes. They looked at Wasser, expecting him to put me in my place or fire me, but Wasser didn't. Instead he said, "Now the oil lines," and before the others could respond I grabbed a wrench the other chief had been using and attacked the line. I soon had it off, but not, I learned afterwards, in the prescribed manner. Now we had to get the little monster out of the engine room and up on deck where it could be hauled away to the shops. This was done with a chain tackle, new to me, but easy to understand and operate. With a chain tackle we hauled the pump off its bed. I began to see how we would haul it out with two tackles, then I had an idea. I asked Wasser if they had another chain tackle. It was out on the dock, he said. I ran to get it and soon had the three placed strategically, for I saw how the chiefs would do it and I saw that another way would be much faster. I was quick and very enthusiastic. Before the shocked chiefs could lend a hand I was moving the pump through the cramped areas of the engine room, up and down and over equipment, then up, hanging the third tackle at an odd angle. A little pulling and slacking and the pump was out. The engineers were indignant—a pipsqueak trying to run things. They looked to Wasser to lower the boom on me but Wasser stood rubbing his chin, caressing his mustache, and then said to no one in particular that the job had been done in less than half the time it usually took, and after giving me orders to clean up the paint locker and coil down some lines, he left. Later, I was to learn how important hierarchy is to any group effort. It reached its peak in the navy and the great sailing ships in their eternal battle with wind and sea. From them, the tradition of hierarchy was carried to steamers and finally even to ferries like ours that plodded back and forth across San Francisco Bay. As for me, I got away with what I did because I didn't know better and because Mr. Wasser, the port engineer, had a quiet sense of humor.

The next days were not eventful, but soon one of the deckhands on the *Eureka* hurt his hand and I took his place. I came aboard and stood by the gangplank with the others. The second mate whistled and we hurried out to a string of baggage trucks being loaded onto the ferry from a train that had just arrived from up north. These were placed on the port side of the ferry with the tongue of each truck chained to the rear of the one ahead of it, like elephants in a circus parade. Then the waiting automobiles were allowed to fill up the starboard side, with the passengers streaming in along with the cars.

They walked down the great gangway of the ferry slip, six and eight abreast. There was an infinite difference in them, and yet a sameness effected by the prevailing style of body concealment. They were hurried and animated, though around this moving band were no drivers with whips, no dogs, no arrogants on horses. No Judas goats led them, no siren beckoned. Yet all this was there and more as the dapper men and jaunty women moved briskly down the gangway and—concealed in clothing, deodorants and attitude —stepped to the deck of the ferry for the 7:15 a.m. trip to San Francisco.

The big gate banged down and stragglers scurried aboard as the massive, uniformed officer, whose other duty was to bellow the euphony or dissonance of the names of towns and stations up the rails, waddled impressively down to where we deckhands were lifting the heavy apron of the gangway. Into his eyes came a combative gleam. "Who looks upon me sees a man," he seemed to announce as he searched out men's eyes among the passengers on deck. Then he stepped on the lever of the apron's counter-balance and his near three hundred pounds of lard brought the apron up off the deck.

The deckhands cast off the lines. The seagulls on the pilings winced at the whistle's blast. Great paddle wheels began chopping the water to froth and out of the slip moved the *Eureka*, biggest ferry on the bay. Those seagulls that had so silently stood at attention on one leg as the brisk parade marched past their pilings took to the air with rasping cries and sailed over the stern, where old John, famous among all dishwashers for his heroic bouts with canned heat, would soon dump overboard the garbage from the ferry's restaurant.

The *Eureka*'s big engine turned a huge double crank and, by means of this, the paddle wheels. The sounds and visual movement of this simple, massive mechanism was a rich knowledge to each man among the commuters. It was one of those few things they really knew in this world of indirection, of complicated cams and gears, of completely enclosed machination. They knew, deep and bone-satisfyingly, how and why they got to Frisco. The throb of the forced draft in the smokestack, the slow, rhythmic pound of strokes in the big cylinders, bit secretly and deep into each man's hidden reaches and, touching that which was purely him, broke the streaming cobwebs of herd concept, the twining but brittle filaments of convention. And free, the man's heart rode the rhythms of the engine far from the water-crawling, time-tied thing, the *Eureka*.

On the windy bow and on the forward saloon deck strode the deep breathers, singly and in pairs. They walked back and forth from port side to starboard, from starboard to port, and on the drafty stern the same vigorous thwartship promenaders were always on the march. While on the lower deck, up and down the broad roadways that ran the length of the enclosed part of the ferry, walked the men who did not care for the buffeting of wind and yet who needed a daily constitutional. And all of these found that, in spite of themselves, their marching always became involved with the beat of the engines. It was often said that, had the exercising passengers been put on a giant treadmill geared to the paddle wheels, the engines could have been removed and the boat would still have beaten her own time to Frisco by six minutes.

To protect myself from their amazing singularity I often saw the passengers as a mob, for if I looked closely I became too involved, too scattered of my force, almost bewildered by the welter of impressions I drew from their faces. Guessing back to the why and how of it, compassion would grip me more often than assurance, for travail marks deeper on a face than happiness. We humans are equipped to make surmises of the faces of those who pass us by, as a matter of necessity, but too much reading of philosophy and the budding psychology made me ponder far too much those locked in with me by the Bay as we plowed toward Frisco.

When I first became a deckhand I was twenty-one. The year was 1924. The flapper reigned. Women's dresses were rather short. Their shoes were blunt and high heeled, but the heels were ugly and gave their walk a rather stumbly effect. They had strapped down all evidence of breasts and the straight lines of their dresses hid their hips. The whole posture was hard on women. And the men, well, they toddled! Men's pants were very full, pressed to a sharp crease in front that almost covered the tips of their shoes. They seemed unaware of how terribly encumbering their trousers appeared. Standing in these immense tubes, men had no legs as women had no breasts, and when they walked, the mechanics of walking was wholly hidden. They just toddled along, while, alongside them, with legs bared to the knee, the girls galumphed on their heels unattractively. Then suddenly the men discarded cigarettes and all smoked small-bowled, thin-stemmed pipes. They would come down the gangway and, instead of going into the seats, would stand around on the deck perched, it seemed, on their tubes while caressing small neat mustaches, their graceful little pipes between their teeth, standing like men's clothing dummies while the girls stumbled by walking sort of behind their legs more than on them and wearing felt helmets, closefitting and protecting the back of the neck closely as if felt could ward off a blackguard's cutlass. And the music! "Jotta, jotta, she had a little jing, jing, jing." Anyway that was the way the hep Irishmen on our crew sang it, and for me it was the anthem of the rather unattractive pageantry of that time. And then, unobtrusively a waft of fashion came from another direction. Women's dresses changed, the skirts were a little longer and molded to their hips. The hats were still soft helmets but had become little flashes of bright color, and many colors accented the skirts and bodices and there was again a vague hint that women had breasts. Now they walked almost demurely— almost, I say, for they articulated the hips slightly, more than was necessary. Still they seemed creatures of the downcast eye— graceful, Dickensian creatures—many of whom wore the perfume of that opulent lady, Miss Crippin.

One day I was standing on the stern I guard where law demanded against careless children and suicides. It was the 5:15 trip out of San Francisco. A few passengers walked back and forth, thwartship, on the afterdeck. Eventually they began to leave until only one, a very large Chinese, was left with me on the stern. He was dressed in black silk and wore their strange shoes, but did not shuffle in them as they do. He was carrying a small basket of fruits that were brilliant vermillion. I watched him as he strode up and down, a tall, muscular, very vital shave-headed Chinese, wolfing the fruits. He saw me eyeing them and held out the basket to me. I took one—a very large ripe persimmon. I ate it with relish as he was doing, threw the bright skin over the rail as he did and thanked him. He shook his head that he didn't understand and proffered the basket again with a great grin. We each took one and devoured it. We were passing Alcatraz. He waved toward it most grandly and laughed a great buoyant laugh. I tried to work up a duplicate. He waved to the receding city and we laughed. He reached in his basket and took out the last persimmon. I shook my head refusing the last one. He hefted it in his palm a moment, then threw it far over the water and beamed at me. He was such a thing of exuberance and such a finely clothed animal, his innate ferocity somnolent. The gusto of his devouring, his stride, his laughter and the giving of his companionship are still brilliant in my mind. I asked where he came from, pointing to him. "Mongolia," he said and shouted with laughter. I had to leave for other duties, as my relief deckhand approached. He waved to me as he left the boat in the crowd. How long ago, and yet he comes before my eyes with his basket of persimmons. The vermillion of the fruit transfers to the lining of a cape he seems to wear, breeze-flecked so I can see, though I know he wore none when I saw him. Maybe I put the cape on him as an honor from the dim recesses of my psyche. What a marvelous thing one of our species can be who, towering over the norm, can laugh with abandon in our mob presence at some Promethean joke we others fail to see. It breaks down our tightening boundaries for a moment before convention, at our own acquiescence, begins hauling the ropes and the fences a little bit tighter, and though we find it almost insufferable we smile at one another and speak of our sense of community.

Well, I paid my dues and became a member of the union in good standing, but to become a member of the crew was another thing. The captains and the mates on the ferries were Scandinavians, the deckhands, Portuguese from the Azores, with an Irishman or a Swede for seasoning, and once in a while an American down on his luck. So I was, from the crew's standpoint, terribly out of place, but learning from them, I was soon adept with the big ropes at midnight tie-up in the dolphins and a year later was number one deckhand by crew acclaim. I grew to think as a Portuguese, talked their terrible English and was pretty well accepted as a paisano.

At each end of our short voyage we worked at a run, straining at trucks of freight up or down steep gangways and then stood on each side of the gangway's lip bathed in our sweat as the passengers came aboard. Underway, I rolled open the heavy forward doors for passengers. In this position I watched Alcatraz come abreast in the ever-changing light and then looked on toward Sausalito, nestled in the hills of the Marin shore. Often on an evening trip as we brought the commuters back from a hard day in the city, a fog bank would mount the seaward Marin hills and come creeping over their summits above Sausalito. Like a great hand it would materialize on that high horizon and slowly reach down for the town. The passengers, staring out at it, were, I'm sure, as I was, struck with our puniness and with mystery and wonder. Often I saw people cross themselves. When we arrived at Sausalito that reaching hand of fog would have moved down and engulfed the town so that sounds were muted. The streets subtly darkened and in a hushed way the passengers disembarked and hurried to the train anxious to be at home amongst small familiars, away from wonder and a certain unease at the vast airs that the wind and sea could force upon the land.

Deckhand on a ferry boat! How uninteresting, how demeaning, how boring. Not at all. An unthinking laborer receiving poor wages? Yes and no. There were all manner of people to observe, many I soon counted as friends, who came to me at the forward door each day for conversation and laughter. Demeaning, some of it, sure, but I didn't want to be one of those who avoid the ugly aspects of our civilization. I wanted to relate to it all and I enjoyed physical work more than physical games. I knew I was useful. I worked like a mule and loved it. Thousands of people surged around me each day. A hundred beautiful women passed me by. Many old and infirm received my help. Children and tourists asked endless questions, and the ferry and I tasted a thousand changes in the weathers of the Bay.

Sometimes tule fog would come down from the deltas of the

San Joaquin and Sacramento. We would ask the passengers to leave the bow as we crept toward San Francisco, but I would be out there with the mate staring into the gray blot of it. Under us, we could hear the hiss of our bow parting the water. Alcatraz' whistle would be ahead and to port, while astern of us, bellowing its way, a too-fast-moving oceanliner, free of the Gate, would move up on us. A tug with one barge astern would signal its condition with a long and two short blasts of the whistle, while one of our own ferries, the *Casadero*, would signal it wanted to pass us to port as it neared. There were more signals as we moved slowly along. Fishboats appeared beside us with mouth-blown foghorns. We would run into a riffle, the bow wave of a vessel not signalling its presence—probably a rumrunner stealing in to unload beneath some fogshrouded wharf. Suddenly the oncoming signals of the liner would be too close. We would drift, listening with open mouths hungry for the message. It would come from above us and out of the fog a towering bow would cut the water and the ship's great side would pass not fifty feet away as our paddlewheel swept us astern and our skipper howled abuse at the ship's pilot high on his bridge. On we'd creep and eventually, with horns and bells and whistles all about, each telling its story, we would ease into our slip, and so would end the six-forty-five trip to San Francisco.

At length, Nordi became fed up with Mrs. Bland's brand of religious cant and quit her green thumb job there. The studio seemed inadequate, so we rented one of the houseboats, then called arks, that had been dragged above the high-water mark of the salt lagoon. It was only partly furnished, but with what we had it was comfortable and pleasant.

On my days off, Nordi and I wandered the hills or rented a boat and rowed across our side of the Straits. We became slightly acquainted with an Englishman who made his living with his pen. Adventure fiction was his niche, but we found him one day at his diggings broke and without food, so we asked him to join us in the ark. We figured we'd like a writer in the house; I myself hoped to write someday if it didn't interfere too much with life. So over he came to tutor me for board and room. The tutoring never happened; I was much too busy to sit still for that.

His name was Fitch. He was a middle-sized, middle-aged fellow with crew-cut gray hair, a small mustache and the harried air of one beset by weighty problems that bordered on being insurmountable. We found he'd once run a trading post in Africa and that he'd been trying to make a living writing about it ever since. He wrote with a lot of bwanas and cobras and leopards and witch doctors, about fierce natives and doe-eyed Nubian virgins, about fever and gin fighting for a man's body and soul, about the letter from home that never came and how this fellow had a very stiff upper lip beneath his crisp mustache, and about when a native uprising destroyed the post. Or when a letter did arrive from home stating that his baby sister, because of an inevitable change of calibre, had been thrown out of a London brothel where she had worked for years, or when an Italian scientist had invented a plastic billiard ball that would threaten the ivory market. Fitch's trader would mutter, "Gad, what a day!" and pour himself two fingers of gin and call for his pipe. The editors of the pulp magazines he wrote for railed at him that he wrote only one story and badgered him to write something different—how about fierce maidens and doe-eyed warriors? But Fitch just couldn't bring himself to do that, so he went broke instead and, with a somewhat limp upper lip, wept on our shoulders—more on Nordi's than on mine.

Our other free boarder was named Pete. He had a room somewhere and ate breakfast in the local restaurant, but Nordi put up his lunch for work and he had dinner with us and was always to be found at the ark if he wasn't sleeping or working. He was a squat, tubby guy, gray hair scant over a round head and with the expression of one who dealt perhaps in cabbages. Wasser had hired us both the same day, and Pete immediately began sizing me up. When I told him that my last job was in extracts and flavors, a look of disgust took over his face, but he quickly put it away and asked if I had "the makings." When I handed him my cigarettes, the look of unyielding disgust appeared again. "Tailor mades, eh? Say, ain't we fancy," he said as he took one and held it strangely, not as the Chinese do, but as if it were Sunday. Still, we worked together and I became entangled in his lore of sailing ships and of the sea. He taught me the knots the sailing ship man uses, beating me with the rope end as I tied them, so I would be able to tie them under stress of storm. He told endless tales of the lost world of tall ships, of calms and storms and mutiny, of falling spars. He told of the great voyages made across the Pacific and the Atlantic, of the Horn and the China Sea. He had a packet of items cut from the newspapers of London, Sidney and of Sao Paulo to substantiate his claims. I could not get enough of his stories, and as I say, he soon lived with us in the ark except for sleeping.

Fitch and Pete took a very dim view of each other. They adored Nordi and she took them under her wing. We ate well, though how we did it on a deckhand's pay I can't understand.

Pete and Fitch were both ardent sports fishermen, but having no boat they fished from the bridge at the entrance of the salt lagoon. There they fished with many others for striped bass—the noble fish of the area. A Portuguese had shown me how to spear silver perch at very low tide around the pilings of the dock when the perch could be seen eating the weed and such from the encrusted piling. They were often sixteen inches long and over half as broad—a fine, meaty fish. I could spear half a dozen of them in an hour. The local fable about them was that only degenerates or very base people would eat them, for they were deemed unclean. The condition that made them so, or so the story went, was that they bore their young rather than lay eggs as a proper fish did. Unclean, unclean! Now I was and am a very naive person, but I am not, nor was I ever, exactly provincial, so I speared the fish, put them in a gunnysack and carried them across the bridge, where our guests, with others of their kind, were intent on hooking the splendid striper. No one would see me, as I crossed the bridge with my gunnysack of fish, for each man would suddenly be intensely interested in the tip of his pole. Two hours later Fitch and Pete would be at our table eating Nordi's stuffed perch, flavored with garlic and spices, baked in a paper bag, a food for the gods. This tickled us as phony, but we never spoke of it, for we enjoyed their inconsistency as much as their wisdom. Fitch, the Englishman, removed the bones from his mouth, delicately, daintily behind his napkin and with haughty disdain looked the other way as old Pete spat them out on the tablecloth in a rim around his plate and glared at Fitch for foppishness.

I bought an old round-bottomed boat of some sixteen feet and decked it over for a sailboat. I put a keel under it and made a rudder and hung it on its stern. Then, planing a long time, I made a mast from a four-by-four of pine. I was working twelve-hour shifts on the *Eureka*. I'd come home feeling pretty weary but my darling would feed me a big breakfast and put on a record of Richard Strauss' *Don Juan* and we'd wind up the old Victrola and let fly with beauty. It would revive me. My ego refurbished, I'd work on the boat for several hours before Nordi led me to bed. I still looked like an adolescent but was twenty-one and enjoying myself immensely.

Nordi became acquainted with the woman in the ark next to us. She had been tutor to the king of Italy for many years and was full of knowledge about the world and food—Italian food. Soon Nordi was feeding us very spicy dishes. The smell of olive oil and garlic was in the house and was very fine.

The tutor lady's husband was one of the most genial persons I've met—a man of wide experience, a puffer of pipes, an absorber of sunlight, a taster of breezes and a connoisseur of lounging. He worked for a big interior decorator outfit who paid him good wages to drill tiny holes in sound furniture to give them a worm-eaten ancient look. "You gotta drill 'em deep. They stick needles down 'em," he said. "You gotta drill the underside and everything —that's for the shrewd ones who make their little inspections asking to see the sofa or chair upside down. They see those little worm holes I've drilled there just for them and, satisfied, pay double and triple." I can't remember his name, but to his wife he was always Gimlet. "You know," he smiled, "the tool I bore the little holes with." It was fine, really splendid, to sit with him out on a small dock he had on the lagoon. He made little throw nets that he sent to a brother in Italy, who sent them back to America as foreign—for a better price. With my work done for the day, I'd sit with him out on his dock and he'd tell me about Algiers or the marshes on the lower Danube or Paraguay. I never smoked when I was with him—the rich, drifting smoke of his pipe was fragrance enough. I'd be sitting on the old driftwood planks of his dock, my legs flat out before me, my back against a post. The sun would beat down through my trousers so my legs felt they were in direct sunlight. His short blunt fingers would be busy with the twine as the smoke from his pipe drifted down to me where I stared at the lapping waters of the lagoon or at my feet or the sky, hearing his story as if he were telling it to someone else, soaking up the sun, half dazed with contentment, full of the most lazy regard of the world about. How utterly good life was in those days!

About this time I got a six-month run on the *Tamalpais*, my favorite ferry. The one problem on the *Tamalpais* was the second mate, Flounderfoot Hansen. Flounderfoot was a Norwegian from San Francisco who, for reasons unknown to me to this day, took an instant dislike to me. Perhaps I was too eager, too innocent, too young. He began complaining about my work and, when I strove to conform to his standards, followed up with insults, unwarranted dressings down in front of the passengers, and finally profanity against my mother. It was then that I warned him. I wasn't about to give up the job; I was just where I wanted to be at that time in my life. But real hate began to grow in my heart. It was so completely unfair, for I was an excellent deckhand. Often he brought tears to my eyes, but I knew that if I knocked him down I would be fired. So, when he kept it up, I went to him again. "I warn you again," I said. "Cut it out. I won't warn you after this." He laughed at me, so I decided to kill him and be rid of him, but in such a way that no one would ever be wise. After much thought, I found a way.

At the time of which I speak, we unloaded the big stuff with a jitney—a small tractor that hauled the long lines of baggage and freight trucks down the road that ran inside the length of the ferry building. Other ferries were landing from Oakland and Richmond at the same time on this particular trip, but we always landed a bit ahead of them. When the driver of the jitney stopped short to let the passengers from the Oakland ferry march across in front of him, there was always a place where the press of trucks coming down the steep gangway slammed into those already on the roadway. The result was a loud crash, but the trucks were constructed for this with a heavy metal overlay at the corners. I noticed that where this happened could not be observed from the ferry, nor by the crew, who were always on the opposite side of the lined trucks. It was there that I decided to kill Flounderfoot Hansen. I would grab him where he stood—always near this point—and thrust him in the space between the trucks the moment before impact. He would be crushed to death the next instant. That particular day, he outdid himself in abuse, but I laughed. In a few moments he would be Norwegian carrion. It all worked like clockwork. I was there on the split second and, grabbing him, shoved him in and held him there.

It is a truism of my life that my failures always help me, save me, while most of my positive ventures fail—usually (but not always) from incongruous accident. On this day, of all days, the Oakland ferry was late and the line of trucks didn't stop, but went on without mishap. In my hands, Flounderfoot turned wild eyes on me. "You tried to kill me," he screamed as I jerked him out and let him go.

"Where's your witnesses?" I asked. He looked around and saw we were alone.

"You tried to kill me," he said again in frightened tones.

"I warned you twice," I said. "You've been asking for it for weeks. Report me if you want, no one will believe you."

"You tried to kill—" he started to say, but I cut him off.

"Next move is yours," I said, and left him to get the mail truck on board.

Flounderfoot never reported me. Nor did he find fault with my work after that, though once in a while our eyes would meet and it was a cold perusal that I gave him in those momentary contacts. He grew thinner. One day he didn't turn up. He was on sick leave for two weeks, and when he came back I treated him like an old companion and, finding he was a collector of stone, brought him a piece of highly colored quartz that is found only on the Tiburon Peninsula and in Japan.

Sometimes the Bay would be a mirror, and Alcatraz an enchanted isle. Sometimes the swells from the seas of some forgotten storm swept through the Gate and made a big surf on Angel Island and on Alcatraz' stony shore. Sometimes on the 5:15 from Sausalito we came along past the many docks in the stench of the sewage of the city that an ongoing tide was carrying to sea. Then the water would be bronze with it, bronze in the early morning light, and one forgot the stench and marveled at the beauty of it.

I was a laborer, a mopper of vomit, a scourer of toilets. My companions in work were illiterate, religious and superstitious, and rather tricky, but somehow I felt at home with them, for we were doing something very simple and very useful. Lifting the apron of the gangway was a heavy chore, and as we strained at its ironwood and oak we always muttered in unison, "Viva la Figa!" ("Hurrah for woman's sexual organ!") It put more force into our lifting, and for years no gangplank was lifted without this inspiring phrase. Then one day a nun, who was herding sweet young Italian girls from some seminary in the hills to their homes in San Francisco, overheard our grunted salute to nether parts and informed the presidents of the several railroads that owned the ferries. Orders came down from on high, denouncing the mentioning of that lush place in unison, and also requesting us to wear neckties. How they got neckties related to that locale of joy I don't know—some puritan executive, I guess, vicariously throttling us for our hoarse reminiscing of pleasures.

Late one Sunday evening when the crowds had thinned I was standing at the forward door when a bundle was laid down at my feet and the man accompanying it said, "Will you open that door just a crack? It's stuffy in here." I complied and then noticed that the bundle was alive, the eyes staring up at me. I gasped. "I'm a doctor," the man said. "She just had both legs cut off by the wheels of the train. They stopped too late."

"But she'll live," I said.

"No," the doctor said. "She'll never live to see Frisco."

"You shouldn't say that in front of her," I said angrily.

"It doesn't matter. She's in shock," he answered, "and I gave her a shot."

"But she mustn't die," I said. He looked me over almost sneeringly. "Too late," he said. "She'll die before I can get her off this boat."

"She must live," I said. I knelt down by her. "You're going to live," I said. "I am a healer and I will not let you die. Do you hear me?" I waited. Finally she slowly blinked her eyes. "Fine," I said. "Now listen. All through this night you've got to hang on. Don't let go and I'll be with you hanging on too. Everything that I am will be with you and we won't give up and when morning comes you can rest, for you will have won. There will be difficult days ahead but all that I am will be with you. Every moment that I can I'll pour it out to you. Do you understand?"

Slowly she blinked. I wiped the sweat from her forehead with all the hope and love there is in us humans. I don't know what it is, sometimes it's just not there; other times, like this, it flows from the strong to the weakened by whatever reason.

The doctor spoke up. "You said nothing about God!"

"I'm an agnostic," I answered. Then I added, "God, if you are and if you love humans, help her to keep living, God, as I am trying to do."

The girl was looking at me. I said, "Together." She blinked at me so slowly, but she did. "We'll win," I said. She seemed very sleepy, but finally she blinked her eyes once more.

The doctor said, "You're nuts!" When I didn't reply, he spoke louder. "I said I think you're nuts!" But I was being with her, conceiving of my vitality pouring into her and giving her strength. Though there were many people on board, no one came within fifty feet of us, nor did any of the crew come up.

We soon reached the ferry building and I went on about my duties, though in my mind I was with the girl. Soon we were under way again, and near where she had lain I saw a big drop of blood. I fainted. When I came to, the crew, laughing rather sheepishly about my hovering over her like a long-lost brother, asked why I fainted over a single drop of blood. Old Bony, an ancient Swede whom the rest of the crew teased but respected, came up. "Leave him alone, you bastards," he said. "He was in there pitchin'." And we all went off to our stations.

Four days later the doctor, commuting to San Francisco as usual, stopped by my door. "She lived," he said. "She's over the hump." He looked me over. "You're a healer," he announced. "Why, you could make a mint. You're wasting yourself here."

"No, I'm not," I answered. "I help people across the Bay."

He sneered and left. He must have moved soon after that, for I never saw him again. I didn't know how much of what I'd done was a matter of psychology or how much was the moving of energy across conventional boundaries. I thought of going to the girl, but I didn't know her name and no message had come from her. I wondered, but did nothing about it.

We wanted to make a garden. Nordi wanted to have green peas

and beans and all that could be grown locally. In our wanderings we came upon an old dilapidated house—the home of a recluse around which was a bit of cleared soil. We made several visits before we found the owner, a small wiry man with a bulbous head and a very furtive, frightened air. I had seen him on the *Marin* often. His name was Smithy and he lived on bananas and filet of sole. Because we loved people it wasn't long before we added the third old man to our entourage. Smithy lived in a decrepit house on the extreme northern end of Belvedere. The land belonged to the country club. He was given to understand that he guarded that uninhabited end of the island, though from what was never clear—mating velocipedes perhaps. He stuttered in talking but not in singing. We found him to be honest, bright in many ways, fond of music, a reader of sorts and full of somewhat funny jokes that he stuttered out, always blunting the point. I do this unfortunate thing too, so from the start I felt close to him. A garden seemed good to him and he pointed out an ancient well. So we spaded up the loose rich soil—actually an Indian shell mound—around the well and watered the eventual garden with water that we hand-over-handed up forty feet in a wooden bucket. About every fourth day we would walk down to work on our garden and visit Smithy.

Anyone who lives on tidal water is fascinated by what the tides bring to his door. A great deal of driftwood came on Smithy's beach—boards and boxes and old grapefruit halves and dead seals too, but Smithy only searched among this stuff for moldings, the decorative straight pieces that finished a room or a doorway. He looked everywhere for this. It was the first thing he spoke of when we met.

"Hi, Smithy! How's it going?"

"I f-f-found a m-m-molding." Or on other days, "J-just b-boards today." He had quite a pile of molding under the house. He would offer us a banana and then turn his dark sunburnt back to us while he slipped the very filthy straps of his little accordion over his shoulders. When they were set right he would strike a frowsy chord, look over his shoulder toward us, but not quite at us, and say "Mother Macree" and, playing badly and singing somewhat like the tune, he would regale us for a quarter of an hour, announcing each song before he sang it. Oh, it was a formal occasion. He faced his back most directly at us and sang while the sunlight coming in a broken window picked out his cot with its bedding of many old overcoats. He brightened up with our persistent company and told us of his past. In England he had been a patternmaker, then in this country an accountant, and, last, he had helped on the local garbage truck, where he had picked up his overcoats.

Fitch and old Pete, while they hated each other, joined in disliking Smithy. A simpleton, a nut, they said. Pete had made sails for my boat and though they were constructed with all the craftsmanship and strength for great emergencies, they were far too heavy for the usual light airs. Still in a good breeze we bowled along. On my days off we sailed around Belvedere Point and north up the inhabited side of it until we reached Smithy's, where we would work in the garden or strip and lie in the sun. We were becoming more and more interested in the fishboats of the Bay and from what I heard and saw I thought it would be a very good life for Nordi and me if I owned a stout boat and trolled for salmon up around Shelter Cove. Every chance I got I would hang around the shops of the several boatbuilders of the region trying to learn by watching, fascinated by the simple arrangement of, say, a forty-footer, of the shaping of the keel, the chamfering of the timbers of the stem and stern, and the steaming and bending of the oak ribs. Just looking, seeing how everything was fitted together, the craft of it all, caused in me a delight akin to that found in listening to great music.

Smithy, Nordi and I often sunbathed between the two rocky promontories on Belvedere's west side. These abutments of the island kept the prevailing wind off the beach. Once, on my day off, Nordi and I rowed down to it only to find a fishboat anchored there. The crew were laying out a net attached to the beach. I offered to lend a hand to the two young fellows who were crewing for an older man. They looked to him for an answer. He was an enormous hairy Greek who considered me for a moment and then agreed. I used Smithy's skiff to help and when it was set they said we would have to wait until the tide was right to bring it in. Nordi, meanwhile, had hidden herself in the rocks for sunning. The Greek and I began to talk of fishing. I told him of my desire to own a boat of my own, then to fish. He spoke to his men and they took their skiff and rode back across Richardson's Bay to Sausalito.

"Come on," he said, "I'll show you my boat while we're waiting."

Man, what a chance to really get on a fishboat and see the arrangement of the trolling poles and the mast and all the rather complicated gear that is on a thirty- to forty-foot, all-purpose fishboat. Nordi rowed us out and we hoisted ourselves up and she rowed back to shore.

Though ponderous, the Greek was quick and agile in getting aboard. The boat was spotless, its intricate paint job of reds and blues and buff brilliant under the sun. We drank a tall glass of sweet wine as we talked of fishing, of ports, of Fort Bragg and far north of Shelter Cove. He said he was glad I hungered to be a fisherman for the two men of his crew were lazy and if they didn't shape up in the next week he might have a spot for me. He mentioned what one trip to Fort Bragg would bring. It seemed a princely sum from my low profile in finance. I was thinking of a blue ocean with eight-foot seas, not twenty-foot seas trying to tear off a wheelhouse. The view was brisk and sunlit where you never had trouble with the engine; it was just the faithful motor and the fish—man!

"Yeah," I said, "you get a problem with the crew, let me know." I was very offhand. After all I was nearly twenty-two. "Of course, I'd have to give the railroad a week's notice, if I resigned."

"Resign," he bellowed at me in disbelief. "Tell those fuckers to ram it."

I felt foolish but I tried a swagger of my own, "They can take their job and shove it," I said, but suddenly I was thinking of the fatherly regard of Mr. Wasser. "That is, some of them," I said, and had another swallow of the sweet Greek wine.

"Tide'll be about right in an hour and a half," the Greek said. "It's hot in the sun. I usually take a nap but I got a little work to do on the engine. Grab a spot of sleep yourself."

I looked around for Nordi. We had pulled the fishboat out to the other end of the net, some distance from shore, and anchored. The skiff still lay on the beach but she had gone back to work on the garden or was sunning up on the rocks. The Greek had gotten into his tiny engine room, which his great body filled. I looked around, trying to learn what I could of the rigging, but the wine made me sleepy. I laid down on the deck. It was far too hot, so I stepped down into the cuddy cabin and lay down and fell asleep. I was dreaming of bright seas when I awoke. My pants were quietly being pulled down. I leapt up and out the door of the cuddy and his lunge missed me. Reason didn't help me, just instinct. His hands brushed me but missed and I was at the opposite end of the boat before he cleared the cuddy door and I had his loaded rifle and hatchet with me. He was in an insane rage, growling like a dog and bellowing Greek, I suppose. As he came around the edge of the house I aimed the hatchet at him and he stopped.

"I'm real clever with one of these things," I said. "Make another move and I'll split you right between the eyes." I could and I guessed he sensed it. He growled something and I cocked the gun and we sat glaring at each other. I fired the gun in the air to bring Nordi. He crouched to jump me. I aimed the hatchet at his nose and he retreated behind the pilot house, so I ejected the spent shell, reloaded and sat waiting. A quick glance ashore showed Nordi on the beach and I waved her out to us and she launched the skiff. When she got near I told her the situation.

"He's a maniac," I said, "and perverted to boot! Come up behind and get me off here."

"What's your hurry?" she asked. She was rowing in a circle around us, smiling.

"God damn it, Nordi! Get me off this boat. I'd rather be caged with a mad dog than with this sex-crazy Greek."

Still she rowed a circle around us, smiling. Finally she spoke, "Clyde, every so often you are inconsiderate in your sexual usage of me. Now you're in my shoes for a moment. I probably won't see such a scene as this again and I want to enjoy it while I can." She made one more stroke with the oars and changed her mind. "I've seen it," she said, and placed the skiff where I could step off.

Before me in a basket half covered with wet burlap was a nice striped bass. I tossed it in the skiff, then, watching him closely, I stepped into the skiff.

"I'll leave the gun and the hatchet on the beach," I told him. "Don't be in a hurry to get it."

Nordi rowed me ashore and I stayed on the beach until she had rowed out of sight around the north end of the island, then I left the gun and the hatchet and climbed up in the deep brush and over the top of the island and down to our ark on the other side.

That evening I told my tale to Fitch and Pete as we fed on the filched bass. They both said I was in a dangerous spot.

Fitch said, "It's obvious he's criminally insane. I myself have known a few queers, but this is not simple homosexuality. They wouldn't rage like that."

"This guy's crazy and from what you say he could pick you to pieces," said Pete. "Watch out for him."

Well, I went to Frisco and bought a hunting knife in a sheath that hid all of it but the immediate top of its antler handle. I found I could wear it under my pants at the groin with the belt hiding even the top of the handle. I put a razor edge on it and never was without it for the next ten years. Several times when straining hawsers had to be cut, I cut them quickly but always shielded it in my hand so no one knew I had it. I believe it saved my life several times, but it never in that time drew more blood than a scratch to signify intent.

Several months later in a crush of passengers coming down the gangplank the Greek appeared, towering head and shoulders above the crowd. He saw me, let out a growl, bellowed something and came at me. But there were two men with him who held him back. Anyway, the oak of a brake stick was in my hand. They passed me and I never saw them again. A year later a fellow that knew of him showed me an item in the *San Francisco Examiner*. My Greek friend had been hanged at San Quentin for the death of two other young men, each strangled in the cuddy cabin.

Anyway, that is how I met a monster. I've met a score more of them since, several of the most vicious accoutered as ladies, but that Greek was the most immediately dangerous one I ever came upon.

By now, author Fitch hung on my wife like an old shawl. After months of weeping on her shoulder about his rejection slips, he started fondling her ears and speaking not a word of literature and its problems. Now, with the evidence I've laid before you, you cannot doubt my child-like open trust that if a slice of bread falls to the floor it will land butter side up. I'm one hell of a tolerant guy, and I like to see casual affection between the sexes. When I came in one day and he was kind of sitting on her lap, I didn't mind too much. Probably an orphan and still needs mothering, I mused, and I told myself how lucky I'd been having a mother, two grandmothers, aunts and an uncle who exhibited himself. But several days later I came home to find her in *his* lap and not looking exactly distressed. I knew a moment of fury, calmed myself with difficulty, and asked him to find other lodgings. He agreed with me, saying he just couldn't leave such a delectable person as Nordi alone. We missed him after he left. Thinking about it I felt that maybe I'd been a little inattentive of Nordi outside the bedroom. I knew following his lead with the ears would make me look an uncreative person, so when I remembered to I'd tantalize her eyebrows. But it seemed only to make her fidgety, so finally I began to feel that a fellow doesn't have to be creative everywhere and I started fondling her ears, seeing they were handier than other parts, and it soon seemed to help her forget our former author-in-residence.

We began to spend more time on the hills of the Tiburon Peninsula, really the backbone of it. In the spring it was lovely up there with a fine view wherever you looked. We would hike up, strip off our clothes and run jumping through the meadows. We had a game where we threw cow pies at each other—while nude, of course. Cow pies come soft like oatmeal mush or, after they've dried a little bit, have a crust that encases the softer interior. Or they can be completely dry and be used for fuel. Then they are called buffalo chips. The trick in this game of ours—really a battle—was to catch the other fellow with a cow pie dry enough to pick up but with a splattery interior. We became tremendously clever at throwing them and dodging. If hit, we repaired to one of the numerous brooks of early spring to scrub off all clinging dung. No one ever caught us at our game, and we enjoyed it.

One early spring day I was up there alone in a saucer-shaped meadow with a springtime brook running over the grass in the lower end of it. I had stripped and was wandering over the grass or lying on it to feel the sun's rays reach deep in me. I felt consciously alive and happy, often raising up and gazing out at the vast Bay and its islands, when I noticed a skunk wandering the meadow. He had come over the rim and was busy sniffing about. I went over to him and he raised his tail, so I retreated a bit and, when he dropped it, came toward him again. After a dozen passes of this kind he let me come closer, where I quietly sat down. He gave me one more suspicious look and then went on about his business. He was hunting and sniffing and listening for something beneath the sod, and when the signal was right, he dug a little funnel-shaped hole and brought out something that he ate with much crunching. Whenever he found a place to dig I went over near him and sat down and soon he let me sit so close I could have reached out and touched him, which I certainly didn't. Now I saw that his prey was seventeen-year locusts, ending their years in the earth and working themselves slowly to the surface. After he lost his fear of me he didn't mind his audience at all and we went companionably about while he got his meal. There was without a doubt a communication between us. His hunger sated, he left and I decided to bathe in the brook that ran among some bushes of willow and other wand-like growth whose emerging leaves were somewhat pink and oily. "Full of the succulence of spring," I said to myself. I bathed and dried myself and left.

That night, before I went to bed, I began to itch between my fingers and in my eyebrows. Sleep soon engulfed me. Later in the night a fearsome dream awakened me. I must have called out in my dream, for my lovely's arms were around me. "What is it?" she whispered.

"Bad dream," I answered and clung to her until sleep and her bosom were one. But far after midnight I awoke again, this time on fire. It was between my fingers and toes, but most inflamed was that sack, residence of my testicles, the scrotum. The skin of the scrotum has great elasticity and sensitivity and something was testing the limits of those qualities. By then Nordi had me in a cool bath of sodawater.

I went to work in the morning but begged off at noon, wild with the itch. The crew and some passenger friends said that the drifting light oil of the poison oak could be gotten out of the pores of the skin by rubbing gently with gasoline or boiled mint leaves or eucalyptus buttons brewed as a tea. I chose gasoline. Anything to stop the itch. The *Marin* seemed to stand still in the water, but finally I got home, procured a gallon of gas, poured a large bowl half full and stripped, and standing in the middle of the kitchen floor, lowered my grossly swollen appendages into the cool liquid. "Yow!" I hurled the bowl of gasoline out the open window, grabbed my outraged parts, burning as if the gasoline had really caught on fire. "Wow!" I ran around the room, I ran outside and into the street with Nordi running after me with a basin of water and wet clothes. She tripped and fell, spilling the water as I hurtled on and into the house, jumped into the tub and turned on the water, frantically splashing it on myself until finally my swollen beauties were immersed. Eventually she got me to bed with my hands tied behind my back and we faced a night of writhing, itching madness. I ended up on the floor, spread-eagled, while Nordi fanned the inflamed equipment.

Nordi, whose sympathy was unbounded, looked more the worse for wear than I did in the morning. She took an early ferry to San Francisco and came back before noon with a yard of soft silk, a soft pair of mittens, a pound of talcum powder, powerful sleeping tablets and an assortment of salves. She made a sack of silk with two handle straps, put a half a pound of talcum powder in it, and helped me lower my poisoned parts into it. Holding the sack by its handles I could walk around and I put aside the idea of buying a small wheelbarrow for the chore.

Next night I put my hands in soft mittens and tied them behind my back. Nordi got a little sleep in another bedroom. A week later I was back at work, looking on the verge of collapse, willing with what will I had left to keep my hands out of my pockets, the prelude to furtive scratching.

Three weeks later, after much thought by both of us, we attended a symphony concert in a public service building. I've forgotten what the particular symphony was, only that it was one we were thoroughly fond of.

As we took our seats far from the aisle, I noticed we were being packed in with a solid phalanx of serious, independent, almost grim people who I thought probably owned hardware stores, funeral homes or were veterinarians. Two very large, very buxom ladies followed us in and took the seats next to us. They were talkative; so am I. They were from Fallon, Nevada. They had come down to hear a symphony. I mentioned that I knew a fellow from Fallon named Ed Storts. They knew his family. "Ed was such a nice, clean boy," one said. "Not like his brother." "Now don't carry tales," the other one said. "Willie will settle down someday."

They both were quiet for a bit and then the one nearest me said, "I wouldn't ask you this, young man, except for you knowing Ed Storts, but would you change places with me? You see, if Chaleese and I sit together, we crowd each other, both being rather large. But if you sat between us, it would be more comfortable. That is," she said, with ponderous archness, "if that sweet little wife of yours won't mind?"

"Oh, she won't mind," I said, always eager to be helpful to others even if only slightly distressed. So we changed places—a matter of her enormous bottom banging a bald pate in the next row and my elbow sinking deeply into her stomach. But then it was done and we considered our programs and, within a moment, I knew I'd made a mistake. For that great bulk of bottom balanced an unusually large bosom that jutted out toward the stage. Nordi was behind it somewhere. I scrunched down in my chair and after a bit so did Nordi, and under the lady's porch-like projection I saw Nordi's sweet face and her reassuring smile. My darling winked at me. God, how I loved her. We felt the large ladies looking down at us, wondering why we were in these strange positions, so we straightened up.

"They're certainly slow in starting the music," I murmured.

"Yes, ain't it a fac'," they answered in unison, at which one of them simpered, "We're sisters"—intending, I suppose, to explain the unison. While I was trying not to notice that it was exceptionally warm in the auditorium and say something pleasant about sisters, the orchestra filed in, which was all right, as the only thing I could think of about sisters at the moment was a pornographic joke.

The musicians were soon tuning their instruments—an ecstasy that at times transcends for me all the bombast and cunning, all the soul and piquancy, of the great masters' music. The lovely chore was soon over and the conductor walked up to the podium, stepping carefully on each side of his long black beard. After the bows and the tap-tap of his baton—signaling, it seemed, a few fine chords—a violin and a harp began telling us how a butterfly feels about tulips and spinach. Then the conductor began to stir up a

stew of sound that we knew and were hungry for, but which surprised us when we tasted of its orchestral richness. That far I got
with the music, but now, as I listened, I also felt the loom of the
ladies' bodies and they, as they ceased to strain toward the music,
began to become rather sated with it and settled back in their seats
and oozed all over their chairarms at me. I felt encroached upon—
attacked. I began to perspire and, worse, to itch. Soon I was
drenched with sweat. Furtively, I worked my hands into my pants
pockets to ease the tension from the massive itching fire now
resident south of my navel. I couldn't do this without bumping and
rubbing against vast arms overflowing into my cramped area. I
scrunched way down in my seat, but it didn't work. I couldn't get
my hands quite in my pockets unless the large ladies moved. I
could have mentioned my poison oak for their understanding but,
though never a very modest man in any manner, I had turned a
complete prude. Like the girl who was a little bit pregnant, I
wanted no one to know of my condition. I tried to listen to the
music. Impossible! Trying to will myself away from this torment, I
started counting the lights, only to encounter the stares of both
ladies. I should have said, "I'm counting the lights!" but I
scrunched myself in and wished I had nerve enough to pitch them
out in the aisle. The itching was giving me a chill; perspiration was
cold on me. The orchestra was doing something with long graceful
swoops. I dwelt in them for a moment—that is, part of me dwelt in
them, the other part wiggled and twisted in my seat, rubbing and
forcing the big fat arms to allow me to put my hands in my trouser
pockets. The swooping melody was in trouble now. It kept getting
tripped and I noticed the fellow with the kettle drums was getting
ready to operate. Sure enough, to a man, the violin section began
earning its keep and the trombones were allowed into the fracas
and when in this maelstrom of sound I saw the kettle drummer at
long last beating hell out of his drums, I reached both hands into
my hip pockets and over to the center of my agonizing itch and was
one with it all. God, the grandeur, the sublimity of the music
blending with that scratching! Then suddenly I was without support, for the crashing sound was gone and a flute was pleading for
its mate, who was off somewhere having an affair with a piccolo,
though they finally got together and invited a French horn to

accompany them. I nudged my itching self from both sides as I practically lay in my seat and again—God!—I looked up. Both those pink monsters had eyes only for me, and with great disgust in their expressions. I had an urge to tell them that I wasn't playing with it, but kept silent. The symphony drew to a close very reluctantly, even for a symphony. In the roar of the applause I did manage to shout out, rather clearly, "poison oak," for the one on my left bellowed that she had a brother that got it "there" once. Then the applause was over and she said rather quietly, "poor boy."

Finally in the jammed aisle Nordi was pressed against me from behind and reached out to encompass me. "Nordi," I said, mashed into that multitude, "let's hurry and get a taxi. Hurry! Hurry!" The slow flow of that aisle full of people poured into a greater mass movement in the foyer. Like cooling lava we moved. Finally, we were in the street where one look at the taxicab situation made me look madly for other sources of surcease.

I rushed off toward Market Street, dragging my darling with me. I hurried along and back of me came the staccato tapping of Nordi's high heels. In my madness for concealment in which to scratch I stumbled on. I was remembering several dress shops on the south side of Market Street with deep foyer-like entrances where one might hide oneself for the divine moment of an otherworldly scratch. With such goals I rushed faster, crossing Market Street at a gallop, Nordi's tapping behind me sounding like she was losing the race. But she was right behind me, holding the slipper from which she had torn the heel in the streetcar track. She wasn't faltering, she was just covering more ground between taps. The first shop entrance was being used by a little German band with tuba and bass drum laying on the tiles as they shared the night's collection. We hurried on to the next. A young couple tarried there, examining hats and cloaks in the windows. Just as they were about to leave, something caught the eye of the girl.

"Look, Sam," she said. "Lookit the hat."

"Yeah," he said, studying it. "Zugerman has nice merchandise, but Wanders has got 'em for less and the fedduh is real pheasant."

"Uh, uh! It's offena toikey!"

"Nah, offena real pheasant."

I couldn't wait to see who would win the debate, so, with Nordi at my heels, I rushed down Market toward the third store. We got there and I hurried in past the island in the center, only to confront a short, middle-aged Jewish couple. They faced the far window studying some damn thing there. I drew aside my coat and slipped my hands in my pants pockets. God, the overwhelming satisfaction was too much for me. My legs turned to rubber. I started to crumple to the floor but my spouse, my wonderful Nordi, grabbed me under the armpits and held me draped against her, staring dazedly at the startled couple as they hurried past us to the street. A taxi and two ferry boats later we were home in Tiburon and, under Nordi's soothing ministrations, I fell asleep.

About six months after her train accident, the girl in whom I had poured myself so deeply came back. She came back on artificial legs that clicked and snapped as she slowly creaked up on me. She stopped and glared at me with utter loathing, then turned and went painfully on. She never approached me again, but often when she came on board her eyes would seek me out with that malevolent stare. The other deckhands noticed this and told me it served me right. Her life, they said, had been in the hands of God. Why should a kid like me butt in? I knew I had done wrong in not following her to the hospital, and I've never been able to forgive myself for it.

It was strange, my near adoration of the Bay region. Somehow, some way, it sustained me in those years. San Francisco was little like most cities when you get into them. It had the San Francisco difference—its great park, its many views of the Gate, its cat-a-corner Market Street and Columbus Avenue, a million things of interest in a thoroughly unique city—but it was still its outer aspects that intrigued me endlessly, and thousands were with me in this view. San Franciscans were wont to leave on weekends, take a ferry in whatever direction and, ascending the hills about the Bay, turn and stare fondly back at the outer garment of their beloved city. In this I felt related to the hikers who came each weekend to cross the Bay and tramp through the Marin hills, for I myself still searched for my fuller being in solitary marches up canyons, along promontories, over rock piles and noble meadows. I suppose I was trying to break through the restraining tissues of my segmented self, and sudden vistas seemed momentarily to remove those utterly logical lies of our culture that hampered me. By now I knew that I was making a religion out of a romance I was having with the environment. Did I ever in those times hunger for more money, a different place in any hierarchy? Did I think of the position with my father or yearn for that block of stock and the position Catherine's father offered? Not once. I still had my reading. I knew by now I would never be good enough as a painter to allow myself to be called a painter. I wrote a bit, but the writing was as bad as a great deal of what I saw in print. In writing, as in painting, I didn't want to disgrace the art or craft of either with my additions. Still, a driven urge to say, to state the majesty of the seen world, the nuances and thunder of the heard world, was in me—driving me often to desperation. I would jump up from my chair and be off into the hills. From the ridges I'd look down on the Peninsula. "Yes," I would say, staring out at it. "Yes," as down in some ravine's bed of autumn leaves I would lay, shielded from the north wind.

It was about this time that a man from South Dakota came to Tiburon and fell in love with the country around. I couldn't blame him for that, but for some reason he decided to buy the arks—all of them—and we had to move. I had made friends with the second mate, Ole Borg—a dynamite Swede who had built his own house above the cove just east of Tiburon. I'd heard he'd built an apartment under his home and asked him if it was available. It was, so we moved our belongings once more. The apartment's three rooms were airy and had a fine view of the cove, and we were quite happy, though a bit lonesome. Pete visited us much less often after that, and the distance from Smithy's made our meetings become rare. Our few friends among the people of the arks were scattered, so we were thrown in upon ourselves.

Spring came again and, avoiding the poison oak bushes, we played naked once more in the sunshine, once more at our cow pie game. It is strange that the people of San Francisco came each weekend to walk the hills about the Bay, but the people who lived adjacent to the hills seemed never to show interest in their contours. But once we did meet a neighbor walking up there. We were busy chasing each other around one sunny day. Nordi ran shrieking from me and the cow pie I had poised to throw, when a head appeared above the rise in the meadow, well ahead of her. I stopped and when she stopped I pointed him out. He hadn't seen us so we dipped down and scuttled through a slight draw. Our clothes were off behind him, so we looked for cover, but the brush we saw was full of poison oak. There was a little, bushy bay tree near us, so we scrambled into it and waited, then we saw that a trail passed beneath us. By then it was too late to run for other cover. He came, a very solemn little man, his derby hat shining with wear, and walked beneath us. He could have touched our feet, as our glowing bodies shone in the leafy gloom of that little tree. On down to the village he went. Had he looked up I'm sure our contorted bodies with the foliage and bits of sky back of us would have resembled a ceiling done by one of the great Italians. (How much we miss with eyes straight ahead.) After he had gone we dropped down from our perch and made love in the soft spring grass. In fact in this time we were always making love. I worked on the ferries and when I came home there was my pink and white darling ready to feed me or make love. I knew how exquisite that pink blossom was beneath her curl, I knew how it glistened with the honey of rapture and I loved her—Oh God, how I loved and adored her. Maybe this time we might reach that paradise that other joinings promised, that we struggled toward with every jot of our young vigor. Was her cry at the last sated or was it that, while within the gates of paradise, all suddenly faded and her cry was anguish at being cosmically fooled by a larger, more calculated design than ours? Of this she would never speak. "We," she confided, "should never look at orgasms direct but only from the corners of our eyes." She said this looking at me from the corners of hers, so I kissed the backs of her knees and the small of her back and under both arms, now salty with perspiration, and we ate the cold dinner, then snuggled away the hours until it was time to sleep.

We knew no one in the neighborhood except our landlord and we felt we should show by our reticence that we had moved in under him, not with him. We would sit in our living room on my day off and stare at one another. I'd say let's do so and so, or Nordi would suggest something. We would both agree at once and go about it—whether it was to go to San Francisco for dinner and a show or to sail our little sloop up to Paradise Cove—but the enthusiasm with which we agreed and did these things was a wee bit forced, for though neither of us would admit it, the edge of our pleasure in discovery of the means and extremes of the adult world was dulling—not to any great extent, but we were losing that first excitement of being free from parental supervision. We had become Mr. and Mrs. So-and-So, who lived next door. I certainly was aware of it, so I strove harder, and with the stimulus of my encounters with people on the job, it was easy for me. Nordi took renewed interest in everything to offset her vague ennui.

I've always been wild about boats, particularly rowboats, and I had a few ideas I wanted to incorporate in the design of one. Having designed it, I decided to build it—worry it together is a better description. The only place we could find to build it was a quite steep hillside, but we spiked a plank between two small oak trees and went to work. The grass was dry and very slippery on the slanted places and our tools and the boat and lumber and sawhorses and paint and nails were continually careening away from us down the slope. Still, with Nordi hanging onto the boat while I, with my feet sliding out from under me, worked on it, we achieved a lovely shaped hull. It was small with a v-shaped bottom, high sides like a dory, and both ends rode clear of the surface of the water. While bringing it down from the hill to the cove, it began to get away from me, so I jumped in. Wow! The curves of it flowed over the undulant ground through and over the dry grass and in a flash or maybe a flash and a half we were down the hill five hundred feet, its bow buried in the soft sand of the cove. It leaked a bit at first but was easy to bail. If you reached your hand over to touch the water, it might turn over on you. Tippy it was, but the easiest rowing boat I've ever encountered and a marvel in rough weather. I could go out on the Bay when small-decked power boats were in danger. It had a flair to the bows high up that kept the heavy spray off your back going to windward in sloppy, stormy weather. Nordi grew to be very adept with the little v-bottom boat. We had another toy. After a long interval, it too became stale, so we yawned a lot as we read the newspapers. And then one evening she went to bed early and after a while, when I had nodded several times over my reading, I decided to call it a day too. The light was on in our bedroom. On the bed, arranged for love, lay my darling, smiling her sweet smile at me. A timeless period later she stared up into my eyes for a moment and then, with the most puckish grin ever, said, "I didn't take any precautions, Clyde, because I want a baby." That was the end of our apathy. Soon Nordi was pregnant and we knew we must get a place of our own.

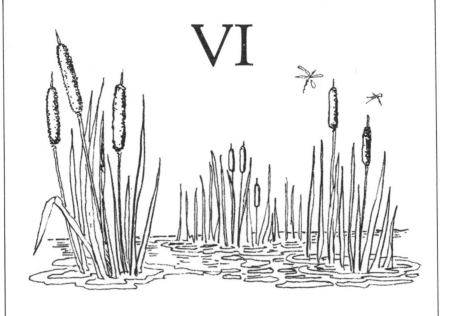

VI

In Which
I Find Life Very Rich But Time Consuming,
Am Given And Almost Lose A Son,
and
Am Horrified At What I've Become

◇ 1926 ◇

I had seen the lame man on the *Marin* for over a year, lame and bald. I had noticed more than once the marvelous shape of his head. His chin was not large but jutted out with a determination almost grim, but his thin tight mouth seemed to always have the remnants of a smile or a new one aborning in the corners. His eyes were brown, large and heavy-lidded and set under a brow that swept up and then over in the large curve of his great brain case. One thought at once of Roman generals, of Caesars and the Jewish merchant princes of a slightly earlier time. His clothes were nondescript and his lameness forced him to sit in a manner that did not lend dignity to the rest of his body. One day he accosted me on the *Marin*. We had just left Belvedere Landing and I had coiled down the spring and was leaving the forward deck when I bumped into him by the pilothouse from where he had been watching me. I murmured an apology and would have passed him when he spoke up.

"Say, aren't you the one who moved into Ole Borg's place?"

"Why, yes," I said, "I did."

"Uh huh," he murmured. Then, speaking up, he said, "my name's Bob Drake. I'm a neighbor of yours. I watched you and your wife building that skiff under the oaks and must offer my congratulations for a splendid feat of balancing."

Well, I liked him at once. We talked until we arrived at Sausalito and he invited Nordi and me to have dinner with them several nights later.

Drake lived in a large old house that was land-based but stood out over the water on pilings. Bessie, his wife, was a friendly person and I saw that she took to Nordi at once. Bob and I found we shared a passion for boats, large and small, and we were soon drawing our dream ships and talking scantling sizes, dead rise and the pressure a mast exerts on the keel when stoutly stayed.

Pet theories tumbled out as we talked, while our wives in the kitchen were doing much the same with the culinary equivalents. The dinner was plain and very good. During dinner, Bessie, in whom Nordi had confided her pregnancy, mentioned to Bob that we wanted to establish a home of our own, preferably near the water. She seemed to know of something pertaining to such property and Bob said he might have interesting information by next week and asked us to come down for coffee the Wednesday following.

I had rented a stout riding horse the week before, for I thought I might be able to make extra money trapping in my spare time. I remembered the skunk I'd spent the afternoon with. We'd been friends. Still, I might trap him. So far, even with spittoons and all, I'd lived an integrated life. It all hung together. Now my code and my need would be split apart. I was confronted with a "both." I had avoided "boths." My mother had died in an attempt to prove a simple, ordered universe and I hungered for such a stand against duality. I loved all animals very much and now I was not only going to prey on them, I was going to torture them! No, not me! How could I? How else will you provide for your son, I asked myself. Go back to Portland to proffered jobs? No, the die was cast. Here by the Bay I might soon own a bit of land. Back home, with the infinite variation of atmospheres, one could live simply with one's hopes. But down here the strident muscularity of the hills, the beaten metal glare of the Bay, the brittle harsh leaves of these trees belied softness and I had become Californian. Then accept the paradox, I argued. Kindness is after the fact of killing and of eating some life, be it green or red flesh. Pain is a part of living. The trap may numb the foot or leg it catches. You hope so, but you don't know. Good God, I know I didn't. But I had to go on.

"He's stubborn, Blue is," said the owner of the horse, as I led him away.

"Well, I'll fix that," I announced. The owner looked at me with a smirk.

"Skin him alive," he said, "if you think that can break him of his tricks."

By week's end, Blue, a tough little animal, had shown me all his tricks. They were well thought out to produce the ultimate in exasperation. Blue was smart. Most horses haven't the brains of a gopher, so we can enslave these great animals for our uses. Some refuse to be slaves, bucking and running away, kicking and biting. Acts like that could make a man want to slit a horse's throat. But not Blue. The way Blue worked it, you'd end up cutting your own. It was with the little things that Blue drove you mad. I was beginning to curse in my sleep when Wednesday came around, the Wednesday we'd been waiting for.

We had our coffee around a warm fire in Drake's big fireplace. "We have friends," he said, "Madeline and her husband, who are buying a waterfront lot, and we're thinking of getting one too, but the owner won't sell either unless the lot between is sold. We were wondering if you might want it?"

There was a silence, then Nordi said, "I'd like to see it. Is it near?"

The Drakes said it was, so out we went with flashlights, found it and stumbled around over it. It was on deep water, had a little road at the top and was only forty feet wide. Nordi was trembling with eagerness when we got back to the fire. She kept staring at my face with both apprehension and hope in her expression, waiting to see what I would say. I realized it was the moment: they were waiting on my decision. I wanted to act thoughtful and judicious. It was a chance to stand, to strike a figure. I knew this, but I tripped on the rug, spilled hot coffee over Bessie's knees and, when it was mopped up, said, "Yeah, I guess we'll take it."

We had enough in the bank to pay for it and in a week all three of the lots were sold. We met Madeline and her husband, Linwood, a writer of sea stories, and a friendship developed between the six of us that lasted long, long years after poor Linwood's death.

Now we needed money, for I had only a little over a hundred dollars left and I wanted to put up a cottage of some sort and there would be hospital bills and all manner of stuff. The hills of the Tiburon Peninsula were alive with skunks. I hated to trap living things, but if I wanted to make a home and provide for a son I was going to have to do it. I knew that in a short time I would be second mate with a raise in wages, but in the meantime I decided to go on the extra board and substitute for those laid up with the winter problems of colds and flu.

I got in touch with a wholesale fur dealer in Sacramento and told him I could only provide green hides, not flensed and with a bullet hole through the head. Skunk furs were in short supply and he agreed to take them in this manner for $2.75 apiece. I felt I was on my way. First I had to break Blue of his tricks and tantrums and balks. On my day off I ate lightly, dressed lightly, and went out to the immense field about half a mile square that was Blue's pasture. Blue snorted as I came close, but instead of wooing him with oats and more oats I threw a rock at him and ran at him. He swept way down the field and I trotted after him. When at last I came close to him I hit him with another stone. He snorted and tore away again and I trotted after. Every once in a while I'd get him cornered and make him gallop madly to get by me and always I threw pebbles at him. The first hour or so he enjoyed giving me the slip, and I was weary. I walked up the hills but ran him down them and always trotted after him. He grew alarmed and started to sweat and soon his coat was covered with foam, but I never let him rest. He ran the perimeter of his field and I ran inside his perimeter, so he went farther, but if he tried to turn back I rushed him so he would have to expend himself to get past me. The dark horse was now pretty well white with foam. In a little over two hours I was worn to a frazzle, but he was undone. He came up to me but I hit him between the eyes with a piece of limb and we went on again, but he moved slower now and the next time he came to me I allowed him to put his heavy head in my arms. Then I curried him and walked him and gave him sips of water and handfuls of oats and then I washed him down and dried him and fed him well. Next day I rode him and he didn't play a single trick—no balks, no rearing over nothing. He carried me about all business and I had no further trouble with him. So, a man can run down a horse if he can make the horse upset about it.

After a week of endless trudging, using every moment off the job to seek the dens of the skunks, I found most of them. Many were in ravines. I could ride the horse up the backbone of the Peninsula leaving him at the head of each ravine, for they were too steep for a horse, then drop down in great leaps, shoot the animal in the head and set the traps and come muling up with the stinking carcass and climb on old Blue, who'd been grazing patiently on his picket. I'd trot him on to the next ravine head and repeat the process. The last two miles I had to go by foot for I couldn't get Blue over a massive stone wall, built by Indian slaves across the Peninsula. Down the road on the east side toward home I'd go, then head up the gullies a bit from the bottom for the last trap sets. It was about a seven-mile trip. Looking back I don't know how I did it; it was a twisted course, the ravines steep as ladders. I hated to kill the animals. To trap them and hold them in pain was hell on both me and the skunks. I threw them a piece of apple to eat before I shot them and I always told them why I had to take them. Many, many times I was in tears, but I kept on. I'd get home exhausted, only to go out in an old abandoned shed and skin the six to ten skunks, wrap the skins up tight in a burlap parcel, trot down to the American Express office in Tiburon with them, come back to the shed, bathe in kerosene, sluice it off with sudsy water, then come in the house, bathe and shampoo to get all the skunk odor off, eat a quick meal and head for an eight- or twelve-hour job on the ferries. Working on the extra board paid off. I got many extra shifts in a week and this, added to the trap line, thinned me down. After a couple of months, I got an eight-hour run on the *Tamalpais*, twelve more on the *Eureka* and eight more back on the *Tamalpais*. That was twenty-five hours on my feet—all the time in extreme tension, for animals were in my traps, suffering those extra hours.

A big storm was approaching as I got home at dusk. I had a hurried meal and began my trap line with a carbide lamp attached to my head and a flashlight. Good old Blue was getting fat in my service while I was getting lean. I couldn't find him. He'd gone under some trees I knew not where, so I did without him in the very windy, rainy night. Cascades of water leaped down the ravines. The flashlight played out, soaked with rain, but the carbide held on. I shot the skunks and carried them in my pack and I put sticks in traps still set so nothing could get trapped, for I knew by now that I too had the flu. In these groves, not in ravines, cattle had gathered to get out of the storm and on my approach in the pitch-black night they hurtled out in all directions. Several times I saved myself by leaping behind a tree as they charged past. By four in the morning all eighty traps had been sprung and I could start back on the road with my pack, but then I fell in a puddle and couldn't get up. I lay there for a while and finally got to my knees and up. The next time I fell I rested for a long time and when I could get up I dropped my pack of six skunks in a ditch alongside the road. I fell several times more, but eventually I got home. It was almost nine in the morning. Nordi was unstrung with worry. She put me to bed and it was several days before the fever was down enough for me to sit up. That was the end of the extra board and the trapping, but we had money enough from these endeavors to start the house and also lay away enough for the maternity hospital in San Francisco.

I came home one day to find the place in a turmoil. Bessie Drake had persuaded Nordi to move into the downstairs part of their house. "Pay me rent and get ready to build." They were actually moving when I turned up. I felt pretty much left out of things, but saw the sense of it and acquiesced.

Soon we were ensconced in the Drakes' lower floor rooms. Here we stayed until I could get a loan from the bank and build three rooms of a small cottage, run a long, long pipe across the country to the local water system—the same with electric wire—and we moved in. It was a little house, but ours. We could bring our boats in through a rocky approach to a very small sand beach —ours too. How Nordi reveled in it. She was growing pretty big with our child, still she would row down to Tiburon a half a mile away, shop for groceries, haggle in the meatmarket and, with the tide figured beforehand, glide back and land on our bit of sand only a few steps from the door. Soon there were flowers coming up around the house and we added on a room and always Nordi got bigger. I made arrangements with her doctor and the hospital in San Francisco and, as her time neared, with one of the launch people in Tiburon and with a taxicab outfit in San Francisco. When her time was almost up, there was always somebody on hand at the dock waiting for our call. Bessie had nurse's training and had been a superintendent in a hospital before her marriage and she was going to make the trip across the Bay with Nordi.

Our luck was good. The preliminary pains started before midnight when I was home. I phoned for the boat, called Bessie and the taxicab company and a few minutes later I was rowing Nordi and Bessie out to the big forty-footer waiting for us. Towing the skiff, we headed across the Bay, my friend Joe at the wheel. Nordi was unconcerned and even enjoyed the trip. The cab was waiting at the dock in San Francisco and soon Nordi lay in the hospital, smiling up at us between pains. They took her into the delivery room where Bessie (she broke horses on her father's ranch in Nevada) threw the doctor's nurse out, showed him her credentials and told him she was going to see that her friend got every care.

I went to the waiting room. I could hear Nordi screaming through the walls. I was guilt-ridden and as the screams went on I became beside myself with grief and guilt. It was I who jetted that seed into her, now all the pain was hers. If only I could share that pain. The screaming went on and then I remembered that I had a hole on my shin from the fall on sharp rocks. It was deep and didn't heal well. It was always getting banged open. Now it had a proud flesh rim around the little crater. That was what I needed. I took out my pocketknife and carved out the proud flesh. Jesus, what pain! But in those moments I was somehow in my small pain with her, in hers. I swore I'd never put her through this again, and I never did. Nordi was radiant when I saw her in the morning. They brought the baby—a boy—in. I was unimpressed. My poor darling had suffered because of this interloper. She laughed at me. "I feel fine," she said. "I can barely remember what happened. Rejoice, Clyde, here is your son!"

So I looked at him. He looked like they'd taken him out too soon—sort of underdone. I knew that we all do—that in this we are like the opossums and the bears. But it just didn't seem fair to my son.

A few days later they were home. But something was wrong. I went to see the doctor. He was all smiles: "Well, Mr. Rice, how does it feel to be a father? A fine bouncing boy!" The usual stuff.

"There's something wrong," I said.

"All you fathers are the same," he went on. "He's barely been born."

It wasn't any use. I reached across his desk, grabbed his shirt and dragged him up out of his chair. "Something's wrong," I said again, "tell me about it!"

He looked down at my hand as I let him go. "Two turns of the cord around his neck at birth," he said. "His esophagus is big enough for a four-year old. He hasn't got much of a chance."

"What can I do?" I asked, staring woodenly at him.

"Well," he said, sitting down again, "your wife says you live over in Tiburon on the beach. Put him naked in his bassinet out in the sun and wind. He'll either live or die. If he lives he'll grow up around that larnyx and by the time he's four he'll be normal. Your real problem is whooping cough. If he gets it this winter or the next you won't be able to save him."

So there it was: Clyde Jr., as we had named him, had only a fifty-fifty chance to survive his first two years.

I went back next week to get more information, but the young doctor, an already famous obstetrician, had died of an infection in his sinuses that had flared to his brain. I did as he advised me. The big basket in which the baby lay protected him from the buffeting of the wind. The sun poured its radiance down on him and we hovered around with love and hope. You could hear his breathing throughout the house, but the doctor had explained it, so we were not frightened. He turned tan and vigorous. The doctor's wild guess had worked. Each day when it didn't rain he was out in his bassinet which was lined so that the wind couldn't blow directly on him. He had been a four-pound baby at birth. Now he gained under our rapt gaze. Fall came. We had to cease the outdoors treatment. We lived only for him that winter, very worried that I would bring the flu bug home. I washed my hands and arms in mercury derivative that probably could have harmed me. I only used it before coming home and, as Bunky (Clyde Jr.'s nickname) waxed healthy and spring came, I discarded it.

I had now been a deckhand long enough for a license for the job of second mate. I studied a week, took and passed the exam. In those days the steamboat inspectors were tyrants. The inspection service was eventually was abolished because of their vicious ways with people studying for licenses, the harsh way they treated honest people, and the ease with which payoffs made them okay the most dangerous of common carriers. I passed all right. As I went in to the head of the inspection service to get his signature, a young Italian was waiting for his signature there. He had worked three years in the engine room of a tug and had passed his examination for second engineer on inside waters. In an extremely arbitrary manner the head of the inspection service asked him where he came from. The man said, "Petaluma," which at that time was known for its chicken industry. The head inspector at once tore the certificate up and threw it in his wastebasket. "I'll never sign a license for any damn chicken farmer," he said. "Get out!" The big Italian wept, but he left. He'd studied a long time for that license. I decided at once that if that devil of an inspector didn't sign mine I'd tear his goddamned Adam's apple out, so when he asked me of my background, in a reedy voice I said, "I'm from art school." He took one look at me and signed without a word. We were both lucky that day. Anyway, I got my license. When I brought it to the railroad office, the port captain was out, so I had the chief clerk initial it on the back with the date. Then some monkey business began, compliments of the port captain, a man named Lindstrom. Like most of the officers on the ferries, Lindstrom was a Swede. He knew two of his countrymen were studying for licenses and would be handing in their certificates within a month or so, so he tried to hold mine back. A whole lot of folderol went on, so I went down to the office, asked him to hand me my license, turned it over and showed him the chief clerk's initialing on the back. With great reluctance he accepted it.

Swedes are Swedes. To me they come in two categories: milk-sop Swedes and dynamite Swedes. I suppose there are gray areas between, but my thinking concerning Swedes is Aristotelian. A dynamite Swede—man oh man! Lock up the women! Clear the streets! Hear his shouted laughter! He is a friend of man, a prodigious worker, openhanded and courageous. But his counterpart is meek, talks softly, goes to church every Sunday in blue serge suit and polished black shoes, always wears a conservative hat set dead center on his scarce-haired head. He is the most innocuous ingredient of a kaffeeklatsch. He is useful as a doorman, barber, minister, male nurse or in a dairy. Some are excellent embalmers. But by and large, along with the lemming, they are the strangest creatures to come out of the north. The famous cartoonist, Al Capp, used their characteristics when he created the schmoos.

Well, we had one of the latter on the *Eureka*. He was the watchman, which meant that he went his rounds but did no work. From what we could find out from him, he was a bachelor, all alone in the world, and lived in a boardinghouse where he kept strictly to himself. An ardent Christian, he had a way of inhaling the word "Jesus." It must have been the ultimate in piety where he came from. When we were under way and not too busy, I would engage in conversation with him about religion and watch him very closely when he said "Jesus," for his lips, after he had inhaled the word, were the epitome of deference and conservatism. It delighted me! I was really very fond of him and treated him with respect. In the dusk of the few lights allowed for our night work he always carried a lantern, wafting here and there like a firefly as he carried out his little duties. He was small in stature but had a large apologetic face and he walked slowly and gently on his heels with the toes of his shoes turned up—not as the Turks do, you understand, but so the toes of his shoes were off the deck.

I bid on this job on the *Eureka*, worked twelve hours on and twenty-four off. It was really a topsy-turvy arrangement. Every other shift was all night. It abused sleeping habits and the crews of the *Eureka* had a half-dead air. Still, you did have twenty-four hours to build a hen house or a privy or engage in other creative efforts. The work on the *Eureka* was endless. On weekends all the long seats on her main deck were removed—removed, what a nice easy word for that job! I wish I could explain how we did it. It was unbelievably arduous to anyone under six feet. It's too difficult to explain except to say that it was done with great heavy two-wheeled carts, one to a man. The *Eureka* tied up at one a.m. You worked like a demented mule until three and then were allowed an hour of spot (sleep, that is). This we did in an in-between-deck place where the steering engine was. That big, hot cylinder gave off enough warmth to drive the sweat from our clothes as we lay scattered around beneath it on the deck and in the light of one tiny bulb. One of the crew was a big dark Swede with enormous mustaches. He nearly always had nightmares as he slept among our scattered bodies. He flung his arms about and roared and whimpered, but if you were tired enough it didn't matter if he hit you once in a while, just so long as it was nothing personal.

It was the watchman who roused us at four o'clock to begin again the rush to get all things done before the passengers came aboard at six-fifteen. How often I awoke at his call to see him standing with his lantern at the top of the steps. "Gentlemen," he would gravely intone, "it is the time!" No one had ordered him to wake us. It was a duty he had taken up himself, with the graveness of an usher in a church—that was the quality of it. "Gentlemen, it is the time!" It gave him the only power he ever knew. He awakened the crew from sleep for their own good. But one morning we had all been drinking there under that hot cylinder, and when he made his fine statement, we railed at him— jeered, I'm afraid, at our friend. His mouth flew open. He was astounded and deeply hurt. When next we took our night shift he spoke to none of us and he failed to waken us in the morning. Just as the ferry was pulling out of the slip for the six-fifteen trip, Manuel, my genial sidekick standing on the stern with him, asked him why he had not awakened us. The watchman stared wildly at him, his mouth falling wide open. Suddenly, he turned, took two steps and jumped overboard. The water, very turbulent from the churning paddle wheels, took him down and he was gone. Afterwards, everyone was nonplussed. But I, even in my youth and in those times, knew that many of us hang on to sanity and life itself by the slenderest of threads. Climbing the hills of Tiburon that day, I mourned him, hating myself.

By now I knew every deckhand on our boats. As a deckhand myself, I had gotten on very well with them. They had accepted me, a green outsider, for I did my work just a shade better than they did theirs even though they were all older than I was—many had spent years in the sailing ships at sea. But they all hated me when I got my license. One day I came aboard the *Sausalito* as second mate on the afternoon shift. It was afternoon on a sunny day and the tide was midway between high and low so that the gangway was level. The train from Eureka had just come in. The freight handlers loaded six boxes of fresh iced salmon on each of three trucks. The trucks were extra heavy and made for the job. I whistled for the crew, who were standing on each side of the gangway on the boat, to come out and bring them aboard. No one moved. I whistled three times more—they acted nervous but no one looked up the gangway to me. So there it was, a showdown. The fish could not be left in the sun. Somehow I hooked the three trucks together, with plenty of slack in each chain. Then, taking the lead truck's handle, I started to tug at it. I got it started, then I really muled into it. There was a jar and the second truck started, another jar and the third. I had over three tons of weight moving on twelve big wheels. But to keep it moving took every ounce of everything I was. My feet didn't slip, no pebble under the wide iron wheels stopped my train. I came on pulling with superhuman effort, my face close to the ground. I reached the gangway and slowly brought those heavy-laden wagons the length of it and finally onto the deck. The lines were let go, the gangway raised. I signaled the ferry was ready to leave and out we went. I felt very strange and climbed the stairs and the ladders to the hurricane deck and fell and lost consciousness. The first mate found me and brought me to. I could soon stand and before we reached Frisco was able to go on with my work. They came at my whistle in San Francisco. Everything went smoothly until after night tie-up. They were all in the hose locker changing to go home. I looked them over. "I'm not going to ask the Captain to fire you," I said, "I don't want you to lose your jobs. But any man of you that hasn't bid off my crew in six months will get his brains beat out with a brakestick." No one spoke and at the end of six months all had bid off and the men I wanted had bid on and I had a fine crew.

When I was a deckhand, the skipper of the *Sausalito* at that time was Captain Krendler, a massive man over six feet tall, with seemingly no cranium except just enough to station his scalp. He had a funny toddling walk and the memory of an elephant. One sunny afternoon when I was a deckhand on his crew we were tied up waiting for the afternoon crew to relieve us. We were all out on deck with the engineers and the oilers and firemen, who were Scots to a man, waiting along the rail. I was sweeping the deck and was practically through with it. Captain Krendler was following me around as I did the sweeping, a strange annoying habit of his. I neared the anchor chain locker that was set up off the deck a few inches and stopped, laid the dustpan down by the mass of sweepings ready to whisk them in and dump them overboard. Captain Krendler stood over me, considering the pile of cigar butts, gum wrappers and such as it lay before us and the dustpan. I, too, studied it for a few moments and then, with a quirk of mind, swept it quickly under the chain locker instead of into the dustpan. He let out an astounded bellow at which the engineers of the black-gang howled with delight.

"You asked for it, you old woman," they informed him. They railed on at him; a couple of deckhands snickered. Captain Krendler, who never forgot anything, considered from the corners of his small eyes that non-Swedish, non- Portuguese son of a bitch who had made him look silly. And now I was his second mate.

I don't know what made me so touchy in Krendler's presence. Perhaps because I felt he downgraded me in his mind. When I took the wheel in the pilothouse he spoke to me only through Ole, the mate. For three months he never spoke to me as I worked under him. Then, one busy trip when I was standing at the forward doors with a half dozen commuters, my friends, who engaged me in banter on this trip each day, Captain Krendler appeared at my elbow. "I'm examining you," he said. "Recite for me the rules of the road." (They are the traffic rules of rivers, bays and seas—one set for inside waters and one for the ocean.)

I knew them by heart. Everyone who is licensed to handle boats does—all fifteen fine-print pages of them. And here we were two minutes from landing in Frisco. It was absurd so I said, "If you blow one blast on your whistle it's for me to come up to the pilot house. Two blasts are for tugs." Absurdity for absurdity.

"There goes your job," they said.

"I don't think so," I answered, "though I'll certainly have to watch my step." So I did.

Soon after this exchange, our crew were given the afternoon watch that ended at nine in the evening. Captain Krendler and I lived in Tiburon and we had to wait around for an hour and a half in Sausalito before the *Marin* would take us home. We sat in the depot waiting room for several nights, furtively glaring at one another. I decided to wait it out in the local movie and spoke to the movie's owner about it. Because I would come six days a week and because I would never see the end of the main feature, I wanted a big reduction or I wouldn't come at all. He was a reasonable man and I paid less than a third for the ticket. A week went by and then Captain Krendler followed my example. On went our ludicrous intolerance of each other. It was winter and he wore a long overcoat and, because of trouble he had with his feet, he walked with amazingly short, insecure steps that seemed to emanate just from the bottom of his overcoat. I would follow this tall powerful figure seen in the dim streetlights toddling along to the moviehouse, follow him respectfully to watch the Keystone Kops dive through windows or be chased by a truck, a newsreel and then the feature, sometimes a comedy, sometimes drama, but whatever it was we never saw its end. The story was never resolved in our presence for we had to leave for the *Marin*'s 10:20 trip to Tiburon. In the movie near the screen was the lighted dial of a clock. We kept one eye on it as all hell would be going on on the screen. We were aroused individuals, living others' lives, rife with meaning. Great dramas shook us and with faces bathed with tears or else grinning with laughter we wended our way to the *Marin*, and always I walked behind the Captain. We kept our distance because he had reason to dislike me and he was a man most generous with his dislikes and also because I stood in awe of him—though not as a captain, but as a builder of large models of sailing ships. He built the hulls about four feet long. He decked them and put on the deckhouses, installed the masts, and rigged everything most exactly. Every detail concerning a sailing ship was there in perfection. In 1884 as a boy he had joined the U.S. Navy and had been deeply in love with the tall ships ever since. His amazing memory was fully stored with the intricate beauty of brigs, barkentines and full-rigged ships. Once a finished model of his was being shipped via the great Luckenbach Steamship Lines to a museum in Washington, D.C. The ship was about to sail, hatches were battened down, booms brought in and made fast, when the Line's offices received an urgent phone call to hold the ship at the pier. One of the countless lines in the rigging was remembered to be wrong. They held up the departing time of the liner for several hours while Krendler came over with another captain and adjusted the thread on the model. San Francisco, the great port, thoroughly enjoyed the incident.

And then Captain Krendler's waiting game to get even with me seemed to bear fruit, for I came down with the flu and laid off for four days. The second mate who took my place was a sly fellow on the extra board who insinuated himself into his captains' private lives, bringing them apples and ducks and visiting them on their days off, to help in the yard or paint the front steps. For some time he had been extremely helpful to the port captain in this manner and he'd grown to be something of a white-haired boy around all his superiors. But that was not all. Ole Borg, the able first mate, and a man with whom I could work closely in the management of the boat, was off on his vacation and the man who took his place was far from a friend of mine. Now the sycophant wanted my job and he found what he thought could be a small lever to pry me loose from it.

When I came back to work the port captain, Captain Krendler, and his first mate were waiting for me. The port captain said they had a grave charge against me. In my absence the substitute second mate had found a problem I hadn't observed or was too lax to care about. It was a blister a little bigger than your hand in the paint of the covering board of the painted canvas of the saloon deck. They were all very serious with this silly excuse to fire me.

"What have you got to say for yourself?" asked Krendler.

"First," I said, "I want you to observe that I have tested it with the point of my knife."

The port captain ducked down and studied it. "Yes," he agreed, "it has been tested, all right."

"The covering board under the blister is rotten," I went on, "so I spoke to Sam Weatherby, our ship carpenter, about it and he will dig it out and replace it with sound wood on the layup next month."

"That's a pretty big thing to keep from your captain," said the first mate.

"I look at it in relation to other things," I said. "I hear it said that a captain knows his ship, so of course Captain Krendler knows this one. But, if you're interested in dry rot, follow me." They followed me down into the engine room. With a borrowed flashlight I showed them the underside of the deck overhead. It was in an unbelievably bad state of dry rot. It was a wonder the wheel of some freight truck hadn't broken through. There are times when I say exactly what I want to say. This was one of them. I said, "You as port captain, captain, and first mate are all aware of this, I'm sure. You would be derelict in your duty if you weren't. Coming on new here, it didn't take me long to find it, but it's been like that for years, obviously. So in comparison I felt the blister on the covering board was of no consequence to any of you and made my arrangements with Weatherby to fix it on the next layup." I looked at my watch. "Time to bring the freight aboard. If you'll excuse me, I'll get about it." No one answered, so I left. They didn't fire me, though they would have liked to. The company decided to repair the deck and the *Sausalito* was tied up for two months while they did it. The *Casadero* was put on the run in its place, and everything went along as usual.

Bunky was getting along well. His breathing was loud, but that was to be expected. However, as winter came on he caught several small colds, the last of which hung on and on and on and then got worse. We called the doctor from Ross. He came and confirmed our greatest fear—whooping cough.

"That large larnyx doesn't help," he said. "I think you should prepare yourselves to lose him, for he won't survive the winter." He gave us a prescription and some meager instructions.

"Would he have a better chance in a hospital?" I asked.

"No," the doctor said, "your wife can give him better care."

I looked at our baby. He was beginning to look like a baby. He was sun-browned and so loveable and, before this setback, full of smiles as he rollicked around. Poor little tyke, poor little guy! A forlorn fury gripped me. Fury at what? An accident? I sat staring at my hands after the doctor had gone. Nordi was weeping as she rocked Bunky. What could I do? I'd tried to heal him. I'd gone about it in the same way I'd gone about it with Catherine's brother. I couldn't do it. He was too close, too important, and I was too frightened. I sat there completely licked and then, finally, I accepted it. Bunky was going to die.

That night I tried to help Nordi to see that we must resign ourselves to losing him. "We'll do everything possible," I said, "but I'm afraid it's no use." After a time she came to accept it. We both did.

We didn't sleep that night until dawn. We lay listening to his convulsive coughing, jumping up every few minutes to pick him up and rock him in our arms. After dawn he fell asleep and so did we. Poor Nordi! I could get away from that coughing that tore so at our hearts. But somehow, even at work with all its distractions, I couldn't really leave him, but carried his image and his torment with me.

Several weeks went by. I was irritable and sullen. The crew knew and treated me as if I were sick. At home one night I was walking the floor with him, humming to him, for he was so restless. I began singing a lullaby that my mother sang to my sisters and me when we were babies. It is so beautiful, but it didn't quiet him. I ran out of quiet songs and began singing a loud song, for a basso with many deep notes. It went dolefully along, "Many brave hearts are asleep in the deep, so beware, beware." I'm no basso, but I did my best. I sang it loudly and Bunky went to sleep. Funny, I thought. He slept for an hour before coughing shook his poor tired body. Nordi got up and fed him and rocked him, but he was so distressed that she could not quiet him. I got up again and walked the floor with him. At length I sang the sea song again, singing as loud and deep as I could and in five minutes he was asleep. I laid him in his bassinet. Nordi was sitting up in bed. She looked at me most gravely. "I think you've hit on something, Clyde. He rests after you sing that song and rest conserves his strength. You sleep now and when he awakens, I'll sing loudly too."

But three hours later, his convulsive coughing woke me. "I tried doing as you did," she said, "but it didn't work." He was moving around fretfully in her arms. Another coughing spell shook him.

"Here," I said, and got up. "This time I'll sing 'Thy Sentinel Am I'—it's loud and deep." I did, and in ten minutes he was asleep. I laid him thoughtfully in his bed. Something was happening in my mind. It was hope.

"Nordi," I whispered as I took her in my arms. "Nordi, I think we're going to save him." She clung to me a long time as the tautness and the hopelessness drained from her.

"Maybe," she murmured. "Oh, God," she said, "if only we can!"

I learned to sleep when he slept and walked the floor with him singing when he was awake at night. Somehow he made it through the days much easier than he did the nights. We bought a medicine to put into boiling water and kept it steaming around the clock, and always I sang. I tried to give him my strength through my arms that carried him, to make that wordless transfer that had seemed to work before. Looking back, I don't think that it worked in this particular instance at all and I'd be hard pressed to explain how the loud singing and rather rough handling that went with it did him good. I only know that in a week the feeling that he was losing his battle left our cottage. He still coughed destructively. We could only wonder how his little body could go on, but it did, and the coughing seemed not quite so harsh, the terrible whooping intake of breath not so desperate. And then as the last of winter dragged through the month of February, the whooping slowly lessened and finally disappeared. We three had won. It seemed at first that we could not get enough sleep, for sleep in those winter months had been a sometimes thing—never more than two hours at a time. For almost a week we gave ourselves up to sleep and lazing around. The spring sun warmed our beach and there we lay like pigs, and like pigs we reveled in our lolling. In fact we played we were pigs and tried for that vast contentment that is theirs. Nordi figured that maybe we achieved forty percent.

Bunky began to grow again, adding weight and length of bones and a solemn study of our faces. He began to toddle after those little rock crabs and play with strands of kelp along the beach and Nordi smiled and planted flowers and smiled even in sleep while I made friends with a sea anemone that was attached to one of our low-tide rocks. I began visiting it each morning the tide was low. I'd say, "Hello." I knew it couldn't hear me, I felt foolish, still the desire to communicate was in me. I liked the anemone. The only means of communication I had was to put a pebble in its waiting arms, which it closed upon. I was a daily annoyance, since it couldn't digest the pebble and later had to disgorge it. Still I became fond of my anemone. It grew to be quite big in time. I still wonder if in some way it knew me or only knew my ambassador, the pebble.

I had become good friends with Linwood, Madeline's husband. Bob Drake was a headline writer for Hearst's *San Francisco Examiner*; Linwood did some such thing for the *Chronicle*. We all considered Hearst, who owned the *Examiner*, a despot, and with good reason. Linwood had worked for his paper for years as some kind of reporter. The wages paid were very poor and Linwood and some others organized a union that raised the wages of newspaper workers. Hearst waited to get even. When America entered the First World War, Hearst declared Linwood a syndicalist and had him jailed to protect the government in our war effort. Linwood was an American through and through. He had no idea what a syndicalist was, but he spent four years in the penitentiary on that trumped-up charge and came out a marked man, an ex-convict, but—worse—a man with a broken spirit. He worked for the *Chronicle* and also wrote his sea stories. I saw him often on the ferries where we would talk of boats and camping equipment, as he was something of a woodsman.

One day I saw him come aboard. He didn't seek me out as he usually did and, as I enjoyed his company very much, I looked around until I found him on the stern, staring out at the receding city. He would hardly talk at all. It was unlike him and I asked him why. He turned to me, a bewildered expression on his face. "Clyde," he said, "I have less than six months to live."

"Why do you think that?" I asked.

"My doctor is no fool. He's sure. A vertebra near my skull is diseased fatally. He gives me six months."

I was aghast. Linwood had lost four years because of Hearst's underhanded vindictiveness. Now he was going to lose the rest of his life too.

"Will you see other specialists on this?"

"I will," he said, "but I believe the good doctor is right."

I assumed the good doctor was wrong. Linwood looked in excellent health. I met Madeline on the road about a week later. "It's true, Clyde," she said. "He's been complaining of pain there for months. We thought it was a strain from a fall he'd taken on those slippery rocks outside our lot. He likes you, Clyde. You're interested in the same things and your feeling for beauty is similar to his. Visit us often in the coming time."

"As often as I'm allowed," I answered. And I did, for within two months Linwood found he couldn't leave his bed. They'd taken a great dark house half way between us and Tiburon and I stopped often. Together we designed a packboard long before they were made by others. I talked to him about fishing and he advised me to get an old boat and patch it up.

This was something that had been in my mind for some time and at last I bought a boat, an old Bristol Bay twenty-seven footer. Like all Bristol Bay boats, it was double ended, beamy and for sail only, and open except for fore and aft decks and a narrow side deck that ended in a coaming all around. Inside all was clear except for a big centerboard casing. Its planking was dried and shrunken from several years lying on the dock, so the Alaska Packers from whom I bought it soaked it for three days until it was no longer a sieve. Still it was a very leaky boat. All that came with the boat was the rudder and mast. I could wrangle no sails or oars from them.

I put an ad in the newspaper for sails and received an answer from Alameda. Three ferry trips and a street car ride and I found a low spacious bungalow sitting among fig trees and all manner of berry bushes. It was in the center of a complete city block and on all four sides were the imposing structures three or four stories high of industry. I opened the gate in the low picket fence and walked toward the cottage as its door opened and a small white-haired man came slowly out to meet me.

"You're coming for the sails?" he said in a great voice, grabbing my hand and shaking it vigorously. "I've been expecting you, this morning. Gad! What a lovely day. I used to sail myself. Had a little boat, but do you know the places where I sailed are all filled in. Progress, they call it. Well, maybe! But they'll not get my land, though they try forever. Come on in, young man, come in!" he said. "I live a lonely life. Wife died over ten years ago of the ague. No, that was her cousin, Annie. Consuelo, that was my wife, died of an obstruction in her, well, somewhere about her person. I'm brewing some tea for us. Are you much for reading?"

I glanced at his cherubic face and figured he'd sailed in somebody's duck pond and was sure his sails would be flimsy and way too small. He now brought out from a desk a great open volume.

"My autobiography," he said and opened it to where he was working. "Look it over while I'm getting some cookies. They're out back."

It was good writing. Where I read he was telling of a cruise he and two other young fellows had made to the Sandwich Islands. He came back with the cookies and explained, "We leased this big cutter and almost missed the islands altogether." Then he offered me the book again. His writing was loaded with allusions to Greek heroes, Roman emperors, German philosophers and the views of Thackeray, whom he thought much of, and a lot of talking to God through bits of sermons he remembered, rather in the manner Defoe allowed Robinson Crusoe to maunder on for pages. I finally got the sails from him and wrapped them up for carrying away as he read me more bits from his great book. "Come again," he called after me. "Like to read you how I met Consuelo at the end of the streetcar line that runs south of here." But I was turning the corner past a sullen brick building and thankfully heard no more. I made a vow with myself, that whatever happened to me I would never become a person like him. (And really, I don't often allude to Thackeray.)

A few days later I was telling Linwood about the boat and about the old man and his adventures. It eased his pain, he said, and he told me of an adventure he'd had out of Maine on a big fishing schooner, a real adventure. "Mine are so mundane," I said. "Anyway, some day I'm going fishing, either off Mexico for tuna or up around Eureka for salmon."

"You probably will," he said, "if you don't get hurt before that. You be a careful adventurer, Clyde, and you'll live to tell about it— that is, if you don't become the Ping-Pong ball of fate and get batted around as I have."

Madeline came in. She had quit a very well-paid position to be with him. "You've lived a rich life, Linwood," she said. "I happen to know that every story you sold to the *Post* was based on your own experiences. Here, I've spiced the soup so you'll think you're in Jamaica."

Fretting over the soup he forgot me, so I slipped away. His sickness disturbed me greatly. It was so damn unfair. I despised Hearst for that underhanded revenge he had taken on Linwood— only for helping to organize the union—and I was so frustrated at seeing Linwood slowly dying. It's strange, but the thought never occurred to me to help him as I had Catherine's brother. It seems never to have entered my mind.

After that visit he grew more tense, his anger flailing at everything. One day Madeline stopped me in their yard as I was leaving. She reached out and took my hand. "Don't come again, Clyde. He thinks you're my lover."

"How could he? I haven't given him the slightest indication."

"His mind's giving way," she said. "It tears me to bits to watch what's happening to him." I moved to comfort her but she slipped away. "No, Clyde, no pity, no comfort. As long as I don't let go I can handle all this. Good night!" she said. "You've been a good friend to us."

A week later a fellow hired me to ride a race horse about fifteen miles up country and deliver it. I was out on the road early, easing right along, when a big Buick came hurtling past me. The driver was Madeline. She didn't see me. Her expression! It seems impossible, but her expression was about life and death and strong-willed compassion. It was there for me to see in that instant. Linwood, I knew, lay dying in the back seat. "So long, Linwood," I wept, stunned by the loss. Nothing I've read, nothing the philosophers have said, nothing religion has promised helps me when someone I know dies. I tried to rationalize now as I went along, fighting down the mare's desire to bolt as she'd been trained to do. We leave hardly a trace. We're mostly water. Oh, a tombstone or an urn of ashes, and we leave assets, some of us: insurance, an old sweater, a pocketknife, and of course the watch. And those living go on living and most of those forget—luckily. Still, it is amazing what a gaping hole the death of a fellow human can leave in the world of those around him. I mourned Linwood's death for a long time—longer, in fact, than I stayed out of his bed.

We had sold our small sailboat to Pete and had dragged the new big one up on the rocks of the bank. There, in my spare time, I began working on it. I steamed and bent new ribs and put an enormous complicated shaft log in her and decked her over forward and made it neat under the deck, and built a bunk where I sometimes slept when working the night shift. Bunky's playing, crying and chortling saw to that. If I worked the late shift I would often have a bite at the Owl Cafe, come home and slip into my boat bunk for my night's rest and have breakfast in the morning with sweet Nordi. I have always been a moody person. The moonlight on the Bay would draw me out to row off into the night or to row along following the shore closely, looking down into the water where it met the shore, so fascinated with it, as if a fine message were written there in a language I could never quite understand.

On such a night I had eaten at the Owl and was passing Madeline's big dark house. Thinking of her, I looked up at some trees on the other side of the house. They were reflecting light from a window high up. I went around the house and looked up at the window. I stared up at it a bit and then tossed a pebble against its panes. Madeline's head appeared. I felt rather foolish.

"I'm not sleepy," I said. "The moon is out. Want to go for a walk?"

She looked down and shivered. "Too chilly, Clyde. I've gone to bed, but I can't sleep either. The front door is unlocked. Come up for a chat." We talked for a long time. Her face was so expressive, so completely beautiful in every way. I was fascinated. She sat up in her bed with her arms wrapped around her knees and her long hair was a great blue-black mane flowing down her back and lying in great swaths on the pillows behind. Finally, she said, "my, but I've enjoyed this visit. Still you'd better go now and get some sleep."

I stood up and we looked at each other. "I'm not going home," I said.

She continued to stare at me and then she smiled. "Will you turn out the light?" she said. So I did.

Three times in the night she called out Linwood's name. It caused me no hint of hurt for I felt I had received his mantle, at least for the moment.

Nordi met me at the door when I got home. Her smile was complex.

"You have been with Madeline, haven't you?"

"Why do you think so?

"It's in the order of things, Clyde. A mixture of sensuality, duty and accident—and now guilt."

"You're quite a detective."

"That's from the guilt, I suppose. It's inseparable from the act now. I'm terribly hurt, but had I been you, a man, I'd have gone over there before this. Do you love me?" she asked, very serious for my answer, questioning my eyes most intently with hers.

"More than ever, a hell of a lot more than ever! Oh, Nordi, you grow too fast. I can't keep up."

"I'll try not to, dear. Now your breakfast is ready, but first into the tub with you. I drew it when I saw you coming."

I became an indeterminate creature: Clyde to my wife, sort of

Linwood to grieving Madeline, and a polyglot to myself. Of course, now that I was the buffer for Madeline's sorrow I had to keep buffering. Actually it wasn't too time consuming and I became rather engrossed in it. After a couple of weeks, however, I found that I was not alone in my endeavors, but that several others were intent in driving the pallor of sorrow from her cheek, and Madeline in her very vigorous manner was helping us help her, so I left this great flurry of activity and repaired, as a father should do, to the bosom of his family. I spent more time with Bunky, my good wife, and the sea anemone.

On the ferries things were switched around again. My new skipper, Captain Lenajarvi, was a lean, taut, small-minded Finn who, when upset, jumped up and down on his cap in lieu of using profanity. I don't know what sect he clove to, but, as they usually do, it took more out of him than the tithe. Still, it gave him righteousness that, on the job, was expressed in pettishness backed by the Bible. We didn't get along well, for he had this great need to jump on his cap and Ole Borg, the first mate, and I gave him no chance to do so. Ole and I both rode to work on the *Marin* where we planned the care of the boat so meticulously and so far ahead that there was nothing to quibble about nor even mention. Lenajarvi's main gripe was that I worked with the crew, hauling out the string of mail and freight trucks. I did this when the tides were way low or extremely high, when another hand was really needed, and he was continuously after me about my playfulness and joy in living.

After the night tie-up, Captain Lenajarvi rarely came down on deck but stayed in the pilothouse. Everything that needed to be done was done and shipshape. It should have made him proud of his crew, but it didn't. So when he did come down on deck one night, I was surprised to see him. It was the only time I ever looked up to him. I was walking on my hands the length of the boat—a thing I often did for exercise and to maintain my ability to balance (I hoped someday to walk a tightrope). I saw those shiny shoes and, looking up, saw it was Captain Lenajarvi. I gave a strong push with my hands and stood on my feet. My white summer uniform cap fell off at this and lit in a pile of dust and stuff that had been swept there. I reached down, retrieved it and wiped off the soggy

end of a cigar that clung to it. It smeared a great brown smear on
the snow-white top. I put it on.

"Splendid weather we had today, sir," I said, as I drew my
dangling watch up by its chain and put it in my pocket, grabbed my
keys that hung from my belt and tried to adjust my tie. "Quite a
rip built up off Alcatraz, sir, on the six-fifteen. Did you notice it,
sir?" But he was not even noticing me. He was treating his cap
cruelly—though not jumping up and down on it—and, because he
couldn't swear, his eyes stuck out a little, a phenomenon that
didn't engage me at the moment. I am sure he hungered to throw
his cap down for trampling, but somehow the idea of two caps
being besmirched at the same time didn't seem to him to be fitting.

"Mr. Rice, the Mr. Mate," he gritted out, "you're an insult to
officers in whole fleet. What maybe you think crew figgers us?
Like you, maybe? No, we can't allow it. We all dignified licensed
officers. I as your captain, I, I—I. Go! Go make your crew work,
show them you officer." The rest was in Finnish and mumbled as
he walked away.

That night, going home on the *Marin*, Ole said, "You know the
old man's got something in this carelessness of yours. You've got
to cut it out. Yeah, I know it's hard to be suddenly a strict boss
over your old pals and drinking friends. I had the same thing on
the old *Lollapankus* when they made me mate on short notice."

"Well," I agreed, "I guess I'll have to act like a prick or I'll lose
this job, but why in hell act officious when there's perfect rapport
between me and the crew? I've got this boat running in oil. Results
are what count. Like the time at Christmas we got the six trucks of
mailbags that had to be sorted before we reached Sausalito and we
had to put them on the train for Eureka. They worked like mani-
acs. Do you figure there's another crew on these boats that will
handle a job like that?"

"I know, Clyde, I know. But what I'm saying is you've got to
clean up your act from Lenajarvi's standpoint."

"Oh, sure, I know, be a marionette disciplinarian—and on a
ferryboat at that. Okay, okay!"

Tuesday started as a fine day. I greeted the fusty old lawyer who
had represented the railroad for God knows how long. He was big
and solid—a former sea captain, now a lawyer with a beautifully

drooping white mustache, a silver-headed walking stick and an insufferable air of looking down on people in general. At one time he was going to beat me over the head with his stick, but when I told him where it would end up he calmed down and in the end we became good friends. We got on our passengers and freight and ten automobiles and were soon on our way. I can't remember who the captain and mate were, though I think they were Captain Lenajarvi and Ole Borg. I do know we had in the engine room an assistant engineer who had risen to chief and this was his first trip in control. We came across on breeze-dappled water and were about to enter the slip. The passengers, restrained by a line, were under the saloon deck on the main deck. Two deckhands and I were out on the bow waiting to tie up. I noticed we were not slowing down and I feared a crash. I told the deckhands to get off the bow. They didn't move fast enough.

"Quick," I yelled, "watch out for the lifeboats."

Instead of reversing the engine when he got the signal, the new chief made one more turn of the paddle wheels full-speed ahead. I felt it when he had lost the second chance to reverse. We were going full-speed into the slip to crash. I turned to the passengers standing packed behind the line, "Lie down! Lie down!"

They looked at me in amazement. The skipper headed the ferry into the side of the slip, smashed into it and ricocheted off it and into the other side before smashing into the inner end of it. The 'first crunching collision with the slip side toppled all the passengers on deck into heaps. I jumped in the air at the moment of impact. I turned and saw an automobile rolling down an inner alleyway headed to run over the people on the deck. I rushed toward it, but a man still seated in the wings ran to it and twisted the steering wheel so that it would run into a post. A boy hung onto the post. I grabbed his hands away just in time.

By now the boat was heading into the inner end of the slip. We crashed into it. Down came the lifeboats and the davits, but none fell on the downed people. The great bars with their immense springs that hold the slip together at the inner end were torn out of place and came down on the bow. John Silva, one of the deckhands, stood by me. I told him to sound the bilges for water and to ask the engine department if the engines or boilers had moved at all from their beds. The wharfinger, who had scuttled away as we came surging at him, came back. I asked him if he could raise and lower the gangway. It proved to be all right. The rest of the crew came and we got the heavy rods out of the way and the davits and the lifeboats moved enough for a passageway between them. A long broken mass of piling by the bow looked dangerous, as if it might fall on the boat, but after looking it over I let the passengers go ashore, a few at a time. People lay all over the deck. The first mate was tending to two men who had fallen down the stairs and broken their necks. Ambulance people swarmed on board. The city responded splendidly to the crash. Only the people on the stairs were badly hurt. We were very lucky. It could have been a catastrophe, for it looked for a while as if the sixty new pilings, broken completely off at the inner end of the slip, would fall on the ferry and capsize it.

The company lawyer had come trumpeting out of the men's lavatory ready to kill the captain. The first impact had thrown him so he lit with his face in a urinal. I told him to make himself useful, that all the people who could be gotten to their feet and off the boat probably wouldn't sue. "Get the malingerers off the boat," I said, "so we can take care of the injured." He did a good job.

Ole moved among the injured and, as we waited for them to be moved off, the crew and I searched the boat for injured people, found none, and got the cars and the freight and the mail off. Satisfied that all was safe and sound on the boat and that the gangway was unharmed, we took on our freight and mail and passengers and autos and left only fifteen minutes late. It was, from the standpoint of efficiency, the high point of my life. I had done the engineer's, the captain's and the mate's job in seeing to the safety of everything. I don't think I've ever again been quite so sure of myself as that time. No one was seriously injured. The two neck injuries proved to be of a minor sort, as was a broken back. The Embarcadero, two hundred feet away from the slip, was cracked clear across its pavement. The first crash sheared off sixty new pilings and the second many more. Had the skipper gone straight in, it would have been complete catastrophe with many lives lost.

The following Sunday was one we didn't look forward to. Each summer on this date the Irish held an enormous picnic in some large park up the line. Getting them over in the morning was bad enough, for every man-jack of them awoke on this day with a chip on his shoulder. But hauling them back to San Francisco in the evening, that was an unenviable chore. We kept our eyes peeled for children and drunks who might fall or leap overboard. The ladies of such an outing would come back with a nip or two too many and often got the count of their children wrong and demanded of me to have the skipper back up ("for my son Brian's fall't overboard"). Then a wild scouring of the boat would ensue and eventually, Brian, her ninth, and Elvis, her twelfth, would be found playing in one of the lifeboats and, after more requests of a like nature, we'd reach Frisco.

On this Sunday evening they came on board as from a great battlefield. First came two perpendicular Irishmen carrying a horizontal one. Then came men supporting other men, then two carrying a litter where rode an Irishman with a bandaged head and a nicely splinted upper leg. Then a drove of tipsy mothers with hordes of children and then a body of badly beaten men came aboard. A spattering of swacked Irish poets with flowing ties floated aboard on the fumes of Bushnell's Irish whiskey. And then there were people who were just people, who came aboard meekly and sat in protected corners. Finally we raised the gangplank and churned out of the slip.

We figured the day was going about par after we cleaned up the broken glass where one Irishman had thrown another through the showcase of candies at the magazine counter. Then Manuel, guarding the railings of the saloon deck, reported a very sick woman under a doctor's care on the upper saloon deck. I hurried up to see her, a somewhat young, attractive Irish biddy, attended by a cadaverous-looking man well into his cups who said he was a doctor, and her husband, one of those men whom drink makes limp and silly, and of course the children.

"How do you feel?" I asked her and got out a notebook.

"Name of Clancy," her husband mumbled when he saw the notebook and he gave me the address.

"Do you feel better now, Mrs. Clancy?" I asked her. She started to reply, but the cadaverous doctor said she was under doctor's orders and not to be moved until we brought an ambulance to the foot of the stairs. This in a sepulchral bass voice and with such authority it seemed to me thespian. I knew from past experience that no ambulance could come on board—a law of some sort. I told the doctor, but he was adamant. I hunted up Silva and told him to run ahead of the crowd when we landed and tell the cop outside we needed an ambulance pronto. We could not stay in the slip over fifteen minutes as other ferries would be landing there, and those fifteen minutes would be extremely busy ones even without trying to get an ambulance on board. I told Manuel to take my place at landing and went back to the Clancys and their doctor. Our instructions from the head office were never to do anything that would bring bad publicity to the ferries. This doctor could stir up a rumpus, but not unless Mrs. Clancy showed herself sick and agreed with the doctor's orders. Again I talked with them and smiled at Mrs. Clancy and said I was sorry she was so ill.

"How do you feel?" I asked.

"Dizzy," she answered.

As I smiled I winked at her. "A nip too many?" I suggested.

"I got it doon to keep Tim from making a bigger fool of hisself."

"Do you like to dance?" I asked.

"That I do," she said, "but Tim here is all feet."

"How about a waltz?"

"Aye," she said, "but where?"

"There's an ideal place down at the foot of the stairs. May I help you down?"

"Sure, and you're a gallant lad," she said and took my hand.

The doctor said, "You heard my orders," and her husband simpered. She was drunk all right. On deck I really had to hold her as we began waltzing around and around down the deck. The whole length of it we waltzed and into the arms of the ambulance drivers on the gangway. The crew hustled the doctor and her husband into the ambulance and we were shut of them. And we got out of the slip on time—a feat the first mate was no end pleased with. The only trouble was that Captain Lenajarvi was on deck when, with Mrs. Clancy in my arms, I passed right by him whirling slowly to my humming of "Pink Lady." He was livid.

That was on Sunday. We were off Monday but Tuesday we were again at our usual tasks. We came on at two in the tail end of a storm on the Bay that reflected a big storm out at sea. All soon quieted down except for a very low ground swell that shouldered in the Bay from time to time. Tuesday was the time of our lifeboat drill, so after we tied up alongside the *Casadero* we lowered the lifeboat from the bow, which was nearest the dock, a matter of rotating the boats that we used. We came out from between the ferries and under a heavy hauser we had strung between them to ease the surge of the ground swell, which usually came in a series of seven after long periods of quiet. Then out we went into the night, Pete and Manuel rowing powerfully or executing turns and backing. The three of us were becoming unusually adept in our maneuvers and pleased with ourselves. After the usual time, back we came sliding along under our captain's eye where he stood on the saloon deck. Just before we went under that hauser a surge caused it to dip to the water. Pete for some reason jumped ahead and lifted it over the bow of our boat. I hadn't time to say boo. It hadn't stopped the momentum of our boat so we swept on under it, knocking Pete ass over teakettle. Manuel dropped between the seats and evaded it. There was no place for me to go. Standing on the stern I saw just how I could step over, as, riding on our gunnels, it came at me. Timing it perfectly, my left foot left the grating for a lightning step over it. But the bail of the lantern that was sitting on the seat before me caught on my foot. In that split second I admired the lantern's flame as it hung there, then I leapt sideways off the boat upon the line that now lay on the water as the boat sped on. The line and I went down, down, down in the water, then raised as another surge swayed the ferries. Out I came, up high above the water. Then as more surges came, down I went and up I came dripping like a drowned rat. The crews of the two ferries lined the rails watching, as I had yelled whoopee when I saw that the lantern had undone me, and each time I came free of the water I whooped, laughing at my misadventure.

Captain Lenajarvi, however, who never laughed, felt deeply humiliated that another crew had seen his second mate in such a deplorable situation. He shuddered, grew hot and then cold, and hid himself from what he felt were derisive stares. The boat came back after my third dip and rescued me. We put my watch first in fresh water and then in kerosene and dried my clothes in the engine room and I went home that night, dampish but otherwise unharmed. No one mentioned that Pete, the most famous seaman of the fleet, had produced the mess with his most stupid move.

Captain Lenajarvi kept his daughter home from high school next day and they composed a letter.

There were mists afloat Wednesday as we headed out that I suspected would thicken before we got back to Sausalito. Bony came to tell me that I was wanted in the pilothouse. Ole was steering. Lenajarvi stood waiting for me.

"Mr. Mate, Mr. Rice, I have a letter," and he produced it, "a letter I order you to present to Mr. Small, general superintendent of this railroad tomorrow at the Tiburon office."

He read off a long letter about dignity and the standing of officers far above the standing of the crew. I, it stated, fraternized with the crew. His daughter and the dictionary had been quite a bit of help. He said I could not handle a boat that was necessary for a second mate to be able to do, then he told of my accident of the night before—but not as it happened—and said he wanted a second mate who could handle a boat for the protection of his passengers. I said, "I have taken a rowboat out through the Gate, landed it on the open beaches and taken it off the beach and rowed it home. There's not a mate or a second mate or a captain here can do it."

He steamed up at once. "Anything else?" he gritted out.

"Yeah," I said. "I'm a better all-around man than you are."

Well, there it was. I would have to do some mighty hard talking to keep my job tomorrow.

We came back in fog as I had assumed we would. I was out on the bow with the lookout deckhand. We were past Alcatraz when I felt—at my back and to the port of us—a man leap over from the saloon deck. I didn't see it, I felt it. I ran to the doors and got through and rang the suicide bell before the skipper, who looked down on the whole thing, could respond. I ran aft with the crew and we lowered the port lifeboat. Now in this I had instructed them most carefully. They lowered the boat to the rail and they took the boat painter forward and made it fast to the rail. Then down we went, cleared the after fall first, and then the forward fall, and I shouted to them to let go of the painter and we were free of the ferry that would go on for a quarter of a mile before it could stop. Away we went for the suicide bobbing some distance away. We got to him. "Get in here," I said.

"I want to drown," he mourned, "leave me alone." He swam directly away from the side of the boat. We wouldn't be able to catch him that way until he tired, and he swam well. Our boat was between him and the ferry.

"Go ahead and drown," I said, "they can't see you from the ferry."

"All right, I will," he said, and stuck his head under the water while his hind end moved out. While his head was under, we moved the boat close to him. I held the boathook like a spear. He popped up.

"Why didn't you drown?" I asked.

"I can't," he said. "It's salty."

"I'm going to have to spear you to get you in," I said and aimed the boathook at him.

"Oh, no," he mourned, and swam to the boat and heaved himself over the gunnel. Back we rowed to the *Tamalpais*. We were hauled up and put our man under guard in the fiddly where it was warm. As we brought the boat up on deck I saw a steamboat inspector who happened to be on the boat with his watch in his hand.

"Seven minutes," he said. "You've made the fastest rescue ever on San Francisco Bay. Best one before was eleven minutes. I'll report it to the newspapers."

Well, as a result of that incident I didn't deliver the denouncing letter next day. When I came to work and we got under way, Bony told me I was wanted in the pilothouse. The scene was the same. Lenajarvi read me another letter, this from Superintendent Small, congratulating me on my excellent seamanship, etc., and informing me that I was to have lunch with the president of the railroad the next day. "And he says," continued Lenajarvi, "that I am to congratulate you and commend you."

"Skip it," I said, and handed Ole the accusing letter and left the pilothouse.

An item in the *San Francisco Chronicle* on the thing stated again that I was going to have luncheon with the president. I phoned him and got through to him. "I'm Clyde Rice," I said. "About that luncheon, I'm interested in poetry and I assume you're interested in railroads—locomotives maybe. We might bore one another, so I decline, but thank you for the invitation. By the way, the would-be suicide had rocks and corks in all his pockets. A thing like that, if it spread, could hurt the country."

He laughed, said goodbye, and that was that. It got around after that simple rescue. Borg, the first mate and my very good friend, could not figure how I knew the man had jumped. Captain Lenajarvi had been steering, but Ole had been standing on the other side of the pilothouse, staring out into the fog, and he had seen both the actions of the would-be suicide and mine. We had both moved at the same time: I to the suicide bell and he to jump overboard. When I told him that I had felt the man jump, it bothered him, but he had seen it. That and the story of the amputee—which he hadn't believed but now began to, sort of added up. It alienated him from me. He wanted no friendship with a freak. I saw it and sadly accepted it.

I had joined the deckhand union with pleasure but it was with reluctance that I joined the Mates Masters and Pilots. I was initiated into the organization by an old sea captain. It was the lodge stuff, all about never turning your back on the capstan—a replica of one, marvelously made of wood inlays—their symbol. Under no circumstances while in the room were you to turn your back on the capstan. There it was! One of my great hatreds of belonging to an organized group. They all ask you to act like a fool, give up your dignity along with your sense of humor, and, after you've done that, act out some yahoo monkey business, and they'll accept you as a brother, conveying symbolically that the level of intelligence in a group is that of its dullest member. My father said of lodges that if you lean enough fence posts together they can all stand up. I went to one meeting. They were all talking about an increase in wages, but the avarice in their eyes and the naked greed in their speeches over another few bucks was too much for me. I got up and left and rejoined the deckhands' union.

When I was still a deckhand a new ferryboat—the *Redwood Empire*—was launched and the *Eureka* was chosen to carry the dignitaries and such to the launching up the estuary in Alameda. At Sausalito we picked up a railroad carload of mayors, politicians and noted people from the area through which our railroad ran. The railroad, too, was now to be named the Redwood Empire for publicity purposes. The politicians were easy to pick out as big pot-bellied men who leaned back when they walked. In their formative period, called boyhood, they had always leaned back when confronting work. That plump member of the great late comic team of Laurel and Hardy was a master of this fatuous stance. And sifting through the throng were little wiry college-bred old ladies who lived out in the brush up the line and were authorities on the efficiency of clabbored buttermilk, on dogwood root rot, and on the spindle-shanked Neffra.

The *Eureka* was decked out with flags and well-secured bunting that, when we were under way, flagellated themselves against stanchions and railings as if to atone for some obscure sin. A fairly good band had come on board and as we passed Alcatraz the band leader, who had done time, had his group serenade the prisoners on the rock with a Sousa march that I felt was extremely inappropriate. I got tangled in the possibilities anyway: I was a convict in a cell up there facing ten more years and then the music came into my cell. I looked out through the barred windows at the bedecked ferry while I listened to the band—beauty and torment were in me. Then someone tapped my shoulder. I turned, "Oh, warden," I said, but it was Mack, the mate.

"Fer Chrissakes, let these passengers out. They been waiting five minutes."

Befuddled, I opened the door and let them out. I didn't even rejoice that I was free and not a convict. I just forgot it as I saw a pretty girl among the passengers—nice legs. I wondered what her ears were like and so on. As we neared the slip I opened the door and squeezed through the people, now crowded behind the restraining line, and got out on the bow for tie-up.

I've seen it countless times. The elliptic curve of the bow moving into the different ellipse of the ferry slip, sometimes coming in more on one side than another, but always a thing of abstract beauty and portent like that achieved by great music, and now it was happening. It is not a still thing but a slowly happening thing and the ferry is a boat and, as a boat, it sweeps into the slip. From outside on the Bay it sweeps as ships sweep into the ferry slip and I stand there trying to get it all in. I feel all the people at my back— all members, as I am, of this pageant of landing. On shore people wait on the gangway, important-feeling people. The band is playing. Suddenly I love the pompous, foolish dignitaries, I love all mankind. I know at last that we are gloriously worthwhile. I know this is a manmade moment, not a natural one and, oh, God, I am so proud to be a man and those beautiful elliptic lines keep slowly converging, relationships keep changing and then they meet and we tie up. The gangplank is lowered and, with the band still playing, the people from the shore flow aboard, laughing and calling to one another as they meet the people on the boat. Ah, God, God, God, such beauty, such splendor! I lean sobbing over the rail and play I am sick.

I lost and won when we tied up at the shipyard, for I had to stay aboard and didn't see the launching. But for the same reason, I didn't have to listen to that same old speech they all make, and, best of all, did not have to feel ashamed for all mankind as I watched some pontifical oaf waving his arms around in a sad attempt to be convincing.

Bunky, by now, was starting to talk. The first word he said after *mama* was *boat* and then *fish*—"sish," as he said it. He was also becoming a problem. He wandered the beach where the eddying current brought in all manner of things with each tide. One thing that came in often were boxes. They were his boats. We saw him launch one and try to get into it. Water poured through the slats and it sank. But a day or so later I saw him get into one that sank slowly, so that he was knee-deep in the water. I realized that had that box been a bit more water-tight it could have drifted out several feet farther before it filled and the most important member of our family would be gone forever. Talking to him would do no good. We policed the beach at all times but still several boxes landed that were tight enough for him to cross his Styx irretrievably. By now we had a dog, a shepherd. I had built a nice big doghouse for him, but Bunky got it. That was after he climbed the cliffs of the point and the fire department couldn't get him down. He finally came down by himself. But that and his attempts to put to sea in leaking boxes made us realize we'd have to tie him up. So overhead we ran a wire across the lot and put a harness on him that he couldn't get out of. The leash from the harness was attached to the wire in the manner used for dogs and he had his upholstered doghouse as a retreat from the sun or a chance shower. Poor little devil. He was heartbroken, but his faithful dog never left him and we were with him every moment we could spare.

I had gained a little weight the last year and had ceased those long runs on the ridge of the Peninsula. Nordi was always like sunshine to me. She'd gotten Bessie to take care of Bunky one day and rowed out to Southhampton Light to the east of us. It's an eight-mile row and there are mean currents to buck, still she got back without incident except a couple of blisters. Several weeks later, though, I was in the pilothouse steering when Ole noticed something out in the middle of our crossing. It didn't look quite like a log. He put his glass on it and said, "It's someone rowing." We went over to see if they needed assistance and it turned out to be Nordi on a jaunt to Frisco. We ordered her to turn back and she did. That night at home I was angry and told her a mother shouldn't take such chances, at which she showed me her study of the tides and currents of that day. She would have made it to the city easily and back to boot, using the currents and tides in an ingenious way. Still I made her promise to take no more unusual jaunts.

I was beginning to be noticed. I was the youngest second mate on the Bay and the oldest in seniority. I had done things like the fast rescue and other similar feats. I gave money and backed the tickets of distressed women from up the tracks who had lost their purses or whatever. I never asked their names and the conductors who knew me now winked as I came to the trains with them and said okay and took the lady aboard like a long lost darling. These women always paid me back. I did other things. I was good publicity, they said. The president of the railroad came aboard for a chat with me. So I was taking up more sidewalk than I needed one day, sauntering up Market Street, when, with the light just right, I saw myself in a big window as I advanced toward it. I came close and stopped. I was astounded, then ashamed, then infuriated. What I saw was a slightly swaggering, overweight young man, a complacent, cud-chewing expression on his face. I'd seen that expression before on the faces of well-fed hogs as they moved slowly away from a trough of slops. I had become what I feared most to be, a placid, passive creature. "Jee-sus!" I threw the fine cigar into the gutter. I didn't look again. What I'd seen was indelible on my soul. I decided to quit my job.

I went down to the docks and waited for the next ferry home and spent the rest of the day on the highest point of Sugarloaf. I tried to think. I was stymied everywhere I looked! How come? Why? Why hadn't I been aware of what had happened to me? Even as a boy I had known that I could never belong to the human cattle. I saw now that one must be alert at all times to fend off the warm arms of security. Suddenly I stood up from my rock, from my sightless perusal of what lay below me, from my numb leaning into the wind. "I'll bring it to Nordi," I said out loud and ran down the ridge toward home.

Supper was ready, but I couldn't eat until I'd told her. We ate as she thought about it. We washed the dishes together, then she sat down, crossed her ankles and smiled her warm smile.

"If you hadn't found out for yourself, I wouldn't have told you," she said. "I myself could be turned out to grass quite easily. We have a child now. Still, that's not enough, I hope, to force you to wear the yoke of an ox. I told you how I felt about it when you quit Acme Flavoring. I don't feel the same way about it now. Time and Bunky make a difference—but no, Clyde, no, I do feel the same way. I love you, more than ever. The only security I want is being secure in your love."

I suppose I was the same as I went about my work the following week. I did all the things you do. I was polite, or mean, or compassionate as fitted each occasion. On one of these days a man afflicted with cerebral palsy came aboard. Usually such passengers would have a normal companion to help them, since getting aboard and leaving seemed to make them more nervous and the other passengers wouldn't help them—in fact, acted with loathing toward them. This particular man had no such companion, however, and couldn't seem to find his way to go ashore. I went to him and took his hand, got my arm locked in his, and as I led him, talked to him quietly about the boat. He clung to my hand as he writhed and tussled. When I finally got him off, I told him that the next time he came aboard he could expect to be helped ashore if I was available. As the crew came back after unloading and loading they gathered around me and began to laugh and snicker at my steering such a loathsome thing off. One Irishman who was new in the crew— though not so new that I hadn't already pegged him as a trouble-maker—came close to me, staring me right in the eye. I could tell he sensed compassion, not duty, in what I had done, and to him this could only mean one thing—weakness. His feeling of ascendancy over me because of my compassion bloomed slowly in his broad Irish visage. Backed by the mood of the crew, he was about to broadcast his discovery. He drew himself up, eyes filled with deri-sion, breath ready to explode the information. My timing, howev-er, was better than his. Before he could make a sound, I drove my left at his chin with all I had and down he went, clobbered. I told two deckhands to carry him ashore and leave him. I informed the captain that he was dead drunk and heard no more about it. The crew, though they didn't know the score, wondered who I might clip next and stayed well away from me for a few days. But after that, at my urging, they did help those unfortunate passengers ashore. There was a home of them somewhere up the line and soon five or six would come, timing their crossing so as to meet the ferry with my crew who, proud of their new knowledge and humanity, would lead them ashore.

Shortly after this exhibition of kindness and savagery, my non-plussed crew saw the last of me.

VII

In Which
I Find The Princess,
Get My Bearings But Lose A Rudder,
and
Land In The Zoo,
Where They Feed Every Denizen But Me

◇ 1929 ◇

It was during my last month on the ferries that I first saw the *Princess*. We were pulling out of Sausalito. I was hurrying up to the pilothouse to steer when out before us, crossing our bow, appeared a most excellent fishboat—the beautiful curve of its sheer line as it swept up the bow to the stem was soul-satisfying. Bigger than most fishboats thereabouts, it looked to be at least fifty feet long. Then I saw its name on the stern: the *Princess of San Diego*.

I entered the pilothouse with a wild gleam in my eyes.

"I've got vacation time coming," I told Ole. "I want four days of it, starting tomorrow."

"What's the sudden rush?" he asked, staring at me.

"I'll let you know when I get back," I said, and took the wheel.

Next day I searched the Sausalito waterfront and that of San Francisco. The second day I went south of San Francisco, and across the Bay and Alameda Estuary. The third day I was up searching the Richland waterfront and came over and wandered along the banks of Green Bay Slough. The fourth day in the afternoon, with blistered heels and a slowly dying hope, I went on to San Rafael and out to their small docking space and then, before I was aware of it, I was standing on the dock looking down on its deck where it lay between two overhoused, overdone motor yachts. Oh, God, its broad decks and the fine hatch to its hold excited my admiration. Its small house was well forward, its fore-castle up in the bow was partly joined to the pilothouse in an ingenious and workmanship-like way.

I climbed down the ladder and stood upon its deck and, after more gloating over high bulwarks and rail, I entered the open door of the pilothouse. Down a hatch there was the sound of tools being used, wrenches banged together. I hallooed down the hatch. The sound of metal upon metal stopped and a head appeared. The face in the dim light smiled and said, "Hello, Mr. Reesa," and coming up the ladder into the light he turned out to be a former deckhand

161

of mine—Manuel Perez. We grinned at each other like a couple of apes, then went out and sat on the hatch. There he told me his story. He was buying the boat from an uncle in San Diego, who was building a really big one. He had a partner who was called back to the Azores—something about an estate. They had been fishing off the Mexican coast for bottom fish—waiting for tuna season, as the boat was a tuna boat. The two of them had brought it up the coast to spend some time with Perez' family and to have the engine gone over by a highly esteemed machinist in San Rafael.

"And you, Reesa?" he said. "Why you here?"

How to explain to him? "I'm going to leave the ferries," I said. "Another year of that and I'd have to shave in the dark."

"So?" he said.

"It's too easy," I went on, "it makes your cock and your belly and your head go soft."

He grinned, but murmured the questioning "So?" again.

"So I want to buy in on this boat," I answered. "You say your partner left."

His grin widened and he slapped me heavily on the shoulder. He held that stance, still gripping my shoulder for a moment longer and then said, "I'd like that, Reesa, but another fella come yesterday who's s'posed to be a fine navigator—captain's papers, any ocean. Maybe we split it three ways."

I thought a while. Three partners didn't appeal to me. Still, I asked him what he wanted as a down payment on such a venture.

"The other man offered four hundred and fifty dollars for a third."

The boat carried five men in tuna season and with a good navigator we could find banks and sea mounts at sea where the excellent fishing was available only to an expert in celestial navigation. So I offered the same on the basis that I meet the man before I put my money down. With such down payments on this fine boat we would have to agree to take only living expenses out of what was made until the boat was paid for; Perez had gotten the boat, which was only three years old, from his uncle for six thousand three hundred dollars. We could pay it off in less than one good season. I was elated, to say the least.

I met the third partner—a big, powerful man who had papers to show him to be what he said he was. We hit it off very well.

"Glad to see another white man aboard," he said with a heavy German accent. As we got to be more chummy he confided to me that we were going to make more money, big money, not the kind of money you get from fish—this derisively. I saw him several times after that as the boat engine was overhauled. One day he came over for dinner with Nordi and me. After we had eaten we went out on the beach to smoke. He mentioned again the big money we'd make.

"I know my way around," he said. "I've been around the world three times and the money ain't in fish. Fish will be our front. Now booze—and I got connections—and drugs is better. You any idea what we can peel off in a couple of months?"

"No."

"Well, I ain't going to tell you yet."

I didn't like this at all, but was further startled when he said the Portuguese would have to go. "You'll be steering some night and I'll ask Manuel to step aft and see something. It's easy. I'll club him with a wrench and pitch him overboard. Man lost at sea, leave it to me!"

"Perez's all right," I said. "He's a good worker."

"He ain't my style, Rice. Here we got a chance. I tell you I been looking for a boat like that for a long time and I can use you, but no greasy Portagee on my boat. There's a Scotchman I know and a Norwegian and we're ready, and through working for wages."

I will never know why he told me, why he trusted me on such short notice, but then a lot of strange things happen to a fellow. I told Nordi about it. She was horrified. She said he had extremely cold eyes. I saw Perez next morning and told him what the German had said. It frightened him out of his wits. He told his wife and mother, and horror and suspicion reigned in their house. They stared at me as if at any moment I might twitch a machine gun from my pocket and—

"Look," I said to his family, "Perez has known me for years. He knows what I'm like. I propose to buy the heiney's share and enough of mine to make me half owner with Manuel. Then the guy will be out."

I left them to think it over and the next day we drew up the papers giving me half. Then I hunted Klaus up and told him I'd bought his interest as well as my own. I'd waxed the inside of my knife scabbard for the occasion. We were standing at the bar at a joint on Columbus Avenue. He looked me over for a long time, but he didn't make the move I expected. He thought it over and finally turned on his heels and left. I was very careful how I handled myself for a while, but I never saw him or heard of him again.

The people on the ferries deplored my move. The port captain was angry. "Hell, Clyde," he said. "The way the retirements are lined up, you'd be a captain in less than four years. You own maybe the best waterfront lot on the Bay. Why go down there, when you can stay here and build on something solid?"

It wasn't any use. That smart aleck look I'd seen in the mirror still sickened me.

With Nordi it was a mixed bag. She loved our place on the beach. She said she'd rather stay there until we saw how it worked out. We parted with many tears and hungry clingings with salty kisses. Bunky could say, "Goo'bye Da."

Then Nordi rowed me out to the *Princess*, anchored out a ways, and I piled aboard and the smell of diesel exhaust fanned through those last tearful glimpses we had of each other, the last caught-breathed good-byes. Manuel steered as gentle Nordi, and then even the Point, became distant and then nothing as we headed for the Gate and the long run down the coast to San Diego.

We met a placid sea outside that built up after us quickly until we were racing down its watery hills or plowing into the backs of them, with a feeling of falling back while we waited for the next surge to hurl us on our way. It was my first experience with the sea, and its over-vivid deep blue was startling. As for Manuel, who was born in the Azores and as a young man crewed on those big oared whaling boats, it received his casual regard. He was engineer and I, captain. I kept off shore about ten miles during the day, intensely interested in my situation. Perez was a good companion, cheerful, honest, simple. With the wind behind us, we coasted down the seas, making good time. That night the lighthouse beams were hidden by fog, so we held off the coast. Several ships overhauled us in the night, disappearing into the fog ahead of us.

We consumed the lunches—our last link with our wives—and then proceeded totally on our own. Steering in the little pilot-house, I saw the crest of each wave that lifted us in the race forward from each side window as it passed. The tumbling broken water of the crest lit a brilliant, greenish-white with fluorescence. At first they were startling, even frightening: a wildness, a coldness toward man I had never experienced on land. But after an hour or so I began to find my place in it and feel more comfortable in a new rhythm.

At dawn we could not see the coast for haze and turned our course inshore and came at last into a roadstead of San Luis Obispo where we anchored and slept for several hours. After that we rowed ashore at very low-tide to get some abalones. We had pried a few from low tide rocks when an elderly gentleman came along and asked what we were doing. On being told he brought out a badge and arrested us for unknowingly poaching on an abalone reserve. We said we were unaware and very sorry, but he was firm.

"How do I know you're that ignorant?"

"Look," I pleaded. "How could we know? We've never been here before. We just came in this morning."

"How?" he demanded.

"By sea. We were way out and came in to follow the shore closer, and it looked interesting here so we anchored."

"Well," he said, and stopped hustling us along the path. "Could you be the boat that came straight in earlier this morning, name of *Princess*?" he inquired.

"That's us," said Perez. "We own the *Princess*, me and Reesa."

"You know," said our captor. "I'm the lighthouse keeper here and I watched you from being a very vague something until you were close enough so I could see your name, with a glass of course. You've got a beautiful boat there. Here now," he went on, "throw those things away. Come on down. I'll show you where to get the big ones."

Well, we tried to cook them but we didn't know how and only made shoe leather of them and went ashore again and gathered limpits off the rocks that Perez ate alive but that I felt I should cook. I finally got several down, fried as hard as rocks.

We awoke in the night to find an onshore wind building up and our anchor dragging. We saw we were way too close to some rocks. Perez started the engine, a big three-cylinder diesel that you started with a blowtorch. The noise as it started up was terrific down there in the engine room and Perez reached up into the pilothouse and put the engine in gear to soften the noise. I was out on the bow hauling in the anchor and had just gotten it clear of the bottom when we started making way toward the rocks. One of my hunches struck me—no one at the wheel. I made fast the anchor chain and rushed in and spun the wheel hard over. We just missed the rocks and the anchor hanging thirty or forty feet down didn't catch on the bottom. I headed out to sea, then stopped and hauled up the anchor and we went on south as before. That was a close one. We had been very, very lucky. He had done it once before in the Bay. Now I asked him why. He was distraught and said, "If I know then what I know now," and threw up his hands and that was all.

We had some coffee, but we had neglected to bring bread. We had beans and rice aboard but didn't know how to cook them. As we passed Point Saul the wind freshened from the north. The western wind that had tried to dump us on those rocks faded and after several hours we were racing before white-capped seas. Just before Point Arquilla the brisk cold wind seemed to lose a little of its strength, and we came abreast of Point Conception. Here we left the northwest wind behind and plowed along in warm tranquil water and the sun warmed the decks. We brought our bedding and mattresses up out of the forecastle to air and dry. We reveled in it, for it was a cold winter wind that had followed us down the long coast.

Now in Santa Barbara Channel, between the islands and the mainland, we turned our boat's bow east and on we went for an hour or so when we began to meet a ripple on the still water that soon made up into wavelets coming our way. An hour later we were charging through a stiff chop that became worse by the hour. We had planned to go ashore for a meal and some easily cooked provisions at Santa Barbara, but the chop coming into the harbor made it an unwise venture. Perez looked worried. Neither of us knew we were burrowing into a Santa Ana—an offshore wind that arises in the desert back of Los Angeles and is famous for its force in Santa Barbara Channel. All that day and most of the night we plunged and reared back and plunged as we moved forward slowly into that great steep chop. As we neared San Pedro Harbor in the dark, Perez, who was steering, said, "I been following another boat in by his masthead light, but I see a better one to follow now—real bright and red."

Bright and red—bright and—I leaped for the wheel, tore it out of his hand, spun it hard over and avoided piling up on the jetty by only a boat length. His feelings were hurt. "Why you no tell me? I turn boat fast as you."

"Perez," I said, "there just wasn't enough time. You've got to watch stuff like that."

"Oh, you right, Reesa. If I know then what I know now."

We rounded the jetty and were in a thick dust storm, but I had made a careful study of the harbor charts while I was in Tiburon and was able to tie up finally—well up into the harbor. It was then about two a.m. and as we had had about four hours sleep since we left Tiburon, we hit our bunks and were soon engulfed in much-needed slumber.

Slowly I awoke. The engine was going. Yes, we were underway! I climbed out on deck. It was still dark. We were running in a rough sea and Perez was at the wheel. "Where the hell are we?" I demanded.

"I think about fifteen miles west of San Pedro."

"Why?" No reply. "Well," I said, "the first thing we're going to do is get back under the land. This is an offshore wind. It'll be smooth a couple of miles off the beach."

Land, when I first saw it, looked like Oregon. It appeared out of the dusk as groves of larch in winter, but a few more minutes and I saw they were oil derricks, thick as trees. It was Huntington Beach. Under the lee of the land it was smooth as a lake. We headed down the coast. Several times we got behind kelp beds and had to retrace our windings to get out. Oh, we were a weary, hungry couple of fools, but the engine was made of sterner stuff and kept forcing the boat ahead and we kept making turns, keeping the *Princess* headed south, paralleling the land about four miles away. It would have been very pleasant if we hadn't been half dead for lack of food and sleep. Finally we rounded Point Loma. We had arrived inside of San Diego Bay and, once inside, Perez ran the boat into the shallows close to shore and grounded it, but with the tide rising we were soon off and anchored in front of the Portuguese settlement, where he visited while I hunted up a restaurant where double ham and eggs gave me strength to row out and sleep aboard. Perez stayed with relatives ashore.

Next day I tried to find out from Perez why we couldn't stay in San Pedro and get some canned goods, steaks and much-needed sleep. But he wouldn't or couldn't explain himself—or the fact that we left home with no provisions to speak of. When I had asked if we were okay for the trip, he said yes. Months later a friend of his who knew why told me.

Three things had been the cause of our strange trip. One, Perez and his wife and mother were terribly frightened by my disclosure of Klaus' plan. They had been in this country only a few years and viewed all blond people with suspicion. Two, Portuguese fishermen from the Azores fished out of San Diego for tuna; out of San Pedro was a group of Yugoslavs, also fishing tuna. They didn't mix. Perez' wife, a big woman who dominated him, had written him a timetable showing him where he would be at what time and what to do to avoid the German if the German and I were in cahoots and he was following us on land for some dire deed. Three, he was really scared in San Pedro where the Slovacks live. How he got the boat out of the old harbor in San Pedro in the dark and in a terrible dust storm, and why he went ten miles out into the full impact of the Santa Ana will always be a mystery. He tried manfully to carry out his wife's schedule and, when he ran the boat aground just inside the harbor of San Diego, was beside himself in anguish because, as I later learned, he should have arrived eight hours before. About the food, I was to blame as much as he in not checking up on him. It may have been a part of his wife's strategy. Anyway, I liked him. I like him still as I remember him. He was honest and open with me, except when his wife's wishes interfered. He was a hard worker, clean and pleasant. My problems with him were that he often reacted quickly without consideration of more effects than one from his action. He was good with our engine, serving it carefully. For all his excitability, I found him a good companion.

We laid up several days resting from the trip and then took on ice and fuel, bait and gear and, as I carefully watched, provisions, a barometer, and a fair-sized fire extinguisher. This, Perez deplored. We also went down to Ballast Point for several skiff loads of stones, about twenty-five pounds in size, to be weights for our set lines.

San Diego was then a small sleepy city with some naval and army installations and a remarkable zoo. I didn't see much of it for we left soon for bottom fishing. We went about thirty-five or forty miles down the Mexican coast and then out about twelve miles. Under us at this place lay a sixty fathom bank. Here we set out our lines. Each line reaching to the bottom had about thirty hooks arranged separately on short leaders along the bottom end. The rock on the lower end held it down. A five-gallon tin can painted red held the upper end of the line floating on top. We set about twelve of these in the same manner around a light cork raft that held aloft a slender bamboo pole that flew a red flag. We used it to orient ourselves with our circle of cans, for if it was even slightly rough, it was difficult to come on the cans. After we got all our circle of lines down we lifted the first one. That's three hundred and sixty feet of line to hand-over-hand up. Eventually I saw a pale green glimmer in the blue-black water that, as we hauled them closer, turned to white and then pink and then brilliant vermillion as our catch came to the surface. Fourteen beautiful red snappers lay on the water and one head where a shark had made a meal. The line was now all twisted in knots from the struggle of small sharks we had also hooked, so we cast it on deck and dropped another in its place. Then, orienting ourselves by the flag that appeared when we both were on top of a wave, we went west to the second can and repeated the procedure. We lost many fish to sharks, but in our primitive way we were bringing many fish over the rail. I began to get seasick. I had decided to start at the bottom of this fishing business, which was baiting the hooks with smelly mackerel. Being bent over a tub of spoiled mackerel is not conducive to a settled stomach, especially if the boat rolls overly much, and the *Princess*, a sweet hull built to travel a long way on a minimum of fuel, rolled. Lying dead in the water above our lines, she rolled her deck under first on one side and then on the other. There would be a small

chop on the banks and the *Princess* would do everything but som-
ersault, and yet she was a safe boat, so I became seasick and stayed
that way for the first two weeks whenever we were on the fishing
grounds.

We stayed three days the first trip and were very pleased with
our catch. Next trip we took on a couple of extra hands. We
worked from dawn to dark and after four days brought in what I
thought was an excellent load of snappers. Perez said there was
another bank farther down the Mexican coast where we might
better our catch.

The following trip was to be only three days and we went alone.
We hadn't got to our fishing bank before Perez spotted a Mexican
gunboat coming after us.

"We run," he said, speeding up the engine.

"But we're fourteen miles out," I said, "they only have jurisdiction over three."

"Not way they figger," Perez answered. "Any boat they get,
they keep!"

Well now! The sleek lines of our boat paid off for us. Straight
out to sea we plunged. They started shooting at us. We could see
the shells bounce near us.

"They got small cannon," Perez said, but they were soon too
far behind us and turned for better hunting elsewhere. So we got
on our grounds and made our set quite late. God, I was seasick,
and the bad cold I had gotten before I left San Francisco dogged
me, but neither annoyance weakened me for I felt very alive and
happy with what we were doing. I did well that day and, though I
coughed a lot, spent a fairly good night.

We were fishing before daybreak and doing very well, but the
sea was rumpled with wind and swells from a disturbance to the
south that sent its troubled seas toward us. I could now stand on
the boat's narrow rail, balancing to the boat's bobbing and rolling
and the sudden rise of bow as, beset with tumbling water, it fooled
the hungry seas with a curved deflection of their forces. The sky
was clear blue and full of light. The water under us and around us
was intense bluish-black, except for wave tops where whiteness
was unsullied. I stood there on the rail, completely unconscious of
balancing to the boat's wild movements, staring down into the

black water as I hauled on the line that would eventually bring our catch to the surface. Vague, ghost-like greenish-white flutterings came to my notice, to change color with every fathom of hauled line until, all scarlet and vermillion and iridescent green, they lay on the black surface or disappeared for a moment in the startling white of a breaking sea. Then onto the deck with them, working the hooks out of their mouths, as the new set of baited hooks slid down the folds of that strange dark sea to its rocky bottom sixty fathoms below.

We were going great guns, vermillion all over the once-tan deck. Then, looking for it, we couldn't find our flag, nor the next red can, nor any can. We stared around, no longer interested in what was below but on what rode the surface. It was a white-capped, jumbled sea around us. In the brilliant light a super-vividness colored and explained the detail of all that was about. And then, far off toward the coast, we saw a flash of red and white that disappeared even as we glimpsed it.

"You see it?"

"Sure, I saw it. It's heading away from us. They must have our gear."

We turned and tore after them. We saw them as we each were lifted on top of a wave at the same moment. They were running for the Mexican port of Ensenada. They had to have our gear. With those big swells coming in and the steep chop they had followed us around our circle while we peered down into the depths. It didn't seem possible, but they were running from the scene of our loss and we were after them. In a little over an hour we caught up with them and could see, as their boat rolled, their deck with our gear cluttered there. We came close.

"Give up our gear," we yelled and were answered with a shotgun blast that didn't quite reach us. As we came closer again I had to duck behind the house as the second blast peppered the deck and broke a window. I got out my thirty-thirty and, when she rolled so I could see a lot of her bottom, I put several slugs down there where the leaks would count. We called to them once more to throw our gear overboard and were answered with another blast.

Through the open door of the pilothouse I could see the steers-

man and in front of him a large compass. I shot and the compass
flew to pieces. I don't think the helmsman was hurt. There was
some blood on him; probably some fragment of the compass did it.
Anyway, he ran out aft and helped the others pitch our gear
overboard. They got the hell away from there toward where Ensenada would be if you kept going, and we hauled our matted gear
aboard disconsolately. After a brief consultation we headed south
for another thirty, forty miles, taking turns at steering and cleaning up the tangle they had left after they had unhooked our fish.
Well, out here it was every man for himself and the devil take the
hindmost.

We anchored about four miles off the coast. Dangerous! But
Perez said it was not supposed to be rough in that area. Still, we
rolled and pitched all night. High up on the mountain above us I
could see a tiny fire where some goatherd squatted in sleep. How I
envied him his stable world! That night and every night after that I
was unable to sleep lying down and propped myself up to sleep,
troubled by endless coughing fits. But morning found me willing
and eager for hard work. We had a great day. So good we left the
gear down and anchored beside it, and though the sharks had been
very busy, we made a small haul the first time around.

It was such a satisfying life—a little hectic away from law and
order, but rewarding—and its beauty was imperiously demanding.
Such sharp contrasts, such vivid changes of color. The blue-black
sea reached up and up until you could see light through its strident
greens and blues, as it held a plume of broken white water against
the sky for a second, and then would be a dark hole, a black pit the
boat would lunge down into, only to be borne high aloft, again to
see the sea around for miles as black against the marching white of
combers.

I vomited everything I ate except the evening meal. That I lay
down with and it sustained me. We made it of a red snapper I cut
up into big square chunks with a hatchet. These we placed into a
great pot over our little stove. To this we added potatoes, tomatoes, onions, celery, salt and pepper and freshly ground cumin.
When it was done we put the pot on the pilothouse floor and sat on
the floor all around it and put our feet against its sides to keep it
from slipping and dipped our bowls into it, downing three or four

bowls before loosening our belts. Then a smoke, and I went below with the only sustenance I would have in twenty-four hours. And always I coughed. I slept leaning into the curve of the bow, jammed into the bow in a half-reclining position, but still I was strong and keen, and things in general were going excellently. Soon I could go up and get Nordi, for we were making good money and had paid our payments on the boat four months in advance.

Soon the tuna fishery would start, and then we would really be busy. We decided to take on two more hands and go south about a hundred fifty miles to a bank near San Martin Island. We took more than sufficient stores, bait and fuel and away we went. I was cooking rice and steering when, just outside of San Diego, Perez, coming in the door of the house, noticed there was no flame under the rice.

"Hey," he said, "the flame's out under your rice. I fix," and before I could stop him he lit a match and applied it to the burner. Up sprang the flame and spread down into the lockers under it. In a flash the flames were by the door. We could not get out. I reached out and jerked the new fire extinguisher from the wall. A half dozen strokes on the extinguisher and it was all over. Somehow the stove, a kerosene one, had gone out and the kerosene had been running down into the food stores below it. Perez did not ask himself how long the stove had been out. That was past his ability. Except for the extinguisher, Perez and I would have been dead in another two minutes, for all the windows of the pilothouse were too small to get through, and the crew would probably have been lost with the boat. Perez patted and patted the extinguisher. "A fine ting," he said over and over as we headed back to port to get a new food supply. We laid over until the next morning while Perez extolled the merits of the extinguisher and we cleaned up the mess of a gallon of kerosene soaked into everything. The stove, on being examined, was found faulty, so we put a new one in its place and headed south.

We had exceptional fishing on the bank north of the island. I was now over my seasickness, but the cough was worse and I slept now crammed into the bow down in the forecastle. Lying down seemed permanently out of the question. Several months had gone by since I had come down here and all that time the cold had been with me. I felt I should see a doctor. I'd had colds that held on for a month before, but then at least I could lie down. Seeing a doctor might tie up the boat for a trip, but would have to be done.

The next night we anchored sixteen miles out at sea on a forty-fathoms bank. Perez and the crew wanted to tie the rudder hard over during the night. I had a disturbing feeling and equally disturbing vision of what would happen if they did it, so I asked them to lash it dead amidships. They said they would and, chock full of fish stew, I went down to my peculiar bed and fell asleep.

In the morning we brought up the anchor and spun the wheel to turn to where we would make our set. The boat wouldn't respond to the rudder. While they went over the steering cables I took a shaving mirror to the stern and, holding it in an awkward position, could see under the fantail. We had *no* rudder. When questioned, they admitted they had disobeyed me and tied it over. "That is the way we all do it," they said.

My psychic hunch that one in the tens of thousands of small cross seas would hit at the moment of crossing against the rudder was correct. In front of the rudder shaft and bolted to it was a three-inch strip of wood that streamlined the rudder shaft into the main area. Some low clouds came from the north—a good sign—but high up maretail clouds were sailing in from the south at what must have been a great rate up there. I looked at the barometer. It was moving down, not fast but not slow, from what it had been at early morning glance. I stepped out on deck. "Am I the captain here?"

Perez laughed. "Of course, Reesa."

"Okay, we are heading north to San Diego. A big storm, not a short chubasco, is heading this way." I showed them the storm clouds coming high up above the low ones they looked at. I showed them the barometer and how it had dipped down from dawn's marking. "Without a rudder we cannot survive such a storm. So as captain, I am going to do what I can."

I had on the *Princess* the steering oar of a life-saving boat—a fine ash oar of perhaps twelve feet. I broke up an applebox and, taking the heavy ends of the box, nailed them through and through on each side of the blade of the oar. The *Princess* had a hole in the center of the stern rail—the afterchock. It was four-and-a-half inches in diameter. We let out the oar and then brought it back in the hole. Two men standing on the hatch could, by raising the handle of the oar waist high, steer with it. We started out and got her aimed in the right way and we did have some control, but at times the handle would kick the man off the hatch. Still, we were heading north. The sea was quite moderate, waiting, it seemed, for the coming fury. Fussing along I found that I could steer a bit with that forward edge on the rudder stock. I kept fooling with it and soon I relieved the men at the oar. I could go on for an hour or more before a deflecting wave would put us really off course, and we'd have to resort to the oar to get her back on so I could take over again. It was delicate work and took constant concentration. We found that I was the only one who could do it.

At Cape Colnett in the evening, Perez and the crew decided we would go in and catch a few enormous jewfish to at least pay the expenses, but I would not let them. The barometer continued to go down and those high maretails had closed the sky, making a listless, leaden, waiting world underneath it.

When we came abreast of Cape Colnett Bay, we were about four miles offshore, but by standing on the house we saw a four-stack destroyer-class vessel—one that Italy sold to Mexico—coming out with a fishboat in tow. They didn't chase us, but we would have been taken had we entered the bay. After that the crew's solid opposition to me stopped—direct danger they could understand.

A bit before daybreak we slipped into San Diego Bay under a very vindictive sky. I tied up on what I figured would be a lee side of a dock and an hour later big hundred-footers were carrying out the same chore, as the storm pounded San Diego with a ferocity I had been expecting. I was pleased that I was alive and, when the boat was in drydock and I had gotten as much of my peculiar sleep as I could, I went to see the doctor who represented the Maritime Hospital in San Francisco. After an hour of tests he asked me if either of my parents had ever been tubercular.

"Both were," I answered, "but they both overcame it. That was how they met."

"Well, I don't know about that," he said, "but you, Mr. Rice, have active tuberculosis."

I was rattled. "What do I do? Where do I go? Arizona?"

"Wait a bit," he said. "Tell me your story." And when I did, he said, "My advice is to go back to Tiburon and lie on that beach of yours and consume enormous amounts of milk, eggs, greens and beefsteak. Lie around for six months—and I mean, just lie around. Then go over to the Marine Hospital in San Francisco and take tests. I believe anyone with the vitality to do what you have been doing in your condition will show the disease arrested, and with proper care you will probably not have another recurrence, but don't wait. Stay away from fishing. Those forecastles are the breeding places of lung diseases. And hear me now! Walk away from that boat! Don't make another trip. You're in no shape to do anything but rest for a long time." He held out his hand. "Good luck to you!" he said.

I went out into the street trying not to look at the old picture but at the new one he'd laid out before me. I walked slowly around the block letting it soak in. I believed that he was right. It explained a lot, like the fact that I'd lost forty pounds in the last two months. TB! If I'm not goddamned careful and lucky, I'll soon be dead!

Perez was not in the shipyard where they had finished installing the new rudder. I finally found him at his relatives' house in the Portuguese settlement.

"Ho, Reesa," he said, "you looka pale. Joe pour a litta wine."

We sat with his relatives in a big clean kitchen. Out with it, I instructed myself, but remained silent. Perez grinned at me.

"I tell them about how Mex try to steal our gear." He laughed boisterously, beaming at the other men. "They make mistake. We still got all our gear." The three men with him nodded in smiling agreement. Then out it came.

"Perez," I said, "I have to leave the boat, quit fishing for good. I have tuberculosis in both lungs."

He'd been sitting with his chair tilted against the wall. Now he tilted it forward and placed his glass on the table. "What's thees you tell me?" he demanded. "You say you're seek. Why," he smiled his broad smile, "you lay over—one, two, maybe tree trip. Get rid of that cough. I take boat on trip. You get half share of boat share. Just sit like old man in sun."

"That's good of you, Manuel. You're a good guy, but you see I have to follow doctor's orders from now on. I want to stay alive. I've got TB. I've lost a lot of weight in two months. I'll be lucky if I pull out of this. But the doctor said, get off that boat! He gave me a regime to follow and, by the powers, I'm going to follow it."

"You say tuberculosis, Reesa?"

"That's what the doctor said."

One of the men left the room. "You no like work with me?"

"You know better than that. Do I need to answer?"

"No, Reesa, we good paisanos!"

The man who had left came back with an older man and spoke to me. "Mr. Reesa, I hear about you. Manuel, here, say you good man." He smiled at me. Warmth radiated from his lined dark face. "This my friend, Manuel Rodriguez, cure many malo, how you say seekness, while we live over on Pico."

"Stand up for him, Reesa," said Perez. "He find what's wrong. Feex!"

I stood up. Rodriguez was a small, woebegone-looking man with an enormous nose and great hands. He helped me take off my coat and shirt, then he tapped me repeatedly on the back and chest while he pressed his ear against my chest and back and Perez told me to breathe deeply. After a time he stood up and told me sonorously what was wrong with me in Portuguese, though he did get out the word *bellows* and thumped me on the chest and threw up his hands in exquisite exasperation and murmured to Perez, who said, "He speak poor Englis but he will tell me to tell you how to cure malo." They talked and talked and the old man got down on the floor and put his face almost on the floor, then got up, dusted his hands, smiled a patronizing smile at me and left. After he left the five of us all took a little more wine and Perez told me of the cure. "He say," said Perez, "you have with the lungs not so good. Pretty seek. This cure we have hundreds of years. It cure the lungs every time. You put on good clothes with white shirt, go before dawn up into the hills, find spring of water where watercress grow, lean over, put elbows in water too. Eat watercress like that, but no touch watercress with hands. Eat like the good burro. Morning dew gotta still be on watercress when you eat. Eat some. Eat some more. Then go home. Soon no more sick lungs, then come back fish with me. Nothing to it. Nothing to it! You do like we do back on Pico. You be ready when tuna come!"

After that—by my not taking a good cure when I saw one and by my being stubborn and rather insulting to their culture—they withdrew from me. I was not welcome. And now, seeking to cut ties with the *Princess*, I took a hotel room for a couple of days. Still I thought I'd try to let Perez understand. I looked in the phone book for a doctor with a Portuguese name and found one, but learned he was attending a conference in Baltimore and wouldn't be back for a month.

My contract with Perez included a condition that I had put in myself: if either of us left before the boat was paid for, the departing person lost all claim on the boat and the catch. I had sent Nordi in that time about one thousand dollars to bank and now, according to the agreement, I had lost my down payment of nine hundred dollars. Our contract was taken care of by the Fisherman's Union. It was to them that I had tendered the down payment and through them that we made payments to Perez' uncle. I sent my belongings home with a note that I would explain later. Then, through Perez' uncle, I learned that the Union representative wanted to see me so I dropped into the Union office. Three men were there. I knew the fellow at the desk.

"How's tricks?" I said.

"I heard about you, Rice," said the fat man at the desk, "and I checked with the doctor. You're smart to quit and you just might beat the rap. Reason we called you in is that that nine hundred dollar check of yours is no good."

"It's from my friend, Bob Drake," I said. "He owed it to me. He's got money in several banks. Runs a bunch of small magazines."

He looked me over thoughtfully. "Like I said, the check bounced, but we kept it. You was doin' real good wit the *Princess* and we'da asked for the money in the tuna season. I kinda like to see a guy bluff his way in, I'll give him room. But you're leaving permanent. Now, get this, Rice, and get it damn good! Don't leave town, don't try to leave town until that check is made good. You're a fisherman, but a lot of our boats don't haul fish. We deal in bottle goods, but hell—you know the score! So we have to have enforcers. Now, Joe and Al here is enforcers." The two lean, hard, blank-eyed characters had let their coats slip a bit so I could see their guns in their shoulder holsters. "You try to sneak out of town and you'll be one more body laying in the ditch long side the road. Stay in town and you're safe and when you turn up the dinero—why, we're quits and you won't have to worry."

"Let's see the check," I said.

"Sure," he said, found it and handed it to me. It was from the State Bank in San Rafael. Bob was making money with his little magazines and because of the market crash earlier in the year had spread the money he had among half a dozen banks.

"Run it through the San Rafael Bank again. I know he's got money in it and I don't understand the tie-up."

I called Bob's office and was told Bob had left with his secretary for a two-week vacation in the High Sierras. They purposely left no forwarding address in an attempt to get away from it all. Did Bob have money in the San Rafael Bank, I asked. His office was not sure. His secretary would know, but she was with him. He was expected back in five or six days. I hung up, feeling as dangled as the receiver of the telephone.

I said, "Natal cord to trouble," and did not know why I said it. "Bum connection," I said of that and swore, "Get off the line." In towering annoyance at myself, I hurried down the street. To where? You're not going anywhere, Mister. You've got to sit tight. A coughing fit shook me. Yeah, I said to myself when it was over, the world's got me cornered. I checked my pockets: two dollars and forty-five cents. I'd eaten lunch but was a little bit hungry. The *Princess*'s last trip would pay off in minuses. I could call Nordi for funds or my father or Perez. No! This was me, Clyde Rice, in this jam. Still, all I had to do was whine. Whines are in short supply, I said to myself. I'll sweat this one out myself.

I called Bob's office again and asked to have him wire me when the check would clear. With the forty-five cents I bought a bag of oranges, then gave my key to the clerk at the hotel and slowly walked into the residential district, staring stupidly at the houses as I consumed half the oranges. Where was I going? Where did I usually go when I was hurting? To the trees, to groves of trees. Not to the goddamned eucalyptus trees I don't, but to fir trees and maples or to lie beneath willows. Oh, to be in Oregon! Yeah, you'll want to be in the womb next! No, Oregon! Oh, forget it. There are fir trees and willows at the zoo. How are you sure? You've only been there once. Uh-huh! Well, we'll see, and see I did.

Sauntering through residential districts until the zoo noises headed me toward it, I finally walked on well-kept lawns, saw peacocks through vistas, smelled peanuts and exotic dungs. I relaxed from my fight against bitterness that clawed to gain entrance. I said, "Roll with the punches," but fell to cursing everything bitterly anyway. No, I said, and remembering the Portuguese cure, said, "Pass the watercress, please!" and giggled weakly as I now lay beneath a cedar, who might have been homesick too.

When I awoke it was dusk. There were only three more oranges. Slowly I ate them and put the peels back into the sack. Under the cedar the falling needles of years had made a dry springy bed. I put out my hand and caressed the rough bark of the trunk and said, "I am most grateful," aiming my thanks into the center of the cedar's trunk. Then I lay my head on a great rounded root that broke through the surface of my bed and slept. No coughing fits, no need to lie in a sitting position. I thought of Oregon, and soon I dreamed of Oregon. No night breeze came to clash the fronds of palms. The moon arose and crossed the sky and I was a boy in Oregon.

I awoke to the clamor of peacocks, cold with dew, and soon the lions roared. As I awaited the sun to dry me, I took the orange peels out of the bag and, peeling all the white lining, ate the tasteless stuff. I searched for a place where I thought the sun would first touch. When it did, it warmed me and I luxuriated in it. I turned myself and turned and turned to warm all sides and then just sat there on the park bench. There was nothing else to do. I started to talk to myself and stopped it. We've got three or four days to wait this out. We'll wait it out in thoughtlessness. It's supposed to be a great thing for a guy. Try it now, you may not get another chance. It was hard, for I remembered Nordi. What was she doing at this moment? And Bunky, what of him? I could see them most plainly in my mind's eye. When I stared they grew distant, but when I relaxed the focus, their smiles, though dim, seemed quivering with life. Oh, to be with them again! I sat there on the park bench while such a panorama of Nordi and Bunky and our life at Waterspout Point spread itself before me. Do all bums see such beauties as this, sitting there in rags dozing? Then shadows fell upon me. I looked up. People were passing—lots of women with children going, I gathered, to see the animals. Coughing shook me, but not badly. I got up and followed them to see the animals too.

When I was a boy many tales were told about the natives of Java and Indonesia. They said that when a native became fed up with the sameness of his life he would run amok, killing all who came his way. We were also told of the orangutan of the same area: as they grew older, the sagacious men orangutans withdrew as hermits, until they became competely anti-social and would kill their own kind in fits of frustration and rage. They were said to sit for days on the tops of palm trees, cogitating, concentrating with great pressure over problems their animal brains could not handle, such as two-and-a-half times three. They would try to work it out with their fingers, using thumbs for halves until they gave up, came roaring down out of their palms and attacked their Minnies and children. And I was told by Linwood before his sickness that far around on the other side of the world elderly men of the Swedish variety in a like situation posed the same problem for their Helgas and offspring before they committed suicide over some metaphysical Swedenborgian concept.

This possible relationship engaged me while I sojourned in the zoo. Seeing an elderly male orangutan several times a day probably stimulated this mental activity of mine. I was concerned whether Sweden was directly opposite Siam through the center of the world and, if it were, what it could signify. I mention this to point out that, though you try to live without thinking, in spite of yourself mental activity of a sort does go on.

People were tossing peanuts to the monkeys. Saliva filled my mouth. I went away from there to see the Tasmanian wolf and the armadillo. An empty stomach and coughing fits and knowing the why of it and wondering how we'd exist while I laid on the sand eating great amounts of costly food, all but gutted me from time to time. And when the picture of the *Princess* sailing south without me came at me I was sore of heart. The day dragged on. Everywhere people were popping stuff in their mouths. They were eternally unwrapping sandwiches and candy bars and dropping the paper; they stared hard at the sandwich as they crammed half of it into their mouths. Such gluttons! So unseemly! I visited the drinking fountains often, but you can't fool a stomach. Finally the people left, and finally the sun went down, and I sat on a bench and on the ground and on another bench. I toddled along taking a little stroll as the peacocks yelled for help, foxes yipped in their cages and somewhere a monkey clanged his swing gently against a steel pole. I sat on another bench, lay on it, sat on it and eventually, in grinding boredom, sought the red cedar tree, crushed some of its green matted needles in my hand and buried my nose in them and strangely fell asleep soon after.

Next day I became interested in some big apes. I shall never know if lack of food and sickness produced hallucinations in me or if they really existed. They were set apart from the other apes and monkeys in a big, roofed, circular cage of perpendicular iron bars the distance of the width of a loaf of bread. The cage was about thirty feet in diameter and around it was a circular lawn and next to the cage were flowers. Spectators were separated from this by a further fence at least twenty feet from the cage. In this fine set-up were three big apes who often stood as upright as we do. They were almost as big as a man and black, and what hair they had was very sparse. Their faces were more like those of men than like that of the orangutan or of the gorilla. They looked more like chimpanzees but were much bigger, and I noticed that they didn't stand as gorillas do.

The keepers fed them loaves of bread, shoving them in between the bars, and sometimes the great apes let the bread just lie inside the cage, too well fed to care. Seeing this, I planned to filch one in the evening when the crowd was gone, for now I was weakening with the hunger, chilled in the nights when cool zephyrs played over my lightly clothed body. Through the nights I longed for the sun as much as I craved sustenance.

I should have been a teacher. Many people have told me so. I live to tell people bits of knowledge I have come upon so that we can all put it into our schemes of things, but this urge can become perverted—by annoyance or an odd sense of humor—into a joy in handing out misinformation. This day, with wrinkled clothes and much in need of a razor, I stood around the orangutan cage and told whoever I could say a few words to that I was a seaman who had lately spent some years in Sumatra and Indonesia and had often "gone up-country" to watch the apes in "their natural habitat." The phrases "gone up-country" and "natural habitat" I let fall with unction and great authority. "Expect a draft from England shortly," I felt covered my seedy appearance. But the thing I aimed at through all this was to speak of the lady orangutans as "Minnies." I wanted whomever I instructed thus to thereafter speak with bland assurance of the females as "Minnies."

The afternoon wore on and I became too weak even for this. I lay on a bench "out back" and giggled over the phrase, for now I was silly with weakness. The sun warmed me and I felt I should look over my bread larder in the great apes' cage. I was standing admiring the view of several handy loaves and idly watching a gardener currying the row of bezalias that rimmed the cage, when one of the apes flashed across the cage, ripped the sleeve off the man's jacket as the man fell back, and grabbing the tool he'd been working with, snapped its handle in two as it jerked it back into the cage. I had seen the whole thing, the incredible speed, the power and the malignancy. Ah, the cunning of the caged ones was there. The handle he'd broken like a matchstick was the size of an axe handle. I found most certainly that I did not want to break bread with the apes and sought the last of the sunlight, to store it somewhere for the night ahead. In twilight I walked slowly down to the Western Union; they had no message for me.

When the sun came up the next day, it came after a night of chills and coughing fits. I was lethargic and weary of the world. I sat on a bench in the sun soaking up its warmth. Off to the left an orchestra was maiming some Beethoven. On the ground before me was a quarter of an orange peel. It had lain several days in the dust and sun. It looked dry, but not too dry, and perhaps chewy. Slowly I was making up my mind to pick it up and eat it. The bench quivered and squeaked. "I hope you don't mind my sitting here," said a man's high voice.

"Not at all," I said. "You'll find it pleasant here." I saw that I would have to forego the orange peel for a while, but I decided that as soon as he left I would pick it up and start chewing.

"Yes," the man was saying, "it's warm for a winter sun. The atmosphere is very clear today. Lets down the warmth."

I didn't answer. I'd slipped into a daze. Nothing was said for quite a while, but he spoke again.

"Do you know anything about music, young man?"

I turned to look at him. Middle-sized, middle-aged fellow with a gray mustache. He looked like the Joneses.

"Yes," I said. "I'm fond of music."

"Can you tell me, then, the name of the piece they're playing?"

I was hazy about it, as about everything, but it finally came to me. "Beethoven's most popular symphony, the Fifth," I murmured and lapsed into my daze and then spoke out of it: "Shame what they're doing to it." As if in a fog, I was behind my semi-conscious shield. The guy was talking again.

"What do you think I did before I retired?" I sort of looked at him again and told him my favorite.

"You had a hardware store in Kalamazoo."

"No," he spoke up briskly, "I was a doctor in Kansas. That is, until my wife died and then I came out to the coast." I settled into my fog again, semi-safe from the insistent demands of my body. His story rolled along about how he had learned to play doctor in the movies and how it was lucrative and easy, until the talkies came to Hollywood. "My squeaky voice ended my career." I understood a little. Perez and I had seen Ruth Chatterton in *Madame X*. "Of course," he said, "I was a saving person even before I got to the coast. I've enough to take care of myself if I live to be a hundred, but it's lonely, very lonely. I never married again after Ruth died. Say, I've got a car here. How about a little spin? It's a pretty town around here."

I'd been thinking about heading north most of the day. I just felt I had to head north. Vaguely I realized that they'd get me, but I hoped I'd beg north of Los Angeles before they found me. I never expected to eat again. "I've got time on my hands," I murmured. "Let's go."

We drove about the suburbs for a while, but ended on a road that went down a canyon. We stopped where a bridge arched high above us. "Pretty here," he muttered and was silent, then he turned to me. "Say," he said, "do you think you could love me?"

I struggled out of my hazy world. "Hell no!" I said. "I'm a lover of women. I really adore them and I have a fine wife waiting for me at home."

"Where?" he demanded.

"In Marin County north of San Francisco."

"Well," he said resignedly after a pause. "Okay—okay. Let's drive down toward town." And then wistfully he remarked, "You know I bring them all down here. I love that bridge, it's so romantic." He sighed deeply and we drove away. He stopped in front of a restaurant in town. "Come on in for a bite," he said.

"Yeah," I answered, "I could use a cup of coffee." It was a cafeteria. I got my coffee, while he chose himself quite a substantial meal. We went to a table. After taking our dishes from the trays he asked me to return the trays. When I came back he was sitting in front of my coffee.

"That double stew's for you, boy. Dig in. I figure you've been in the park without food for days. Dig in, young fellow. Your fast is over. Tell me your set-up when you are through eating." After that marvelous stew with dumplings and the dessert began to take hold I told him. He listened wryly to the ultimatum of the fat man.

"As you know," he said, "I like boys and young men. I find them several places, but the upright stubborn and rather stupid ones I find in the zoo. Sick as you are, you shouldn't stand on your pride. Here," he said, "let's go down and see if your wire has come in yet."

It had. It informed, with apologies, that a certified check had been sent to the union and a one hundred and fifty dollar check to bring me home was sent to the same address. We stood outside the Western Union office. "How can I thank you?" I said. "And at least I can pay for the meal."

"I'll give you my address," he said, "but don't try to pay me back. Help the other fellow."

"You mean the next person who needs help?"

"Well, for a guy that holes up in the zoo, you're a little above par. Sure, you write me a letter the next time you help somebody out of a jam."

I sent him five letters in the next year, one about a lady who gave me something back.

"Where will you sleep?"

"Same tree," I answered. "It's cedar and I want to thank it once again for hiding me in its low boughs each night."

"You better take this lap robe," he said. "It's never been used."

I thanked him.

"I don't suppose you'd want me driving you back to your sleeping place?"

"No, I'd rather you didn't," I admitted.

"Makes sense," he muttered. Then he got in his car and drove away. I can't remember how I got home. I never saw Perez again, though I heard he wrecked the *Princess* on the rocks about two months after I left and that before he died he was the skipper of a hundred-and-thirty-foot tuna clipper.

Otherwise it's a blank. I was pretty sick for a while. I can't remember going to the Marine Hospital seven months later or receiving the news that I was cured. Nordi was shown the x-ray films of the scars. I can't even remember coming home after that, though soon I was well again—well enough to begin to notice that the world I had left had scars of a different sort.

VIII

*In Which I Make
A Poor Thief And An Even Poorer Cuckold,
Manage To Grow Up A Bit,
and
Lose My Job*

◇   1930   ◇

I became acutely aware of the Depression. It was odd—I had lived through a most desperate time in many men's lives, and yet had been completely insulated from it. I had left the ferries and was hunting for the *Princess* in October of 1929, the time of the stock market crash. I was sailing down the coast of California as many great financial institutions crumbled. Everything that happened to the country while I fished off the coast of Mexico was like distant thunder, and Nordi wisely discontinued the paper and kept me ignorant of all that was happening until I was pronounced well.

Now, however, I walked into a rather devastated world. Bleak were the streets of San Francisco, where well-dressed men moved as if without volition about their fruitless business, the strut of affluence gone. Newsboys squalled of fresh disasters as they peddled their papers through oddly deserted streets. When I started to look for work, I had a feeling I was being ridiculous. Firms that were still in business looked at me in disbelief. They were having a hard time keeping on even a small segment of their crews. "Aren't there agencies to take care of you guys?" they asked. Or, "I don't care what you're good at, we can't use you." Some, almost with tears in their eyes, murmured "Sorry" as they closed the door.

I'd been at it about two weeks when Lindstrom, the port captain, appeared on our beach. "In times like these," he said, "it's cockeyed when you won't come to us and we have to come to you. I expect you at work tomorrow morning—extra deckhand." And having said that, he left, mumbling to himself.

Perhaps Lindstrom's offer was his left-handed way of letting me know that I needed him more than he needed me, for there had never been any love lost between us and there had been quite a bit of ill feeling over my quitting. And it was true that returning to the ferries was a come-down for me—a backward step in what little direction I perceived in my life—and just plain anti-climactic. Still, with the Depression foundering the country, I was delighted with the prospect of any job.

There were three other extra deckhands at the same time, though we were soon augmented to six. The company owned four ferries: the *Eureka*, the *Sausalito*, the *Tamalpais*, and the *Casadero*, and of course the smaller *Marin*, one of which was always tied up, receiving repairs or being painted and cleaned. Once a year the steamboat inspectors came around for inspection, which took about a week. As extra deckhands, we helped in the inspection, dusted, washed, painted a little, but mostly we just loafed along on the docked ferry, watching. If anyone of authority came aboard we would go through the motions of dusting and window washing. We were paid less than regular deckhands except when we worked as substitutes. I got a week on the *Tamalpais* almost at once.

The first thing I noticed was the difference among the passengers on the boats: the lack of exuberance was immediately apparent. Now there were two restraining lines across the stern beside the chain, and deckhands were instructed to watch men who stood pensively at the rail. Weepers were to be brought inside.

I also quickly became aware that I was being treated coolly by the Portuguese. In times past I had worked with them, had learned the ropes from them in several ways. Now, however, it was common knowledge that I had left the *Princess* because I would not allow myself to be healed by Manuel Rodriguez' prescription. Evidently Rodriguez was highly regarded by the Portuguese of California. Those on the boats knew more than I did of my sojourn in San Diego, and they went out of their way to make it as hard as they could for me.

But the hostility of the Portuguese was nothing compared to the forced idleness when, after my stint on the *Tamalpais*, I went back to being an extra deckhand. To sit around all day, but to fake work if anyone came aboard, seemed the negation of my manhood. At that time there were five other fellows on the extra board: Tom, a tall clean redhead, just out of the Coast Guard; another just like him without the brilliant coloring, from a freighter, whose name was Oscar; a long-nosed squirming man who was a living representation of Ichabod Crane—really more like Will Rogers as he had played Ichabod Crane in a movie I had seen—sharp nose, little suspicious eyes and a great length of chin; and two Portuguese, both of whom were stodgy and lazy. Finally, I spoke up: "This stalling is something I'm no good at."

The ex-Coast Guard swore under his breath. "Isn't there something we could do?"

"Sure there is," I answered.

"Well, why don't we do it?"

"Yeah," the fellow from the freighter said. "I'd sure like to be doing something."

"Well, I agree. Still, we're not paid enough to do a lot of it," I said. "It wouldn't be right but I know plenty of stuff that needs to be done on these boats and never is."

"Look," said Tom, "you been second mate here before. Why don't you lead us?"

"How about me leading?" said the guy that looked like Will Rogers. "I been taking a course on leadership and the 'zecutive ladder."

"Where you been working?" asked the freighter seaman, Oscar.

"I worked for a firm what went bankrupt. Shoe findings and wax. I could really—"

The Coast Guard man stopped him. "No," he said. "I think you're completely green at this. Rice," he said, "what do you think of doing something?"

"It isn't what I think," I said, "it's what I feel. I never could go for this stalling, this acting, acting like you're working when you're not. We could work a little bit, but not enough to take work away from others. There's plenty to be done that isn't done. For instance I know that there are seven capstans on these four boats that have never been overhauled."

"For Chrissakes, let's do it then," said Oscar.

"All right," I said, "I'll take responsibility," and led them to the job.

We lowered a lifeboat to the deck and used its davit and falls (block and tackle) to haul up the barrel of the capstan. We cleaned ten or fifteen years of rust out of it and had started to put grease mixed with graphite on the gears when Captain Lindstrom came upon us.

"What's going on here," he said. "I didn't tell you to do this."

"I know, Cap," I answered. "But we thought we'd do a little something to pass the time. Look at it, it was barely operable. Look at the crud that we got out of it."

"I tell you, I don't like it," Lindstrom said. "What if this boat had to pull out on short notice?"

"We'd have it back together way before they could get steam up," I said.

"No, I still don't like this. Put it back together and don't start any more."

"Okay," I answered disgustedly.

We went back to our loafing. The Portuguese were jubilant. "The Captain learn you to try to change things. I coulda told you. Listen, never do anything you don't have to."

"Yeah, I heard that in the Army," spoke up Oscar, "and still I don't like it." And, resignedly, "But I heard what the skipper said."

Next day the port captain was back and looking a bit nonplussed. He nodded to me to come outside. We went out on the deck. "You know," he said, "I told Small what you were doing. I told it to him for laughs. He laughed but then he thought about it and finally he said, 'Let them go ahead. If Rice uses good judgment, it might be a useful thing.'" Lindstrom turned to me. "I personally don't think much of your judgment, but there you are. Go ahead. Only remember we don't want any union trouble."

"Okay," I said, "we'll see how it goes."

It worked out better than anyone's expectations. I knew the boats like the back of my hand. I certainly wasn't unique in knowing all the things that never got done, but now I was in a position to do them. I saw to it we worked slowly, commensurate with the wages paid, but I also saw to it that every job we tackled was well done. We painted the hulls of the ferries when they came in, working from long, log-painting rafts, and because we chose to work we were happy at it. We were eight men now and we sang as we painted. We sang a very lewd song and slapped on the paint while we sang and we laughed a lot. Soon complaints came in concerning our language, but Superintendent Small, whose offices looked out on the dock, said, "I've never seen underpaid men choose to do such fine work. Let the ladies who pass by turn a deaf ear."

Soon I went to the head of the union and told him our story. "I'll stay out of it," he said, "but see if you can't get the extra deckhands a tiny raise in wages."

"I've been thinking about that," I answered. "I'll see what I can do."

"Wait a minute," he said reflectively. "On further thought, forget the raise in wages. The way things are going, we better stand pat." And my crew agreed with him.

One day the paint foreman, with a judicious pulling of lip, came to see me. "Say," he said, "last year they cut my crew in half and still I've got to refinish all the passenger coaches. Now if you could see your way to do all that fancy interior work we do in the upper cabin I might get by."

I agreed if he would lend me one man for some of the intricate gildings on supports of the ceiling on the *Tamalpais* and *Sausalito*. Eventually I took over all the work on the boat that the engineers didn't do. On another day, Captain Lindstrom came grinning to me as I was about to board the *Tamalpais*. "I've got news for you, Rice," he said as we climbed aboard. "Yeah," he went on, "it seems you've built yourself a niche and it grew. You are slated to be superintendent of maintenance and repair of the Northwest Ferries. You'll have thirty men: machinists, carpenters, painters and extra deckhands to do the job. The position will become official after the annual meeting of the board, and the pay will be the same as the other superintendents get, but not until the board meets four months from now. Until then we can only pay you extra deckhand wages, plus giving you the keys to the warehouses. Take what you can sell to make up the difference until the board meeting. That's all Small can do for you now. Congratulations."

Nordi was ecstatic. The several months I was laid up on the beach had cleaned out our savings and we were just barely getting by on my present wages. I looked at the keys to the storerooms. They would make the difference.

Next morning I took over my added duties. We were to work a great canvas down under the hull with ropes pulled up on each side of the ship and work it back to midships where we would lash it tight. The center of it would cover the great saltwater intake valve screen that was flush with the hull surface. The screen would be covered with barnacles that impeded the flow of water and had to be scraped away. It went without incident, though while we were doing it the tides would pull at the canvas and, if the currents or tides could move it away from the screen, the boat would quickly sink for we had to remove the great valve to get at the screen.

All jobs went well that day. I found time to hang a gallon of paint on a wire down under the water from the ferry. That night I came down in my skiff, drew the paint up out of the water and took it home. I painted the kitchen floor with it. When it dried I gave it another coat and another and another. Oh, it was a beautiful floor, but I was uncomfortable with it. I bought some paint and painted over it and still I was annoyed, for however my superiors condoned it, it went against my grain. The idea of selling stuff that I pilfered caused a deep unrest in me. Nordi noticed and I told her about it. I was ashamed of myself as a breadwinner.

"Clyde," she said, "I want you to be yourself. Sure I'd like the things we could buy with the money from stolen goods, but it might change you. I'd have a new sofa and a fine table but some of my Clyde would be gone. No, my naive fool, I can't take the chance. Don't you dare come home to me a kind of semi-thief, like the others I see everywhere."

We made a garden, fertilized with herring and small sharks the sport fishermen left on the beach. To grow our peas on, we shoved willow saplings into the ground, and after the peas were eaten we had a willow hedge. When the herring ran we scooped them off the rocks and salted down a keg of them. I continued to spear the big perch. Our garden was successful so we ate well, but had to be frugal about everything else. Still, in those times, we fitted the scene to perfection.

I had to fire the two Portuguese. They were too lazy to ever work on the ferries. The Portuguese on the ferries were by and large excellent workers, very proud of how they handled their jobs. Looking back I see that one of the things that kept me on the ferries so long was their warmth, their frugality, and their dedication to simple jobs, slighting nothing. I esteemed the Portuguese highly. They had not yet been poisoned with the universal mania to spend their lives sitting behind a desk.

I was secretly pleased with what I was doing to the ferries. They were in tip-top shape. We had found a dangerous weakness in the keel of the *Marin* and averted a disaster. We overhauled the *Sonoma*, the company launch, and, scraping and cleaning her bottom, found a leak and repaired it. Slowly the time of the annual meeting of the board drew near. Mr. Small left on the *Marin* one morning to go to the meeting in San Francisco. He smiled as he passed me. "I'll have news for you," he said, "before you go home tonight."

In pleasant anticipation I watched him step off the *Marin* that night and went toward him, but he passed me unseeing. An hour later I heard the news. He had been told to lay off over three hundred men, to leave only a skeleton crew in the terminal, for the Depression was steadily worsening. That ended my job as an extra deckhand and I realized cuts would be made in the ferries too—probably only half as many trips a day. My seniority was nil.

I stared around for a place where seniority didn't count. Perhaps I could get the job running the *Sonoma*. The *Sonoma* was a thirty-six-foot motor boat, then called a launch. It was decked in and had quite a house on it. Starting over the forward engine, it developed into sort of a pilothouse and steering place and behind it a cabin for eight passengers and a cockpit that held six. It was very narrow and its massive engine was ancient. The number on the engine was two-thirty-six, built when the Pioneer Engine Company was quite young.

For some reason the union contract with the railroad called for the crews for the freight trains to sign in in Sausalito, though the freights started up the line from Tiburon. In the daytime the *Marin* carried them over on her regular schedule, but at eleven thirty she tied up for the night. Then getting the men to the job was taken over by the *Sonoma*. In the past I'd had the running of it several times, when the old drunk whose job it was took half a dozen too many. Now he, Osgood, was going to retire. I wanted the job, and so did the white-haired boy who painted the skipper's steps in his off time—the boy with the red apple for teacher. I went to the port captain, Lindstrom.

"Skipper," I said, "I want that job. I helped you when you first came here. As captain on the *Marin* you did such a good job they made you port captain. I was one of your two deckhands. It was partly our sharp practice that brought you to notice. Since then I've had those yard crews cleaning up the boats and that's helped you settle into your position a little more securely. I've been a solid value to you here. I haven't got a red apple for you. I'm a man, damn it. I've earned that job and I want it."

We were in a little paint locker on the *Sausalito*. "Let me out of here," he said. We were alone on the boat.

"I want that job," I said. "I'll let you go when you turn it over to me." He pushed to get out. "Don't get me riled," I said. "Give me that job."

He thought a moment, not looking me in the eye. "Okay, okay, now let me out."

"Sure," I said and stood aside. "Only don't think about changing your mind." He didn't. I was assigned the *Sonoma*.

I settled down to see what I could do with this simple job. The trip between Tiburon and Sausalito was about three-and-a-half miles. Leaving Tiburon, you set a course for Belvedere Point where you passed between a great bellbuoy and some sunken rocks about a hundred yards off, at the end of the point. If you hit either, you and your passengers hadn't much chance. The engine on the boat made so much noise that from the steering position you couldn't hear the bellbuoys, and the rocks awash were far from cozy. Here were continuously varying swift currents and tide rips brought about by the deflection of the floor of the Strait at this point. The next course was from the point to a small harbor past the ferry slips of Sausalito, a simple enough route in daytime or moonlight, but in fog or storm a really tough one.

In a way it was a lonely job and far from safe. Still, it was a job, and I took care of that old boat as if it were a yacht. Every month on my own time I would give it a day of daylight working, varnishing, scrubbing, scouring, changing oil in the engine. As I say, it was lonely. No crew member ever entered my little pilothouse. Most of the time I carried a crew only one way. Oh, sometimes I'd have a few both ways, but usually I came back empty. Just me and my pipe. The engine pounding along, moonlight on the water, the lights of San Francisco on my right and Angel Island and Belvedere looming up ahead. I'd put my pipe away, open both doors, and the fresh night breeze would quicken me and I'd sing—a creature of ecstasy, unwilling to admit the truth about an uncaring world—secure in a miasma of a light-opera love song, my warm clothing, a goal at which to aim the boat, and the beat of the engine making a rhythmic sense of progress toward that goal. At either end of my small voyages I swung the boat in a tight half circle to come up to the floats. It was a far different configuration than that of the ferry landings—the slow turning between high straight wharves and the curving movement ending quietly against the square angular floats and always the beautiful wake following. It was not like, but still related to, the way a seagull approaches a landing. Each time it seemed new to me and like a melodic phrase, though in storm we plunged along, going right through every third wave, and my landings were made alongside heaving, leaping floats. Then the train crews prayed, for they were jumpy when the wind blew or when the fog muted their steps on the wharf as they came toward me. Often coming back from Sausalito I went close to the cliff at Belvedere Point and fought the tide race there to get to some eddies and backwater that moved in my direction. I gained little in this. It was really nothing more than an idle contest with the tides. One night I was amusing myself in this manner, looking down in the water where the lights from the cabin shone. A shoal of small fish scattered away from us and then half of the torso of a woman appeared—an upper arm and half the torso—going down the tide race. It was gone even as I stared, leaving me shuddering and with a sense of loss. . . .

I had known Art Coulter for some time before I sailed south in the *Princess*. He was married to a very beautiful girl—slim with a lovely childlike face and breasts that were full and high. One Sunday Nordi, taking Bunky, had gone to see her brother in San Jose. Bob Drake, going farther south to Carmel, had taken her down and would pick her up next day on his way back. I had been lolling on our beach with friends. Now alone, my head pretty fuzzy from gin fizzes, I was trying to make a drawing of the *Princess* in heavy weather when Art knocked and I called out a welcome. He ushered in his wife, Taffy. They too, they said, were feeling no pain. Though a member of the San Francisco Yacht Club, Art hadn't a boat yet but crewed on other yachts. They had walked over from the club with, he said, the express purpose of arranging for me to paint a picture of them to hang in their bedroom, a picture of them in the act of love—"screwing," he said, "missionary style. What would it cost?"

"Nothing," I said, "but I'm not much of a painter."

"I've seen some of your stuff," he answered, "and I like it. So when can we start?"

"I'd have to make a sketch," I countered. "I've had a bit too much gin."

"Well," said Taffy softly, "we're in the same spot."

"Let's make some strong coffee, and I mean strong coffee," Art said. "Then we'll pose and you can get that preliminary sketch."

I not only drank two cups of that thick brew, I chewed the grounds and soon my hand was steady. I decided to use pastels and set up my easel as they stripped and, using our couch, assumed the position.

God, they were so beautiful. Art, who was quite a bit taller than I am, was splendidly muscled and had a most interesting face—a bit Mediterranean and just slightly Jewish with a clear, well-tanned skin. Taffy, named after the color of her hair, was a lithe, startlingly pale product of Scandinavia with pink cheeks, lips and nipples. I got a fair early sketch, overriding my usual pitfalls. I should have been aroused sexually, but I had learned in art school to subjugate desire. Now, viewing such symmetry, such a celebration of the graces possible in us humans, I was filled with pride and exaltation past desire. An exultation so widely based, so holistic, as to find its perimeter in the not-yet-known, and all this joyful flareup in my mind sparked by the comeliness of bodies. I continued in luck. I applied the slight color it took to nail down the essentials. They gave me four long poses with four short rests before the light faded. They promised to continue next Sunday and left.

A book, *Man the Unknown* by Alexis Carroll, had come out in 1927 and now I read it. What it said fully coincided with my beliefs that science should seriously look into the phenomena of psychic happenings. Dr. Carroll, a prominent member of the Rockefeller Fellowship (an early-day brain trust), pointed out that science sidled away from the psychic because, these phenomena not being

constant or consistent, there was too much room in the field for
fakery. Scientists were obviously afraid they might turn up something that would put a tear in the great web of things that was
making sense. It made me feel that I was not alone. In looking at
everything economic, political, religious or scientific, it seemed to
me they were in the position of a house with one wall missing.
Until we could search and research and understand that other
segment of reality, add it to our knowledge of everything else, and
see the broader perspective's effect on religion, science, and culture, I felt there was not much sense in summation. Of this and
these I thought as we pounded along, the *Sonoma* and I, through
the murk of rainy nights, and the late starry nights when at last the
moon had gone behind the hills.

The Depression was now worldwide. It went down and down
and hit bottom. The remark went around that there was no place
to go now but up, but now there was no go. Conditions stayed
steady at zero on many scales.

Next week, the Coulters phoned to postpone until the following
Sunday.

The seaweed grew long on the *Sonoma*'s bottom. I asked for
bottom paint and three days to haul the boat out and to scrub and
copper paint the hull. I was refused. I figured the refusal was the
result of the stultifying effects of the Depression on people's
minds. Now, with the seaweed almost a foot long on the hull, I
asked again and was again refused. What to do! I scrubbed away
and could rub it off at the waterline but little else.

In between trips I hunted around on the wharf and found among
other things a group of short pieces of steel railroad tie. The least
of them weighed one hundred and twenty-five pounds but I got
several of them down on the float. I got some more down and laid
them along the *Sonoma*'s rail on one side. I must have had almost a
ton of them to tip the boat sharply so I could scrub farther down
the hull. In fact, I was able to get the grass off her three feet below
the waterline, but that was all. Later I thought of piling them on the
bow to raise the stern and work under the fantail. One night I
made the first trip over and back and thought to bring a few pieces
down on the float between trips, so I could be ready when the quiet
time came. I was standing looking at them considering which piece

to lift to my shoulder—I awoke deep down under water. Well, I thought quite calmly, I'm underwater but I want to live. I began to paddle to the surface. It took a long time, but finally I poked out of the surface and drew a deep breath. I came out high and looked about me. I saw the moon through the trapdoor I'd stepped backward into. I was under the wharf. I swam to a piling and climbed it. On top of the piling was a wharf timber. I could get my fingers in the interstices of the planking it supported. Hanging freely under it, I swung along toward the trapdoor. I came opposite it. To get to it I had to do the same thing with the planking. The old planks were separated enough to get my fingers in and over the top to support myself. In that manner, swinging forward as if swinging on rings in a gymnasium, poking my fingers up through the debris, I gripped and swung forward to the next fingerhold of the other hand. Finally I reached the open trapdoor, grasped the edges of it and heaved—one heave and I was kneeling on top of the planks of the dock, safe. I knew I couldn't work in my sodden clothing. I still had time, so I trotted home, less than half a mile away, changed clothes and trotted back. The crew were on board—they'd been waiting fifteen minutes. One smart aleck said he'd report me. Knowing this I wrote out an accident report and sent it in and though I finished out the night I called the office and told them to get a substitute as I was laying off for two shifts. The first day I could hardly move—every muscle was strained. My coat sleeves and pant legs, my underwear and socks, were slit in many places where the barnacles on the pilings cut through, making deep scratches on my legs and arms. Most of the skin was gone off the pads of my fingers.

After two days in bed I went back on the job. I was asked to appear in the office next day. Now Captain Lindstrom thought he had me. In the matter of the mate license I'd circumvented him and I'd pressured him in getting the *Sonoma* job. He already saw his pet—the boy with the apple and willing paintbrush—running the *Sonoma*. Here was something to work up a case on. "What were you doing on the dock? I hear you walk around and go clear out on the end. Why?"

"I use the privy on the outer end."

"Oh, you do, do you! Why don't you use the one in the round-house?"

"It's twice as far and I have to keep close to the boat for emergency calls."

"I hear you walk up and down the dock all hours of the night, why?"

"To keep warm."

"You're looking at that girl in the window above the American Express, ain't ya?"

"Skipper, she does that between eleven and twelve. I'm too far away to see anything. That's for the men on the train barge and the railroad crews."

"Well, let's go over there. I want to see why you was wandering around up there at two or three in the night." I went and showed him the trapdoor. I don't know who opened it. "You allege you fell through this trapdoor and came up out of it. Wait a minute," he said, and examined the planks that edged it. My fingerprints were dug into the wood. "Let's see your hands," he said and I took off the soft cloth gloves. "Yes," he said. "But why was you up here?"

I told him about the rails and the *Sonoma*'s bottom. Still he didn't want to believe but when I put several short sections of the rails on one side and told him to look below the waterline where I'd scrubbed, he gave up. I showed him under my chin where there was now a great scab and a lump at the base of my skull and we reconstructed the scene. When I stepped back I had fallen through the opened trapdoor. I caught my chin on the edge of the hole as I dropped through, hit the back of my head on a fuel pipe a yard below, which stunned me but did not break my neck. I had gone far down into the water, maybe to the bottom where I came to and fought for my life in a much calmer manner than I usually conduct myself. I'm not a very muscular man. I have narrow shoulders, just normal arms, but strong legs and a large chest. There's something missing in this but I can only assume that adrenalin, shot into a system well aware that survival was at stake, produced the effort and control necessary to keep living. It astounds me.

The privy Lindstrom sneered at stood out on the end of the

abandoned dock, the inner end of which accommodated the *Sono-ma*'s float and gangway. It was small and made of rough unpainted lumber and the door opened out on the bay. It was a one-holer, and how beautifully green was the water below its ass-polished hole. You didn't close the door—what for! So you took a crap, but you continued to sit there as errant breezes fanned your balls. You didn't even light up a smoke—you just sat there away from things —all the goddamned things we clutter our lives with. For five or ten minutes out there you were in "Eschrow County" where everything holds still.

Perhaps for a quarter of a century that magic privy accommodated one and all. Then one day a bum passing through found it and used it. He had crabs and left a hundred or so adventurous ones there, more than half of them pregnant. So a fellow waiting for the *Sonoma* one night gathered a few unto himself and took them to Frisco. The next night he brought them back, and the next night there was a similar occurrence. Then Will Buford, who was fishing out on the end of the dock, took a scattering of them home up on the *Corinthian*, and so on. Now in places of good will, as this area was, there is bound to be a certain percentage of promiscuity. Researchers are wont to measure the percentage of this activity by the speed with which a pestilence of crabs goes through a community from a single source. It is often said that promiscuity is one of the positive forces knitting a community together—a diagonal stitch, weaving through the inevitable squareness of the woof and warp. Be that as it may, after the bum's visit to that edifice out on the wharf, we all bought blue ointment, the cure of the day, and slapped it on our nether parts and in many instances into mustaches and kept silent, but continued to smile knowingly at one another.

Oh, Tiburon, I have never loved another town but you. Still, I must admit you missed greatness, for on finding how quickly that itching scourge spread and, deducing from that how cozy was the community, you as a well-knit group didn't buy an open-headed drum of the ointment, where all could dip in openly and take what they needed. No, you couldn't conceive of that, and so, dear Tiburon, I hold you in memory as a lesser grail of a town.

So I ran the night launch, the *Sonoma*, sleeping in the day. With

Ed Harrington and Mr. Davercossin, whose house stood out over the water at the west end of the beach, we had a neighborly group, separated from other houses by a very tilted band of rocky meadows. We visited back and forth daily, shared meals, extra money, a water system and the driftwood of the beach. We all felt it was a very special place. Several times a week oil tankers passed so close to our shore that we could exchange shouted greetings with them. Raccoon Strait was a much-used waterway. We looked out on the Navy's destroyers and cruisers, on freighters, fishboats, regattas of sailboats, strings of rowboats being towed to fishing grounds, and once in a great while an ancient sailing hay-barge would waft past, patched sails swelled out by the westerly. Since my sickness, it had become a place in which to wait, to gather force for whatever might come. So much had fallen to pieces of that world that existed before 1929 that we wondered if the U.S. would ever be the same. People of the Midwest and the South sifted through California's cities and countryside, driven from their land by drought. People with a tireless hunger in their eyes for work to do, food enough for a sense of immediate security, and a chance to grapple for land that wouldn't blow away, land with water on it, land that would raise a crop.

I knew the *Sonoma* job couldn't last long when the company would not let me haul her out, a thing I could do without cost. I knew she was slated to bleach her bones on the muddy banks of some slough. I was saving every cent I could for what was to come. Food had grown cheap—eight cents a pound for a salted ham of pork. Heidi, our goat, gave us all the milk we could use. Nordi and Bessie evolved a pot of beans that I have never seen the like of since: beans, tomatoes, ham ends, onions, garlic and spices again proved that the sum is greater than its parts—so cheap, so nutritious and so delicious. "Come have a bean with us" meant you were invited for lunch, and looking timorously at a far from glittering future, we all wallowed in the comfort and the safety of our haven by the cliffs of Waterspout Point.

When I stepped aboard the *Sonoma* Friday night, there was a note by the compass that informed me I should take the *Sonoma* on the following Thursday to a haul-out facility at Angel Island's Quarantine Cove. The military of the island allowed us to use it in trade for the use of our float and gangway. This message made my job seem more substantial. I would scrub her bottom clean, remove all barnacles and give her two coats of copper bottom paint. Sam Donahue would take over the *Sonoma*'s run with his big forty-footer and also haul us over and back while we worked on the *Sonoma*.

Nordi was pleased with the news and made me a banana whipped-cream cake—the same one I got on my birthdays. I rowed across the straits to Quarantine Cove and looked over the boat cradle and windlass and wire rope on it. My job was precious! I wanted no slip up on the haulout. Everything looked in fine shape.

The Coulters came over late on Sunday—they'd had a squabble, they said. Art was a carpenter and landscape gardener. He built houses, put in pools, did sidewalks and steps and carpentry around the homes of his clients. He'd had three men in his crew and they'd done some beautiful jobs, for Art was a perfectionist. Now with very little of that kind of work going on, he'd let his crew go and could find very little to do himself. Taffy had found a job in an office somewhere that was stable. The reversal of roles was difficult for them. Nordi had patched Ed's, the bachelor's, pants, and he had given her a pint of gin. So we made them a couple of tall drinks and soon they were their usual amiable selves. I abstained. What I had to do with the pastels was small delicate work around Taffy's face and Art's ear and a general touching up of the whole thing.

Before we knew it the sun went down, but I had a newfangled bulb purported to be the same as sunlight, so they took their pose and I began, working carefully as I had planned, and exquisite Taffy waltzed with me between poses, laughing with childish pleasure when we collided with one another and the table. It went well but I had difficulty with the exact color of her lips. I was getting it quite close. Now I didn't need the pose, only Taffy in a chair holding her head and lips just so. Several poses and several waltzes later we noticed that Art and Nordi were not with us. We went outside and looked around and called. They were gone.

"Maybe they went to Ed's to see if he had any more gin," I said.

"They'll be back in a minute."

Taffy put on her clothes and tried to pose her lips for me, but couldn't. "Let's look," she said. We walked down to Ed's house—no lights. We came back and looked at Drakes'—dark and silent. It was near two o'clock now. The beach was deserted. I didn't worry for me but was terribly worried for Taffy. The fire had gone out and it was cold. I started to make a fire but she restrained me and crawled into our bed. I sat on the edge of it. I'd been trying to reassure her but now we both were silent as we thought our separate thoughts. Then Taffy got up and put on her shoes and a light coat. "I'm going to walk over to friends on Belvedere. He's left me," she said. "I'm sure of it."

I offered to go with her but she would have none of it. I allowed her to go alone. How I could do such a thing I can't understand. So many things, looking back, I can't understand. Anyway she was gone. And alone I could only believe that somewhere Nordi lay in his arms. I shook. My hands trembled. It was hard to breathe. Then fury was in me and agony to get at him writhed through me and then, most clearly, I saw Nordi as she'd been when I came home from Madeline's that morning. I saw her sorrow, but mostly her steadfast love. I still shook with rage and loss, but through it all that picture of her stayed. I saw again her forgiving eyes. "I can't beat her," I said out loud. But again the shaking started and the pain. Fury made me grab at things, twisting whatever I could lay hands on.

"Nordi and I are one," I said. "Whatever happens, Nordi and I are one." But Art, what of him? I had liked Art. He was a real good guy. If they came back—and she'd have to come back, for there was Bunky asleep in his bed—if they came back I'd be as reasonable and considerate as I had planned, if this thing, this infidelity, ever again assaulted the bond between us.

When they came back several hours later, I had pieced together again who I was and what my relation was to the world and Nordi. They came in together from the night and blinked at the light and sought my eyes. I was able to smile at Art, for the situation demanded that I either put him at ease or kill him and I no longer wanted to throttle him, but it was Nordi's eyes and mine that were informing each other that no link of the chain that bound us had weakened or broken, that the bond would always be stronger than life.

"Yes," I said, and Nordi nodded her head and looked away. Some strain left the room. We had coffee and I told them of Taffy. I put the blame on Nordi, but Art demurred.

"It was my fault," he said. We sat there sorrowfully thinking of Taffy. But that was really up to Art.

We slept separately in the tail end of the night and Art slipped away before breakfast as did I. I roamed the hills that day thoughtlessly and went to work on the *Sonoma* that night—the routine was good and when my time came to sleep I slept heavily.

I slept alone that day. We were quietly separate, except for our eyes, that strangely didn't cherish each other so much as the bond between us, each glance reaffirming it.

Art came in the evening. He had gone to see Taffy, but she had decided to leave him and would not let him in. He had phoned her, but they had gotten into the spat they'd had Sunday and ended up each blaming the other and agreeing to a separation. "I'm going mining," proclaimed Art. "I haven't had a job to do in almost four months."

"Mining?" inquired Nordi. "Why mining?"

"Well, my dad's a mining engineer," he answered. "He's got a dozen claims in the northern Sierras and he told me to take my pick."

"How about money?" I asked.

"Just enough to outfit myself and five hundred dollars to take care of food and tobacco," he answered.

He and I both thought of broaching the subject of Nordi. We were working up to it when she gave him an extra pickaxe we had and hurried him away. When I got down to the boat and was leaving on the first trip he wasn't among my passengers and he'd left our place too late for the *Marin's* last trip, so I was pretty certain Nordi was again in his arms.

It was a night of torment. Under a full moon with not a breath of a breeze, the boat with all that grass on her bottom was so slow it seemed we were stuck in eternity, as if I were pinned—tied down as the boat seemed to be from all action—and could not go to where she lay quivering in ecstasy, to hurl him away and plunge into her and jet my life blood to prove I was her only one. The engine clattered along. We seemed mired in a thickening sea. I tried to light my pipe, but my hands trembled so I couldn't and my mouth was too dry to swear. I took the torment and eventually we were in between high docks and the curve of landing was happening and I was tying the boat up, as passengers streamed up the gangway—just like, my wounded mind said, just like they did before! And it seemed a truth too wide-reaching for my mind to encompass.

At home, I tried to eat breakfast, but I gagged on it. The table was tipped, chairs flew apart as I grabbed her and dragged her to the bed and beat down on her mad for release and, when it came, wept in adoration of her, as if she were a madonna, and then her fingers were in my hair, caressing me as she murmured of her wronged boy. It seemed as if she were forgiving me for some childish mistake and I fell asleep knowing that her great goodness of heart could not be measured by the tags and ties of convention.

Going over to Angel Island Thursday morning a rare thing—in fact a very rare thing—happened. It was a quiet sunlit morning, the water like glass. We were about to enter Quarantine Cove and were passing Point Ione—we must have been two hundred yards off the Point—when beside us, about eighty feet away, we saw a whirlpool. We could not hear it because of the racket of the *Sonoma's* engine. You could see into it. Harrington, my helper that day, who climbed upon the cabin top to see better, said the hole was about eight feet across, three feet below the surface of the Bay. How far it went down before it closed we had no way of knowing. We were, however, in its perimeter of activity, so I turned slowly away from it with everything the old engine could cough up, and slowly we did draw away and then into the cove. Had we been much closer I think we would have been sucked in, the boat flung around until it tipped over, swamped and then torn to pieces and sucked under. For a rowboat there would not have been a single chance had it gotten within fifty feet of the thing. The strange part is I had been on that spot many, many times—as had countless others, for it was a favorite trolling place—and I never saw nor ever heard of a whirlpool there. I reported it to the geodetic survey and several years later they had the answer. The ebbtide corkscrews through the Strait and, when forces are just right, can create a whirlpool. Whatever is sucked down eventually arrives farther down the Strait at Tiburon, having passed under the Strait. This they proved with certain objects that had the same specific gravity as water and would be easily identifiable.

Everything went well with the haul-out. We cleaned and painted the old boat and in two days had it back on the run, sliding through the water like a boat should.

Art was gone. We received a card from him up Mount Shasta way. "Do you love him?" I asked her. We had eaten breakfast and knew it was at last time to talk.

"Not in the way I love you."

"Then you do love him?" It hurt to say it but I had to know.

"Yes," she said, dropping her eyes from mine and forcing herself to stop fiddling with a fork on her plate, "in a way, yes."

"Why this all of a sudden? Is it his big prong you saw, or why?"

"If you're asking what started it, I can only say I am wondering about it too. I do admire his strong body, and yes, his great penis, but before I saw him nude I was attracted to him. I adored his smile, it starts so slow. Don't be hurt by this. Nobody could take your place in my heart, but he's much easier to be with casually than you. You're a very complex and moody man; sometimes you hardly speak for days. God knows, I love you. I'm mated to you for life, I'm sure of that, and our sex life is perfect. But it's married perfect, Clyde. Do you know what I'm talking about?"

I was about to hit her, mad with jealousy. But I can be rational, so I looked back into my life to see what she was talking about.

. . .*other eyes looked into mine: I was pulling out a stuck drawer in her desk, my arm had inadvertently brushed her breast as we worked at it. At once she raised up, still as a statue, and her blush suffused her face and neck and traveled down the vee in her dress. Her pleading eyes were changing me, changing time. The office and the storeroom ceased to exist for us. She had gone to our trysting place and I followed. . . .*

Nordi was looking at me. Her eyes were pleading too, pleading for understanding. Though now I did understand, I felt mean. All I wanted to do was to strike out and get even. I wanted to hurt her. "Yeah," I lied, "it was one of those tawdry sometime things."

It hurt her. "I always expect honesty from you, Clyde; don't let me down."

"You were damn quick to let me down," I sneered.

"That's cheap of you, Clyde."

"Cheap? It's what you did was cheap, Nordi."

She looked at me with blazing eyes, but she crumpled and laid her head on the table. "Oh, God," she mourned, "the filth of words can destroy beauty."

"What do you mean?" I demanded.

"Any beauty the defiler can't comprehend," she said and moaned as she sobbed that the great beauty she had experienced could be so easily besmirched. I stood beside her staring down, so ashamed that jealousy, like corrosive acid, could bite deeply in me and prove me base metal. I touched her shining hair. She looked up, eyes full of tears of despair. "Oh, Clyde," she said hopelessly, "please unsay it, please unsay it."

"I do unsay it," I said. I picked her up, carried her to the big chair, placed her in it, laid my head in her lap and told her of my abject shame. I told her I did understand but that my love for her had gotten desperate. I didn't tell her of the torment I'd been through, nor would I.

We went on as before. I tried to be gayer and more carefree around her. I realized that losing the *Princess* and the sickness that followed and the general air of the Depression years had taken a great deal out of my spontaneity. I tried—successfully, I think—to be more inventive in bed and let my passion for her have free rein. That took a lot more of my vigor than I liked, for I had begun to gather rocks, big rocks, from all over the Peninsula. I wanted to build her an adequate house of stone.

That slogging work soon took off the fat, the flab I'd laid on under doctor's orders the year before. The stones I gathered from the rocky hills had to be carried down to the roads alongside the Bay. Many weighed over a hundred and fifty pounds and some I had to carry over a quarter of a mile. Often I thought I must be crazy for I wanted the special stones with brilliantly colored granular quartz covering one of their surfaces in colors of green and blue and a sort of bronzed purple. I would wander about studying over fifty of them to find one I wanted. I fixed a heavy carrying rig on the back of my old Buick that would take several and later I bought a second-hand trailer to carry them.

Nordi had made the plans for the house. It would cover all the back part of the lot. Its two stories would face the south and the Bay, where it would be largely great windows. I also made a wooden yoke that fit my neck and shoulders and every day made seven trips from down the beach carrying two buckets of sand that I worked into the clay of our soil in front of where the house would stand. Soon I was mostly sinew.

I had almost enough rocks for our house, then we changed the plans. The revision took a lot more stonework and we decided to make the walls thicker, using the glazed ones where they would be seen on the outside or in the big living room, two walls of which were to carry their jewel-like colors. Anyway you look at it stones are heavy. I got a second-hand trailer to haul them in and started on the program again, dreaming of a stone fort of a house as I sweated. Always I had to carry them to the road. It was a slow slogging business. I wish I knew why there was this appeal for drudgery in my life. Part, I suppose, was my childhood worship of the pioneers who chopped out a farmstead in the wilderness. Anyway, I loved this garnering of rocks.

For a while we received cards from Art telling us about his prospecting and his mine and little things about the birds and animals, of which he was very observant. They came every two weeks. Nordi began to bloom. Her color, always good, became radiant. I went to town and, taking a chance on size, bought her three dresses of subtly flowered gossamer. They were just right for her and in them she was a joy to be with. Kissing Nordi's lips in that time was like biting into a ripe cherry, and though it was in the last of winter, she made it seem like spring.

One day Nordi looked a bit different and several days later a little more and by the end of the week I had caught on. Imperceptibly she had started using eyebrow pencil. I decided to see what would happen and said nothing, but it never got any darker. Still, she used it every day, sure that I had not noticed such subtle changes.

Every morning when I milked Heidi, Bunky's dog would watch.

Once in a while he would jump in the car and come with me rock hunting, but he was really Nordi's dog and watched over Bunky faithfully. With our son now three, and with a goat and a dog, we added pigeons—fourteen big white ones. I built them a cote that was the best job of carpentry I had yet done. I hoped to buy the little lot next to us and doggedly brought in a load of stones every day. The rocks I wanted were not at our end of the Peninsula but five miles away. Sometimes Nordi would go. She would get Bessie to take care of Bunky and he would play with their little daughter. In fact Nordi and Bessie traded the chore of child watching a lot, which gave them freedom to shop or, in Nordi's case, to walk, as she now had taken it up again, as we did at Grandma's house before coming to California. Sometimes I would take her with me rock hunting, but it was very rough work, for they were mostly on top of the hills where other quartz outcrops and springs broke the turf. A year before I would have thought nothing of her rolling one down the hill, but now somehow it didn't seem a thing to let her do. On Madeline's advice she wore a great floppy hat to protect her skin.

Madeline liked Nordi very much and, I assumed, instructed her in women's wiles, for every once in a while I'd notice something a little different in our lovemaking and I once heard Madeline giving what I assumed was intimate advice that was hushed when they heard my step.

On the other side of us, Bessie offered a great deal of practical knowledge. Raised on a horse ranch, she was a true farmer's daughter, besides being an excellent nurse. She could never quite forgive Nordi for not nursing her baby, even if it was on the advice of that ill-fated doctor, nor did she ever feel that Nordi or Madeline were quite up to snuff, for neither had ever taken the bucking out of a horse and broken it to the saddle.

Though they were getting farther apart we received another card from Art, mentioning that he would be down in Berkeley in six weeks and might he drop around and see us? Nordi looked at me worriedly. "What shall I answer?" she murmured.

"Do you still love him?"

"Not like you. I try not to, but I guess I do," she admitted. "I wish he would stay away. Maybe we could just be friends," she said. "It must have disturbed you terribly when—you know—"

"It was kind of rough," I lied.

"I still wish he'd stay away," she said, pouting. "But I guess I'll write that it's okay to call."

Under all the attention I was showing her, and perhaps because she had had a lover and felt the power of her femininity, Nordi had changed in many small ways. Her upper arms that had become slightly plump were slender again, under a regime of daily hill climbing and arm exercises. I fell in love again with the way the muscles and ligaments in her armpits made slight but lovely modulations under her skin as she lay with her arms wrapped around her head. Her breasts that seemed to me much larger than before made sweet curves by her armpits and the nipples and their aureolas were colored like the big delicate petals of flowers of flame and pink and the most subtle shades of warm lavender. In bed she now was instantly responsive to the slightest touch and soon in a near delirium of ecstasy, so skillful in giving pleasure and the proud offering of special charms. Still there was a delicacy in her fervor, a faint sadness that passion so easily aroused had such control over her and a compassionate but reproachful pout for me, the catalyst.

I planned to build a fence around the three properties and the back of the cliffs of the Point. I had spent a few hours making drawings to show to Bob and Zimmie, Madeline's new husband, and to point out the necessity of it. Nordi had gone to spend the day in San Francisco with Bunky. I ate a sandwich, too late to bring in my usual load of rocks. Maybe I should take a stroll and see if there weren't a few stones on this end of the Peninsula. I took the dog along and was soon on the meadows above the town. There were none of the encrusted ones I had found on the other side of Sugarloaf, the eminence of the whole Peninsula. The west side of the Peninsula here was all meadow but from the ridge east it was impenetrable brush. Oaks pushed up through it and much of the brush was the vine, poison oak, but occasionally on steep terrain there were areas of hazel brush. As I came near one of these the dog ran ahead and entered what looked like a solid wall of hazel, then came back out, looked at me and barked and went in again, and, when I came abreast of the place, did so again. Maybe a fox den, I thought, and decided to investigate. Carefully forcing my way through I found it opened up after a bit into a dim trail and soon came onto a tiny camp walled all around by the tall hazel brush. The tent itself was under an oak and beyond it a few feet a water seep had a waterhole dug into it. The tent of heavy olive green canvas was one of the type whose sides can easily be lifted making a pavilion. It was closed. I called out a hello, received no answer and tried again. Then I went to the tent and opened the flap. It was empty. I trod carefully to leave no sign, for I was trespassing. Inside the tent blankets were attached to the ridgepole in bags of oiled silk. There was a small Primus stove and a metal cupboard. The place was floored with deep dry moss. Lying over one end of one of the oilskin bundles suspended from the ridge was a scarf that I knew in a glance as Nordi's. I had to sit down, for I shook and trembled all over. I sat there hardly thinking for quite a time, and when I had control over myself, I looked further in that neat camp. All around the slight opening in which the tent stood were thick plantings of violets and maidenhair ferns. The place was replete with the perfectionist in him. Carefully obliterating my tracks, I left. I was pushing through the brush when, at my feet, I saw a glimmer of white, an envelope. I opened it, knowing I was violating my code. Code! I laughed crazily. It was a letter Nordi had planned to send to Art, but the thick brush had scraped it from her pocket. It said in part: "Darling, please stop coming down each month. It's too long a drive for you, just for several nights and the few hours of the days we spend together. You know how I love it but I've been thinking of telling you to stay away. I should, you know. After all I'm married to a fine husband and I do love him. Only how can I ask you to stay away when we are so wonderfully good for each other?" I put it back where I found it and hurried away from the place, figuring to catch them there and kill them.

A dullness, a deadness of mind came over me; perhaps nature's way of protecting one of her most fragile creatures from the crises that his invention of culture produces in him. I admitted to myself that two can practice deceit. "I can do it too," I said, and the dog looked around. I hated him for leading me where he did.

When Nordi came back I betrayed my hurt in no way and soon was aboard the *Sonoma*, filling the gas tank, scrubbing the salt spray from the windows. I knew the boat now as a refuge. Nothing is so good for bereavement or loss of faith in someone or something as the routine of a job—a job others expect and need you to handle well. I was fairly busy making six trips. As I shuttled back and forth in the mooonlight I knew that man is the most sexual of animals. I wondered if our involvement in sex was inherent or the result of cultural embroidery. The rhythmic beat of an engine can lead a man past his usual perimeters. I was furious at Art and Nordi. "That is what is making me stew this way," I said aloud. God knows I was, but why, why? I came in to Tiburon and went to see the dispatcher.

"They want you in Sausalito, Clyde." Back I went, going the opposite way, and going the opposite way confused the forward movement of my thinking, but I did see and put into a few words something I was aware of but couldn't formulate with words before. I felt it dimly and then I saw it. "Culture and law have to parallel life and living somewhat." I couldn't carry it farther and see the rest of it. I'd been reading along these lines but these things came to me as discoveries in that I saw that the drives of sex, shelter and food and, in colder and hotter countries, of body coverings were the basis for the infinite embroidering—the taboos, styles, laws and the morals. The results were good for business and sometimes—like the waltz—were delightful. I got tired of thinking, couldn't remember what brought all that on, then realized that I was wondering why I hated Art. In a brief flash I hated him again. He made me a cuckold. The word inflamed me—why? Natural tinder fanned by custom, I guessed. I was expected to hate him. They trained me when I was small—everywhere they trained me, but I was no goddamned vine. Still, what would they think of me if I didn't hate him or what would I think of me if I hated him wrongly?

"Jesus," I said to the breeze that was blowing through the open doors, "if I wasn't so sleepy maybe I could learn something from what I'm thinking now!"

So I hauled the train men back and forth and the drunks who missed the last boat and I slept a while, carried some more people across the Bay and I was walking home again. Nordi greeted me with such warmth, such tender regard that for the moment the only part of the letter I could remember was "I'm married to a good husband and I love him."

Was this duplicity on her part, I asked myself, and realized I should think so, but didn't quite think so, and that I should take it to my spot on Sugarloaf and try to figure it out. I didn't go up to Sugarloaf directly. To do that I would have to pass that patch of brush behind which violets and maidenhair ferns spoke of Art's love of my darling. No, I drove on four miles, parked and came up on Sugarloaf from the opposite end of the Peninsula.

Lucky, Art hadn't one problem of most lovers of married ladies, for I was away nights and slept days and every other day Nordi walked through the meadows high in the hills, and nothing really tied Art to his mine.

Before I had gone fishing I'd made a three-sided windbreak out of upright slabs of rock, some of which represented several successive days of dragging and lugging. They shielded me from the sea winds that sped across here, hurrying into the interior valleys of California.

As I sat on the turf of my thinking place I saw a little cross out in front at the end of a miniature grave. A bird, I thought—someone killed a bird and was sorry and buried it. I was curious; what kind of bird? With a flake of rock I dug it up, berating myself as a grave robber. What I found on a leafy bed was a condom of semen. I looked at the little cross. Both pieces of it had been whittled and there was faint writing on the whittled places. It said: "In memory of our ninth child, Roderick. Cause of death—thin rubber." And on the upright piece was inscribed: "The sap of trees holds the sap of man." Was this whimsical burial the work of Art and Nordi or what other lovers? "Okay, okay," I said as I replaced the sod. "I came up here to think," and soon a clarity of mind did come to me. Looking out over the vast bay and the cities of its perimeter seemed part of it. A clarity not of thought alone, but a clearness in between thoughts. No rabbit warrens, no jumble of third-level and fourth-level vague tentatives that caused the usual confused pushing on that is the mode and mood of everyday thinking. It was rather abstract thinking and, as such, carried little of the necessary load of implications. And yet it worked for me.

The problems I brought to this grandeur of scene, this openness of mind, appeared Lilliputian when I displayed them.

I am a cuckold.

It carries no weight in your culture—only in theirs.

Can my wife be a wholesome woman, loving two men passionately?

She obviously is.

Why have I been so full of hate and jealousy?

Fear of losing my complete ownership of Nordi and my status as owner.

Do I want Nordi to be my slave?

Certainly not.

They hide things from me.

Hell, yes! Sex is a most private thing and they were also being discreet as lovers should be. It is not a matter of simple duplicity but a matter of necessary duplicity, to lend grace where awkwardness could destroy.

Does Nordi understand all this?

Of course, instinctively. She is a woman.

What about Art?

He is clean, a gentleman of charm and I like him. He's the kind of guy to take along where the going gets rough.

Shall I break it up? I believe I can.

But if having a husband and a lover makes her seem always brimming with happiness, how can I?

Maybe she should spend the extra love on another baby?

The doctor said no, that she could not bear another baby.

What to do?

Go look in that window on Market Street again and, if you have to, ask her as you did before.

Vastly relieved, I fell asleep in my stone lookout on things. When I awakened I sauntered down to my car, still worried, but no longer in agony, no longer hating.

We ate our dinner smiling at one another, as we always did unless something was wrong.

"You slept in your cairn?" she said tentatively.

"Yes, I did."

"It was a very clear day. Could you see very far?"

"In several ways, yes."

"Do I understand you in that, Clyde?"

"I believe you do."

"I've been hoping you'd go there."

"Nordi, do you have enough love so that he and Bunky and I can feel we each receive it all?"

She waited a long time, sitting so quietly, my dulcet lady, and she looked away from me when she replied. "Yes, Clyde," she said, "I was surprised at first, but I have much more than enough."

"In every way?"

"In every way, dearest."

"Then let's not speak of it further," I said. "I will learn to be content."

Her head was in my lap. She wept, I thought, for many reasons.

When Art came down to Berkeley at month's end I asked for his help with a fence around the three lots. He was over bright and early on a Monday. We both knew the score now. We knew that both of us had foregone that great joy (except for the hour) of possessiveness so inherent in sexual love, because of our love of, but more because of our delight in, seeing the full flowering of our radiant lady. We didn't vie as we dug holes, put the posts in them and tamped them. That would be unseemly in our case; no, we worked away together and we had the wire up the third day and the gates and the stuff out over the water by the fifth. I encouraged Art to stay over as he said nothing was pressing at the mine. The fence building and protecting the place was a good thing for Art and me. After that we weren't so formal with each other. After lunch Nordi and Art were puttering around in her rock garden while I dozed and watched for a while.

"Bunky should have his nap now," I said, "and I'll have a snooze too or I won't be able to stay awake on the job tonight. Put a sign on the door 'do not disturb us' and be elsewhere for an hour or so. How about visiting Drakes or going for a row?"

As they went away, I saw she wore her walking shoes. Soon they would be above the houses into the lower meadows, walking along so jollily. I could almost see her puckish airs, hear her drolleries and her laughter. As they go higher she'll reply to something he says with that sidelong glance, that roguish grin I know so well. It's steeper for them now and then they're up in the high meadows. They told each other the walk was to Sugarloaf, but as they near the hazel brush to pass it, Nordi's face will pale, stricken with longing and her lips will quiver as he helps her to their bower. Jesus! This is one thing, this agony, that I must conquer! If I can conquer this and allow her a lover, I think it will be a better gift for her than a fine house, a shiny new car, all the stuff others have, the stuff I can't get unless I forsake our life as we live it now. Strange, I'm going to clear my conscience of guilt concerning things I can't provide her with by becoming a cuckold. The irony of it pleases me! How funny it would be, how ludicrous, if it were happening to someone else! Now go to sleep, cuckold, damn it! Go to sleep!

It was about this same period that a friend of mine, a seaman named Carl, turned up. He was very well read and had a great sense of humor and an expression that, when you looked at him as he looked at you, would start way in the back of his eyes some-where, gain strength rapidly, and would bring about that same growing gleam in you; for he looked like he saw it, and suddenly both of you would explode into laughter over the absurdity of the human scene. A sardonic man, often sad, his features seemed pressed about his nose, and yet he had a wide mouth equipped for guffaws that he never uttered, being essentially a quiet man. And in spite of this sense of compressed features, his eyes were far apart.

They had turned up one Saturday before noon: Keith Guiness, an Irishman and a great brawler and lover of Shakespeare; Carl, the seaman; Dodd, a friend of Keith's, also from Ireland, the maker of a stout, a dark dark brew with an impeccable white-foam; and Keith's brother, Jerry, a priest. They brought with them a dozen or so large steaks, a dozen bottles of stout and six of gin. Art was with us, having just that morning arrived from the mine. Outside our little house the rain came down the wind in great draperies. Inside we were six hearty men jammed into a little sitting room, all somewhat damp from coming through the down-pour that never let up that day. There was a smell of wet woolens, of tobacco pipes and booze and of oatmeal we had just eaten before they came. The windows were steamy with our exhalations and all this olfactory exuberance wasn't mixed somehow but came richly to one's nostrils each as its own entity. Then Nordi opened the door of the kitchen and from three big frying pans came the wonderful smell of frying meat. From the open oven, potatoes fried in advance and held there piping hot finished that great hullabaloo of fragrances.

We laughed and drank the stout and gin and we sang, the big priest's clean tenor keening through the second-rate singing of the rest of us. After each song there was laughter and the good racket of congenial talk. After we'd eaten and as the smell of coffee and burning tobacco gained dominance in the room, I slipped away from philosophical arguments, laid down in the Drakes' spare bedroom for enough sleep to carry me through the night while the little party continued without me.

It was on such a get-together of Keith's friends—who always brought with them steak, stout and booze—that Annie Marge appeared, not with them but simultaneously. She dropped in to see us before she went to San Francisco. We all eyed her with approval, except Art, whose dedication to Nordi sometimes exceeded my own. Nordi and I had known her at art school and would have liked to talk, but we could see that the trip down from Portland had wearied her, so we fed her and ensconced her in the Drakes' spare bedroom and returned to the party. Everybody was talking to everybody else. Carl was holding forth about Sibelius, a composer who, at that time, was not too well known on the coast except for his *Finlandia*. The rest of us, including Art, were chewing at the priest, concerning the considerations of a French abbé about some of his archaeological finds. Then the talk switched to the Irish rebellion.

Keith Guiness had seen action there as a rebel and it wasn't long before they were sentimentalizing over Ireland and its glories. All was fine. The brothers sang some of her great songs and a tear or two dropped into the stout. Carl and Art were talking of the early history of Northern California when Keith and his brother, the fellow behind the collar, said something disparaging about Scandinavians in general and Swedes in particular. Dodd, who'd been studying the foam on his drink as if it were of great moment, said, "Swedes don't know one foot from another." They had forgotten Nordi's Swedish descent. She came from the kitchen, arms akimbo, leaving a vast frying pan of chicken and quoted a famous diatribe against Irish writers and poets that she had memorized from Thomas Wolfe, following it up on her own in really great style and ending in happy taunting laughter. Oh, she laid them low and with great authority. There was a bellow of applause and Art and I turned to each other from different parts of the room as if we were proud parents of a precocious child and beamed at one another, caught ourselves at it and were terribly embarrassed and were gruff with each other for some time after. Keith and his brother were entranced and for several years after teased her and brought her little presents whenever they came, which was every time Carl circumnavigated the world, for he was a seaman on round-the-world Dollar Lines.

In the morning when I came home Nordi and Annie Marge were having breakfast. As we three had known each other at art school, we talked a while about "where's he now," and "how is she" until we tired of gossiping. Then she told us about herself. About a year after our marriage she had taken a job in a doctor's office—three doctors, in fact. She had done well there and after several years as a nurse she became secretary—in fact, majordomo of the office. She ran it well. They told her so, she said. It was a happy place, but then to their dismay the stuffing began to come out of the sofa, for she fell in love with the youngest and most popular doctor. Her "S.S." she confided to us, her "secret sorrow." At first it was adulation of the great doctor but gradually she fell and fell hard. The two others, sadly, saw it all happen, though she carried her "S.S." deep inside her heart. After all, he was married, a social creature; there were two children and a baby. Then she began hating his wife and eventually she showed it. She wept if the wife called the office and finally sent her a spiteful note. It became too disruptive. Everyone could feel her anguish. The senior doctor called her into his office. He was very fond of her—they all were—but he let her see herself as they saw her.

"It can't go on, Annie Marge, you can see yourself it can't. You have friends in San Francisco. Go down there, fall in love, live recklessly—no, I don't mean recklessly—I mean go out, meet people. You're thirty, I believe, and a virgin I'll wager. That's bad, Annie Marge. Get involved. Look, if I were you I'd, well—meet people. At your age it's absurd to, to—oh, go ahead and do it." He gave her a five hundred dollar check and helped her clean out her desk.

With tears streaming down her cheeks, her arms full of old glasses cases, correspondences, the cover of her typewriter and nine packets of dental gum, the poor girl hit the street. She took a taxi home, where taxis were never seen, dropped her stuff in the gutter, rushed into the house, up the stairs to her room and lay on her bed screaming while her parents closed windows and doors as the neighbors, seeing the taxi and hearing the screaming, came running and stood all around the house. This we got from her after several sessions without tears and in her own rather childlike way of seeing it. The day after the screaming incident, she sat around the house in a wrapper and slippers drinking coffee, somewhat oblivious to the well-wishers and her parents. What she was doing while they stared at her was reordering her life, rending and tearing the "S.S." part to bits and deciding to find out about sex, a commodity she knew next to nothing about, but feeling that with the acquisition of that knowledge she would in some way get even with the wife of her late "S.S."

We told her to make our place her headquarters until she got settled. In San Francisco she found an ailing mother in the room she expected to occupy. She hadn't let them know she was coming. I went over to Oakland and got her baggage. She stayed with us. She slept on the couch and every day she looked for a position and pretty soon she looked for a job. There was no work to be had. When someone got sick or died, the people of the firm closed ranks and the duties were absorbed by those left. Marge got a bit panicky. We talked her into giving herself a vacation for one or even two months living with us. We would charge her four dollars a month as food was cheap and we had to have the other stuff anyway, so she relaxed for perhaps the first time in ten years, as she was by temperament a driver. Marge was on the lookout for a man, but Carl, after seeing her when she arrived, left for another round-the-world trip on the *Stanley Dollar*. That meant that his group would be absent from our place for many months. Art, as I said, shunned any woman but the sainted Nordi. He brought over several friends, however, but she didn't care for any of them. One was too old, and another walked funny. He had recently sprained his ankle. I brought several but she was still enamored with the doctor in Portland. She did like to hike and went along on my rock hauling expeditions and helped, though there was little she could do. She took some of the strain off when I noticed that Nordi would be wearing a little more eyebrow pencil than usual. Finally she found out about Nordi's exceptional love life and had a fit of jealousy.

"How can you do it?" she asked in a very annoyed tone.

Nordi smiled at her as she poured her cup full. "Do you really want to know?" Nordi asked, and, on receiving an affirmative, said "I never make comparisons. I never talk about one when I'm with the other, and I allow my sexual needs and fantasies complete freedom, and, Marge, I happen to love them both very, very much. There's only one thing I hold back from them and that's the time and love and my joy in him—that is, Bunky." And then, pensively: "I wish Bunky had kids to play with. There's no other little boy around for a mile, I do believe. There's two older girls but he needs a chum."

Annie Marge was of Finnish descent and ashamed of it, though if I had been able to choose my nationality, I think I'd have been happiest as a Finn. I consider them remarkable people. Carl was half Laplander. There was nothing unusual about Marge. Her profile was a bit dished, though her face wasn't, which gave her a slightly questioning look. She was fair with light brown hair and she had a very small rib cage and waist that made her look frail. I don't know where she packed the lungs, but she could not be winded on a fast climb. We had rolled down my stones one day and were sitting on them ready to put them in the trailer, when she brought up her ever-present subject of men and, in her remarks, she said she could never be close to a man with a scarred face like mine.

"Oh, ho," I said to myself at that, "you're going to lose a certain membrane because of that." I liked her well enough but I didn't love her, fine companion though she was.

I seduced her, oh yes, I seduced her! Entrapment with wiles. Everything worked out in advance. Oh, I was a devil! I wanted her to get used to my holding her hand. She did so in arm wrestling and helping her up steep places and as we climbed trees. I taught her to row, helping her in and out of boats. I deliberately poured some dust in her hair, a so-called accident and helped her comb it out and then brushed and brushed it. Oh, yes, and as she washed it, I must see if it was really clear of the stuff. It was, but I brushed it some more. She quickly grew tolerant of me.

I found there would be a high tide at ten p.m. on my day off. It would be complete with full moon. I rented a large, very heavy rowboat and asked if she would come with me on a moonlit row. She happily agreed. Art and Nordi looked at me with ill-hid annoyance, as a cheapener of sex, which should only be based on a great and mutual love. Oh, I felt devilish, I admit.

The day before I had stopped at Paradise Cove, as I hauled rock, and cleaned debris from a nice sandy place against a high embankment. I had also cut a quantity of dry kindling wood and some larger pieces and scattered them about where I could easily find them.

Into the boat I put a mat and on that several blankets and a pillow, arranging them so she could lie on them while I rowed. Then to make it more fiendishly complete, I brought along a pair of freshly ironed bedsheets.

Art and Nordi were visiting Madeline and Zimmie when we left. I remarked about the warmth of the night, so she brought no coat. Away we went, the tide helping us on our way. Soon we were off the ancient coaling station and some sailors saw us and whistled and sang. This happened at a time when I had planned to sing the "Barcarolle" from *Tales of Hoffmann*. Of course, then I couldn't. Why in hell hadn't I anticipated this and passed the station from farther out? Well, finally we left their singing and catcalls behind. Quiet reigned again except for the splash of oars and the ripple at the bow. Along in here I planned to whistle "Estralita," but when I cast back for that I drew a blank. I secretly fretted at the disruption of my program.

She spoke up. "Clyde," she said, "I see you're as appreciative of silence as I am. The moon and the rowing are perfect."

"I thought you'd like it," I said, and rowed on.

At least my timing was right. The boat's bow dug into the sand of Paradise Cove at exactly high tide by my watch. I drew the heavy boat up as well as I could and we left it to take a walk in the meadows above the cove. It was a beautiful night. The moonlit meadows and the small groves here and there cast mysterious shadows.

"Let's go to the top," I murmured, and up we went, going in between groves on narrow aisles of grass to other meadows. I grew tired, having hauled two loads of rock during the day. We kept discovering other glades, other meadows, 'til she wanted to rest. We sat together in a way that forced her to lean against me or slide off our perch. We talked in murmurs at the moon's instruction and we said little. When I felt the tide had ebbed enough, I got up and said, "It's been wonderful, still I should get you back to your trundle bed. Rowing you home will warm me. The air is getting very chilly." I shivered and down the hill we went until we came to the boat and, what do you know, it was high and dry. Oh, I struggled and strained to move it toward the water. We both did, but it was stuck. What to do?

"I'm cold," I said. She shivered. "I'll make a little fire to warm us."

I soon repossessed my scattered dry wood and had a blaze going. We looked into the flames as we warmed ourselves. "We'll have to camp here until the tide comes in," I said. I went to the boat and got the three blankets and a bottle of wine and started making the bed.

"Oh, it will be fun," she said, "but we'll keep our backs to each other. You know, even in an emergency, there are certain rules."

"Of course," I agreed, "but I think we should take off our clothes and put them between two blankets to lay on and put the other blanket over us. The cold will come up to us through the sand. I've camped in all kinds of conditions and I know what I'm talking about." The fire was now a bed of coals. "It's an emergency and we mustn't get chilled," I went on, "or we'll spoil our adventure."

"It is an adventure, isn't it?" she said and told me to look away while she took off and placed her dress and other things between the blankets. I did the same as she and crept in. We lay with our backs to each other and soon warmed up.

"Are you comfortable, Annie Marge?" I murmured.

"Am I ever," she whispered. "This is so comfy. And look at the moon. You know, Clyde, this is so romantic I can hardly believe it. It's really just California, though, isn't it?"

I agreed. It was then that she sneezed and sneezed again. "I left my handkerchief in the boat. Look away while I get it."

She was at the boat a long time and when she came back she grabbed her clothes out from under the blankets and put them on.

"Clyde Rice, I found the sheets. Don't tell me they're for sails. You hoped to gild the lily for a joke, decided not to, when everything was working so well. The very idea! Oh, damn your sense of humor!"

When she had her clothes on, she pounded me under the blankets and laughed at thwarting my plans.

It was no use. I admitted my evil aims, so I dressed and hunted along the beach a ways until I found several round limbs and bits of round wood, put them under the boat, rolled her into the water, put our gear aboard and headed home to the occasional laughter of Marge, who said it was wonderful.

"But it wasn't real, Clyde, you imitation villain."

Our dear friends, the Drakes, separated. Bessie went home to the ranch and Bob leased a three-masted codfish schooner and, with some friends, headed for Alaska to salt down salmon. Bessie's brother's wife came to take care of the place. Her name was Lenore, a very pleasant young lady with whom we later developed quite a correspondence. Anyway, she offered Marge one of the lower spare bedrooms that were under the main house and close to the beach.

Then one night when I started the *Sonoma*'s engine a petcock into a cylinder blew off, tying up the boat for the night. The company hired a Sausalito taxi to haul the crews around by land and I was free for the night. I came quietly to Marge's window, she unlocked it and disappeared. I opened it quietly, stepped inside and closed it, undressed and got into bed beside Marge.

Far away in an upstairs back bedroom slept the girl of the house. We were alone with the whole night to spend on one another. Marge giggled and soon we were wrestling, pinching and biting and then we were kissing and Mother Nature took over. We were a delight to each other, for I found nothing in my way. Before dawn, she said, "Though I like you a great deal I don't love you, Clyde, and I think you feel much the same way about me. I suppose I should thank you but I won't for I feel I gave as much as I received. Now at last I am a woman and terribly sleepy."

A few days later with nobody home in the three houses except Annie Marge and me, we were wrestling out in the grass between houses and generally annoying one another when she got one of my small ropes and tied my hands behind my back. I let her, for besides my sheathknife an my pocketknife, I had a small, very thin, very sharp knife in an inner pocket. After I was tied she led the rope end through the top rungs of a long tapering ladder that lay in the grass and then she ran the rope down to the bottom rung and tied it. While I laughed to myself, she searched me and took the sheathknife from its sheath under my trousers on my groin, the whittling knife from my pocket, and continued searching and found my hideaway knife. She put them all in her purse while I howled for mercy. She went to her room, changed to street clothes and left to spend the day in San Francisco.

She had tied the rope too tight and my hands began to swell. It was a beautiful job. There was no way I could get to the rope end and untie it and I was tied too closely to the ladder to get up. I had allowed all this, feeling secure with the tiny hidden knife, and I expected her to return after her charade was convincing enough. I got the ladder over on top of me, but in that position I couldn't get up either so I rolled it back and lay panting. Unless somebody passed on the road I was tied until Nordi or Marge got back in the evening. I remembered how it had started in fun and how I let her do the tying, but as soon as I was tied, she became a different woman; a mean and nasty look came upon her face and she uttered no words, for to her it was no longer a joke. I lay wondering about this when I heard footsteps in the grass and turned my head to look up at a middle-aged couple who were staring down at me in perplexity.

"Please," I said, "will you untie the rope at the bottom of the ladder?"

The man did and I arose stiffly, turned my back to him and held out my tied hands, which he untied.

"Thank you," I said, rubbing my swollen hands together.

"Well," said the woman, "we are looking for a Clyde Rice. He's supposed—"

"Me," I said, "I'm Clyde Rice. What can I do for you?"

They both began grinning. "So you're Clyde," the man said, and his wife uttered a very satisfied, "Well!" Then she said, "Annie Marge Larson is my daughter, and he"—she indicated him with a turn of her head and motioning as if she were hooking him with her nose—"is her Dad. We're on vacation and came to see Marge."

I put my swollen hands behind me and escorted them to the house, and soon we were chatting over cakes and coffee. When Marge arrived home, she said nothing about our little game that had gotten out of hand. A few days later she went along with her parents to see Uncle Arnie in Alameda—or was it Altadena?—and life droned on.

Nordi and I went for a walk one day. I had awakened at noon. We hadn't walked far before we were on a steep hillside above the road to Paradise Cove. We said nothing, just being one, looking down on Kyles Cove below the road. We'd been sitting there long enough when I noticed a movement in the tall weeds, lush anise plants and grass. It kept coming toward the road. I pointed it out to Nordi and we continued to watch for soon it would break cover to cross the road. Finally just a bit of its head showed as it examined the road listening for cars or people. It hadn't a long muzzle like a coyote. It could only be a bobcat. My hand was on Nordi's arm when it burst from the tall grass, ran across the road and into cover on the other side. It was our son, Bunky, all alone, but no! The grass waved again and Bunky's dog followed him into new hiding.

Poor tyke, no other boys to play with. When he got tired of playing with an older girl in the neighborhood he evidently went on long forays with only his dog for company. We'd left him in Lenore's—the Drakes' relative—care, but he'd gotten away. After that we felt if he could travel like that we could take him with us on walks that weren't too long. This to his solemn enjoyment. He rarely smiled or laughed, except when we would cut up; then he was beside himself with mirth. His voyages of discovery went on every time he could run away. At least the lessons on the danger of traffic on roads had taken hold. I took him with me on rock trips, but I could see I bored him when I tried to teach him about oaks and laurel and different shrubs of that country. But if I sang to him when we were looking out at some view of the Bay, he was enchanted. With his dearth of peer companionship, we spent much of our time with him, but of course it didn't make up for the lack. Had we had the sense that God gave the monkeys we'd have adopted a brother for him. Oh, looking back one is aghast at former stupidities.

He always treated Art as an equal, and he loved to be made much of in Annie Marge's lap.

It was really a male society that we had at the Point. There were Nordi and Bessie with Madeline on weekends and now Bessie had gone, while there were Bob and Art and Zimmie and Ed Davercozen and myself and old Pete and our visitors from town—Carl, Keith Guiness and his brother Dodd, and Dave Cartwright and once in a while Harrington. If the talk wasn't political or philosophical, it was centered on boats and boats and boats, or women. In this situation an ordinary woman was treated as extraordinary and an extraordinary woman was treated—nay worshipped—as a goddess. It could have harmed Nordi, but she was too fine, too honest to let things go to her head. With the coming of Annie Marge and Lenore at the Drakes', things balanced up a bit. We often had weenie roasts on the beach. It was here that I discovered that clean old men smoked Bull Durham cigarettes with a different fragrance than young women and men do, and then I found, using old Pete and Ed Harringer, that old men, smoking Bull around fires of rotted driftwood, reached the epitome in that sort of fragrance. We worked it a few times with great success, the old men unknowing of course, but they got into an argument about a certain kind of knot. Old Ed was a beer wagon driver and called the knot a pastern knot, while Pete, a seaman through and through, called it a carrick bend. They soon hated each other and would not come to the roast if the other was to be there. With only one at a time it cut down on volume and we could only achieve that wonderful aroma by waiting for a very still evening and using a smaller fire.

Often Annie Marge went with me on rock trips and sometimes

we didn't get back when we should. We had a jolly time of it. I never saw the snarl on her face again. One day she came home from job hunting with a big cake and a big smile. She had found employment. A doctor in Mill Valley hired her and also gave her living quarters in back of his office. The pay was low but, with the apartment thrown in, it made her independent again. I moved her things over and got her settled and she gave me a kiss and the key —a key I was never to use.

Sunday night I went down to my job. The *Sonoma* wasn't in her berth, but lay alongside the float. I washed the old boat down figuring the company had used it for some emergency purpose. I wiped the engine down and got ready to start it. This you did by shooting a little gas into both cylinder heads through petcocks; then, leaving both petcocks open so there was no compression, you rolled the big flywheel over until it was almost at firing point for the first cylinder; then you closed the cocks and gave the flywheel a heave and away she went. I had the cocks open and was casually rolling the wheel up to where I could close them when she fired, jerking the wheel out of my hand. I was no way ready for that jerk and it did something to my back. I looked the engine over and saw the cause. It had been re-timed. Osgood, I thought. Yes, there it was—his tool marks on the make-or-break arrangement. In one of his drunken wanderings he had come down, taken the *Sonoma* out of her berth, taken her out for a little trip in the dark, brought her back and left her at the float.

It was time now to make my first trip, so I got the engine started—though it was very painful—and took a crew and some odd passengers across to Sausalito. When I tried to tie up at the float, I couldn't. What to do! Well, I thought, I'll take her back to Tiburon and report out. I didn't want to be alone in the steering place going back without someone there if I became completely disabled. Of the passengers only a drunken sailor looked to be of any use. I told him my problem and he agreed to stay with me. With every seat taken I left the float as usual to pass astern the outgoing *Tamalpais*, but a wave jerked the *Sonoma* in a way that paralyzed me. We were headed right into the churning paddlewheels of the *Tamalpais* while I sat there immobilized. The sailor was asleep crouched by my feet. I found I could use my leg. I did and kicked him in the head. He woke up and pulled the reverse lever as I had instructed him at the float and we missed those paddlewheels by about ten feet. I was now useless but he did what I told him to do and we got across and made a very sloppy landing at the float. Eventually an ambulance came and the night crew from the shops got me strapped on a plank and out of the *Sonoma*. Every move was very painful, and it took a long time before I was deposited in the ambulance. At the hospital they found three vertebrae dislocated. I was there many days lashed to a board. Two weeks at home in the same manner and I was transferred to a panel in bed where I could move around a bit. Later, when I could walk, I was given a watchman's job on the *Marin*. "Never to do physical work again," pronounced the doctor—the same one that had said Bunky would not survive the winter in that time of whooping cough. This gave me reassurance of a sort.

I read a lot and I kept trying to do things at home and I continually did simple exercises. Months later I recovered enough to do paint jobs on the boat. I was on the *Marin* one day, standing on the fender painting the outside of the boat, when the skipper called down to me that we would leave in five minutes. Everything was painted before me, even the handrail. I didn't want to touch it, so I got in a very strange position and strained to pick up my paint bucket without touching the rail. There was a clicking sensation in my back and great pain. I was forlorn, still hearing in my head the skipper's summation as I left: "You better figure on being a watchman for the rest of your life."

I felt pretty low, but when I woke up next morning I was in fine shape—in fact, far better than I'd felt since the accident. I subsequently found that the strained, odd position had snapped the dislocated back into its true alignment again and after a few days I got my *Sonoma* job back.

While I was watchman on the *Marin*, I saw more of the great Lonnie, who was a deckhand on the *Marin*. A slender, middle-sized guy with a fine beak of a nose, his thick hair just started to turn salt-and-pepper gray, he had a most beguiling smile and he loved a bottle, though he was far from an alcoholic. Lonnie was an adventurer who had settled down. He had been a cowboy, movie actor, seaman before the mast. He'd been in on an expedition up the

Amazon and spent a couple of years sailing out of Singapore through the islands. Lonnie had stolen his wife, an upper-class Mexican, and brought her over the border with three relays of horses. He told many wild tales and we got to figuring he was all talk, so we were happy when old Pete said that knots were all the same all the world over, but that around Java and Sumatra they tie one rope yarn to another in a different way from the one we all know. "If he's been around Jakarta or anywhere in those islands, he'll know how to tie that knot."

So we doubters got together in the forecastle of the *Marin*. We started tying knots, at which Pete was an expert. When we got to rope yarn knots Pete got the strands in Lonnie's hands and he tied the regular knot.

"You know any others?" he asked Lonnie and Lonnie tied the Javanese knot. Pete couldn't get it right, but Lonnie tied it expertly.

"It's called the Timor Strait knot," he said.

Well, we all sat there looking at Lonnie, now believing every damn tale he told and figuring he was quite one humdinger of a man.

Lonnie was a great mine of misinformation for those he felt wouldn't know what to do with the truth if you gave it to them. He spoke of them as people who couldn't get their asses settled down in the saddle. He loved to tease tourists and while I was a watchman on the *Marin* he used me as a straight man for one of his acts.

Along about five p.m. on a Sunday was the right time for it. It was based on the harbor or hair seals that hang around Belvedere Point. The stupidest of their kind, they do not dive when approached — no sense doing something extra — their hairy dog faces just sink out of sight if you come near them. So now on the 5:15 Sunday trip from Tiburon there would be standing room only on the upper deck. On leaving Tiburon we would hunt out a group that looked to be tourists and stand near them.

Lonnie, to me: "Say, did you see that Johnson fella come aboard?"

Me: "Yes, I did. I tell you, Lonnie, I can't stand the man, I don't know why."

Lonnie: "Instinct, maybe. He's a dog trainer and a mean one.

Remember those two Airedales of his?"

Me: "Yes, I know he has two Airedales but what's wrong with that? He calls them Venus and Pinkus Boy."

Lonnie: "He's training them to swim the English Channel. There's twenty thousand dollars in it for him if either one makes it. He trains them by making them swim from Tiburon to Sausalito. It's all right if the tides are right. I saw the two between Tiburon and Belvedere Landing as we came over. We should catch up with them at the Point."

All this was said loud enough for the tourists to hear. As we reached the Point, Lonnie would crowd to the rail and search the area and see a couple of hair heads. "There's Venus now. Yeah and Pinkus Boy," he would say in a loud and excited voice and point. "They look tired to me and still a couple of miles to go."

As we neared them with our tourists staring at the poor dogs, first one and then the other seal would sink and Lonnie would wail, "Oh, the poor brave dogs, drowned for greed." By this time all was astir on the upper deck. The tourists would want to get at this man Johnson. Outrage would spread around us and Lonnie, mumbling sorrowfully, would leave. Sometimes they'd ask me to identify Johnson and I'd say he's down in the cabin. He's just an ordinary-looking man. It was with these little diversions that Lonnie kept his mind off the fact that he had settled down.

They were building the Golden Gate Bridge. From our house we could see the tower at Lime Point that would one day support the cables, and the tower on the south side was rising too. The bridge would spell an end to the ferries, to our way of life. Ah, the changing world. We yearned for the excitement of change, while we clung to security. Bored by one, startled by the other. I didn't look things in the face, I ran the *Sonoma* and hoped for the best. Far in the back of my mind I began to wonder if living in a small colony might be the answer to our problem. If, say, a group of ten people lived somewhere on the coast in the Pacific Northwest. If they had a fishboat and some land—say, a hundred acres—couldn't they produce enough food and fish for their own needs and for market to make enough money for supplies they couldn't produce? Wouldn't they be happy together in communal life? Nordi and I talked about it.

My strange guilt still stalked me. The ideal life for me was not the ideal life for a woman. Oh, she told me it was fine, that she was happy, and she did glow with life. Still when I looked at what other men, rich men, could give their wives, I was full of misgivings. Finally I concluded she should go on a fine camping trip with Art. I could pay for it if I worked through my own week of vacation. They said it wasn't fair to me. I pointed out that it was the only way we could do it, otherwise she would have no vacation, as I didn't make enough money to quit working for a week. Eventually they agreed, so Nordi got to see the Sierras, Lake Tahoe and Mono Lake. Art was his own boss and he'd been working night and day on his two projects and needed a rest himself. They took Bunky and much equipment and left when I was at work, as I wanted them to do. I came home to an empty house—I saw at once that I was lost without her. A house is a complicated box without a woman in it. Two weeks, that's fourteen days. Good God, why did I do it! For my conscience's sake. Okay, okay, somehow I've got to stay alive and sane until she comes back. Yes, that's all that matters now. Exist until she comes back. I must keep a neat house, eat well, sleep as much as I can, yes, and spend a great deal of my time on Sugarloaf.

Somehow I fed myself and tumbled into bed. I couldn't sleep. After an hour or so I got a sweater of hers, some of her under-things and her slippers, wrapped them up, used them for a pillow, and escaped into a deep dreamless sleep. When I awoke it was dusk. In the dark, I ate a piece of the pot roast she'd left for me, made myself a lunch for the boat and went out. The tide was low. I went down to my sea anemone. She's gone, I told it.

A week later this survivor still operated the *Sonoma*, a hollow-eyed clown. I sometimes felt as though I'd been disemboweled. And then the *Sonoma* began to leak. A side-long blow a floating log had given us had dislodged the butt end of a plank under water. It was down the side where, lying on deck, I could just touch it. Then I could see it; it was barely discernible. It leaked about three hundred gallons in twenty-four hours. The bilge pump on the engine was broken. In the cockpit was a tiny hatch—too small to get a bucket through. A gallon can would go through and with this I bailed between runs and on into noon. I went to Lindstrom in the office. He would hardly hear me. "Rice," he said, "we got problems around here about the ferries and trains. Everything's falling to pieces around our ears. It's up to you. If you knew how things are around here you wouldn't be bothering me."

I went straight up on Sugarloaf to think it out. All I could come up with was that fine sawdust might be sucked into the crack by the incoming water, plugging it, then I could work in larger sawdust and cover the opening with heavy grease. There was such a grease for locomotives. It was like shoe leather when cold. So, holding some fine sawdust in my hands I got the sawdust sucked in and then thrust a hot handful of the grease into the crack and around it. It cut down the leakage to around fifty gallons, though every fourth night I had to redo the process and bail away. It certainly didn't seem right or honest to be without a big bilge pump on board in case the butt loosened up dangerously. As he said, I had to do what was done on my own. I got some oak driftwood boards and some other stuff—piping and two-inch hose—and I built a rough box pump with a plunger eight inches by eight inches. I got a four-foot oak handle to work it with and installed it in the corner of the cockpit and made a canvas cover for it. It wasn't varnished or painted, just smooth oiled oak. It kept the bilge clear and in an emergency I could pump out eighty gallons a minute. All should have gone well, but it was reported within a week by that same anonymous son of a bitch who reported when I fell overboard. They, the train crew, were protected as they had never been before, but there is a type of man (we all know him) who is always waiting to squawk or squeal.

One morning I had put the *Sonoma* in her berth when Captain Lindstrom came hurrying down the wharf. When he got closer I saw he had a check for me with a slip of dismissal attached to it.

"You've gone too far, Rice," he said. "We've had complaints about a homemade pump you put on the boat. You don't seem to realize this is a railroad and you can't stick jerry-built junk wherever you please."

As he talked up on the dock above me, I fitted the handle in my pump and started long easy strokes that brought bilge water gushing overboard. Lindstrom looked at it a moment and then stopped his harangue, came down the ladder and put the deck bucket under the spout. One stroke filled the bucket and ran it over. He was amazed.

"Clyde," he said, "this pumps twice as much water as those four-man bilge pumps on the ferries." He tore up the check. "Hell," he said, "I'll have one cast just like that up in the shop and fit it in here. A wooden pump looks primitive. Forget the check, you're doing a good job of it here."

The next week I hauled rock every hour I could. I think I had more than enough, but didn't want to stop until I was sure I had surplus. I thought a lot about the house, how I would lay the foundation deeper and wider. Two of the walls in the living room would be finished with the encrusted stone. I'd gotten a pamphlet from the state on solar heating published in 1927, and was going to use some of the ideas I found in it.

Three more days and the two weeks would be up and she'd be home, making everything come alive again. I became almost light-hearted. I took Heidi in the trailer to be bred and left her for a week. I cleaned the house most thoroughly. In fact I spent the last of the fourteen days cleaning and varnishing the *Sonoma* and the house, then I waited. She had had her vacation and I had sweated it out. Now, by God, I should be free of that nagging feeling that I was cheating her of the good life. Evening came. At eleven I left for my job and hauled the train crews back and forth. Before I knew it, it was morning and I hurried home. The house was empty. Next day was the same. Hell started then. Had she left me? God! I would never see her and my son Bunky again. I'd find him, but then again, maybe it wasn't desertion. Maybe an early snow had caught them, but how? I didn't know if they were in the southern Sierras or the northern.

The fourth day they were overdue and I phoned Art's father and told him my fears of an early snow. Had he any idea of where they were? I wanted to search for them.

"They gave no indication where they would be," he replied. "You're talking about a very mountainous area sixty miles wide and three hundred miles long. There's nothing to do but wait."

The agony was at me again. The one I thought I had conquered. I couldn't sleep. What food I could get down had to be washed down—my mouth dry and my eyes dry. Hate came spasmodically. I put it away. I tried to be reasonable and calm—to establish an island of quiet in the middle of my anguish. I was so weak I could hardly do my work on the *Sonoma*. Thoroughly stupefied and stunned, I thought vaguely of leaving the job and starting to scour the world for them. The seventh day they came, all tanned and jolly. When Nordi saw me, she said, "Why, Clyde, you look awful! We better get you to a doctor right away."

"Do you realize you're a week late?" I asked in fury.

"Yes," she said, "but it was so wonderful and I thought you wouldn't mind."

I looked at her. I saw that she couldn't conceive of the torture she had put me through. Fury left me. I knew at last that I had passed her. I looked deeply in her eyes. It wasn't there. "Nordi, my dear," I said, "you'll never catch up." But she did, long after.

Life went on as before—a month, two months. One night I came down to the *Sonoma* and opened the shed where I kept the gasoline and oil and tools. Taped to the gas can was a note that told me I was dismissed and that Captain Brockaw and Captain Anderson, with much greater seniority and rank than mine, were taking my job between them on Wednesday.

Next morning I took home my tools and personals and bid the *Sonoma* goodbye. Nordi and I talked it over. Ferryboating was done for. The bridges—the Golden Gate, the San Francisco-Oakland and the Richmond Bridge—would finish it. Progress! Two weeks later, after some fog and a storm, the *Sonoma* was sold for junk.

IX

In Which
Goats Almost Save Me,
We Try To Live Off The Land,
I Get Sealed In Despair,
and
Am Finally Saved In Spite Of Myself

◇   1931   ◇

Nordi and I sat in our living room.

"I should have learned a trade."

"You did, Clyde. It was ferryboating."

"No, I mean like a carpenter or a machinist."

"They're walking the streets just like other unfortunates."

"I don't know how to go about this," I said. "I've got to find work and the city is alive with men—experts in their trades—who can't find work. The chances are poorest there. I think I'll look around in Mill Valley and San Rafael—yeah, and Santa Rosa and Petaluma."

Before the end of the week I found that that was useless too. President Hoover was saying take a chance. "If we all start doing something, investing some of our savings in something that we think might work, it might jar the economy off center. Be inventive, take a chance for your country."

Yes, I could see we had to do something. Maybe I could find some unusual way to make my living, be my own boss. We had saved up a thousand again—a very small nest egg. I went to the government extension agent in San Rafael and got a lot of pamphlets on ways to start a business on your own.

"Build solar water heaters."

"Grow Turkish tobacco in California for cigarette manufacturers."

"How to build a small blue-cheese factory."

"Raise goats and sell their milk."

"Make rammed earth houses."

"Chickens—how to maintain an egg route."

"Trapping—furs." This I inquired about and found there was absolutely no money in it, not anymore.

Blue cheese—that looked good with milk at eleven cents a gallon wholesale. I spent several weeks trying to put that together with a fellow in Nicasio, where he had some buildings and land that were feasible, but he built a store instead.

Goat milk—we knew about that.

I went to the city hall in San Francisco one morning and after innumerable shuntings around found that the city consumed five gallons of goat milk a day in its hospitals. Surely that was a small amount for so large a city. Of goat milk I knew only that the fat globule in it was one seventh the size of that in cow's milk and so it was much easier to assimilate; also it was comparable to the fat globule in human milk and thus valuable for babies and weak patients. I went back to the extension agent in San Rafael and asked him if he could get the figures on the goat milk consumed in other cities the size of San Francisco—Los Angeles, Seattle, Omaha, Houston. Sure he would, he'd be delighted, this was the sort of work dear to the bureaucrat—statistics. Cities of comparable size used two hundred gallons a day compared to San Francisco's five. I pounced on the figures, swore the man to secrecy and drove home.

Nordi thought it over. "What can you lose?" she asked.

"Our thousand bucks and what we'd have to borrow."

"How long will that thousand last if we sit tight here?"

"A year if we hold our breath, but it's no use waiting for jobs on the ferries. They're a gone goose."

"I don't know how you'll do it," she said, "But it seems you've got to gamble. Besides it does look like an opening for somebody who has goats."

"Yeah," I said.

"Then why haven't others latched on to it?" asked Nordi. "Five gallons, phooey!"

So I went back to the city. San Francisco had two milk distributors. They had forced all the small distributors out with threats and mayhem—dirty, dirty pool. I hunted up one of the plants and finally got to the man in charge of distribution—a big Norwegian. Mr. Lorendahl was a rough, demanding sort of fellow. When I told him what I'd found, he belched before he said, "What of it?"

"Well," I said, "it's this way. Either I sell my milk to you or to the other outfit. Do you want the business?"

"Sure," he said, "I'll pay you up to seventy-five cents a gallon and we'll build it up to a hundred and fifty gallons. Sure! Where's your dairy?"

"I haven't got one yet—only a few goats."

"Get out of here," he yelled. "Get your goddamned ass out of here!" He glared at me, then turned on his heel, through with me, and began screaming "Oscar" so loud that Oscar came and they went over some figures together.

I was walking down Market Street heading toward the other plant realizing that I was operating on less than a shoestring. I had only a bit of knowledge to build on. I was sore at that big "Scandihoovian." If he would agree to buy from me, I'd work it out somehow. Goddamn him anyway. I turned and retraced my steps. He was in the same room where I'd left him, standing in the middle of it in a white coat as if he were about to go into the plant. He scowled at me but before he could say anything, I asked, "Will you turn around?"

He did.

"A bit more," I instructed him and the big oaf turned. "A bit more," I said, looking him up and down. He started to turn but stopped.

"What the hell's this all about?"

"Well, I don't know," I said. "I think I could talk to the President or the Governor without much trouble and I'll bet I, a non-Catholic, could wangle a moment with the Pope; so I just wanted to see if you had a third leg or a halo to put you above normal men, so that a guy had to have a goat ranch to talk to you. I found this opening for goat milk in San Francisco and I'm going to build an exceptional medicinal milk set-up. There isn't one around and from what I can see of you, you don't need any special privileges to be talked to about it, do you?"

He looked mad, then amused and finally he laughed. "No," he said, "I ain't no damn pope. You build your goat milk set-up and I'll stay mum until you do and take all you can produce, but it better pass the milk inspector with a near perfect report or you're out. How long before you're in production?"

"A year," I said, "and I'll follow the inspection instructions to the letter."

"Okay, Rice, I believe you," he said, "now beat it."

He opened the door to the production room and yelled, "Emil, Emil, get your ass in here," and Emil heard him over the noise of the clanking machinery and came.

Walking down Market Street I bought a cigar and puffed into the next problem—a twenty- or thirty-acre problem with water and a house that I could lease. It took some time, but eventually I found a place, only a mile north of Paradise Cove, with a broad shallow waterfront. Here was a long low barn, the owner's weekend house, another old house inhabited on weekends, and a decrepit building of one large room with no ceilings—a former storeroom. We put rolled roofing on its leaking shingles—put in an immense window of many panes we found on the place, looking out over the Bay. Now we needed lumber. I went to Sam Donohue and he agreed to have his brother tow a raft of lumber from the San Francisco docks to the goat ranch, as we called it. On the docks my inquiry revealed the fact that two days later a lumber schooner from Coos Bay, Oregon, would dock and unload at a certain wharf. I was there when they tied up and saw the captain.

"What do you get a thousand unloaded at the wharf?" I asked him after talk of Coos Bay where I had a relative.

"Thirty-five dollars, millrun," he said. "The whole deckload is millrun."

"If you unload a towable package of six thousand board feet I'll pay forty dollars per," I said. "We'll tow it away. I'm building some farm buildings up near San Quentin."

He agreed to unload it in the water at eight o'clock next morning. In the package—a kind of raft—was shiplap, two-by-fours, two-by-sixes, two-by-twelves and odd sizes. We towed it over next morning and, at high tide, Sam's brother gave me a rope from the raft. I pulled it and beached it and when the tide went out broke open the raft and, using my shoulder yoke, was able to get it all safe above the beach before high tide came again.

We were about to move when Art, who had been busy at his mine since that vacation trip, knocked at the door. God, I was glad to have another fellow to go over the goat ranch ideas with. When we were done, he said, "You're going to need help."

"I can't afford help," I said.

"I'll help you for food, lodgings and five dollars a month and you provide the tobacco—yeah—and razor blades."

"But not the lady, Art. I know how much you love Nordi, but it wouldn't pan out in this situation and it wouldn't be fair for you to work your head off for her. She wouldn't be able to reward you. No, Art, with the set-up I see ahead of us, a triangle is out."

Art thought a long time. Nordi poured him another cup of coffee. She looked at me most intensely. Finally I got it. They wanted me to leave.

"The way that lumber lays, anybody who saw me bring it in could steal it. I'm going up there and guard it until I can get it in the barn." I took some blankets and left. It brought me pain, but hell, I know about love, the yearning to be together, to be lost to everything but each other. "Clyde," other voices said, "what you're doing isn't natural for a man." "Sure," I thought, "and murder is natural in me? I've proved it and I've suppressed it and I'll suppress whatever I choose. Tonight I'm suppressing bonding and ownership and dog in the manger. It's a rough row for a man to hoe, still I'm not ashamed to work at it."

It was a bit chilly beside the lumber, but after a while I slept. Next morning Nordi and Art and Bunky came out. Art spent an hour looking over the place. At noon as we lunched, Art spoke up: "I'll make my offer again, minus the lady. You know how I feel about Nordi, but you don't know how I feel about you. Well, I like you, with many reservations, of course, and I like Bunky and the Bay country. It's winter and the river is high; no placer now, no panning, and what you're going to do is an adventure I'd like to be in on. How about it?"

"Yeah," I said. It was all I could say. The back of my throat was an arch I couldn't control. "Yeah!"

About a month after I was laid off I heard that Lindstrom and Superintendent Small had said that I had taken a great deal more of things than I was entitled to when I left. This got under my skin, since I had been meticulous in my dealings with the company. I got drunk one night and, tying down the horn on the car, I drove into the terminal, turned on the lights that lit up the whole place, opened up two or three of the storerooms with the keys I still held, loaded up with what I could use of canvas, and rope and tools and nails and paint, closed the place up, turned out the lights and drove away with my horn still blowing—an extremely foolhardy stunt but nothing was ever said about it. Perhaps they figured they owed it to me. I thought so too.

First we got the lumber in the barn, then we went to the old building we'd re-roofed. It had no ceiling so we sprayed whitewash under the whole underside of the roof and walls, then we made a partition about ten feet from the end from floor to rooftree and put a ceiling in it. That made a loft with a barn door to it into the main room and a ladder to reach it. Nordi and I slept there. Under it was the kitchen with a breakfast nook and many innovations of Art's devising. One was a little window in the outside door down low for Bunky's view of things. Art made a big closet in the other end of the room and on top of it he made his bed with a unique ladder cut into it. Then we papered the walls and put cheap linoleum on the floors. A dry log on the beach provided our winter's wood as winter, after faltering, really came on, but by then we were settled and snug in our new home. We rented the cottage at Waterspout Point to a lady from New York, but that didn't quite pay the mortgage payments on it.

After Art's coming in with us we decided we should try to get our food wholesale. Art said that some of the small mining operators who fed from six to twelve men were able to get a great cut on their food costs. Art knew of a mine that hadn't panned out and was abandoned—the Florabelle. We went over to Oakland in Art's car and hunted up a big wholesaler. I came into the cash sales department and told them I had a crew working the Florabelle and that this mine up there bought their grub wholesale and I was sick of buying mine at the retail price. Well, they looked up the mines I said were wholesale and found that they were their customers and that there was a Florabelle mine and agreed. We bought enough for a year of flour, beans, prunes, Crisco, rolled oats, sugar, pepper, spaghetti, coffee, and cases of canned goods and slabs of bacon and raisins, tobacco, razor blades and hard candy. Must have been eight hundred pounds we jammed into Art's big Hudson and left for the goat ranch. It worked so well that I went to a big plumbing and sheet metal warehouse in San Francisco. This time I acted the half-witted son of one of their plumbing accounts who had been told to get them to sharpen their pencil or "Pa's gonna deal elsewhere, 'cause we're gonna pay cash this time and the price is gotta be right." I ordered all the plumbing material we'd need and a dozen big sheets of galvanized iron for the air washer and a half dozen rolls of fencing "for our Aunt Lulu living up near Petalumar." The whole thing came to a third of what I'd have to pay otherwise. Art and I took off in a borrowed truck with our spoils, both feeling tremendously clever.

Art was in his glory planning things. I'm not stupid in innovation, but most all of ours were his. For example, in that great barn we had nurseries for kids, two delivery rooms, an isolation room, areas for goats to be out of the weather, areas for hay, a room for sacks of concentrates and oats. Then we began building the milk house. It consisted of a milking room where four goats could be milked at the same time, a hallway between this and a room with a milk cooler and storage space, and a room for washing all equipment. All these rooms were separated by the hall. Our money soon ran out. We got a loan from my father but it was paid out slowly and held us back most grievously. Later I learned that the delay was entirely unnecessary and without his knowledge.

To save money I made gravel for the cement floors and foundations by pounding up bricks from ruins of a powderhouse that had once stood on the place. I hammered every day all day for a week to make enough. The sand for concrete we got from the beach.

Art now had a girl he visited in Mill Valley, which relieved me of the dog in the manger thing. Every month Sam, the bootlegger's man, would arrive with a gallon of whiskey, take what was left of the present bottle and depart. I never used more than a pint, nor did I ask for it or pay for it. Sam was from Malta—a great country for goats I'm told—or maybe he liked me, anyway once a month a new, full, gallon bottle was deposited in one of our cupboards. Eventually, eight months later than it should have been, the building was done, the tanks and cooler, the metal equipment bought and ready to install. I had twenty-five goats and needed one hundred more—all would be registered animals. I arranged for a plasterer to cement plaster the building inside while we purchased the necessary goats in Oregon and Utah.

It was after we had everything done but the air washer that Art left. It did not concern Nordi. It could have been from some inept remark of mine, for my foot is never far from my mouth. Maybe it was the long waits we had for money from my father with the job just crying to be worked on and finished—maybe that did it. Anyway, we had a disagreement and with spring coming he went back to his mine and the elusive source of that coarse gold dust. We missed him.

Then I picked up the newspaper one morning and read that all milk coming into San Francisco must be pasteurized or certified. A certified dairy was at the top of the heap in fine raw milk producers, its requirements superior to Grade A and guaranteed. The city had had a scare of bovine tuberculosis in its milk and was trying to eradicate it, but the Grade A dairies and guaranteed raw milk dairies were doing all they could—at least as much as the certified dairies. The latter were under the jurisdiction of the American Medical Association and practically all their stockholders were doctors. To pasteurize goat milk would ruin it for what it was—the most easily assimilated milk other than human. I went to the milk inspector and explained my problem. I went to the head of the certification group office and asked if goat's milk was comparable to cow's milk and as fine a food for babies. I asked why certification was necessary and they said, "Better milk for babies."

I applied for certification. The milk inspector went with me to the offices of the certification group and explained that we far surpassed their requirements.

"You should see it," he said. "It's the ultimate for producing milk for hospitals."

They had a meeting and voted on whether I could be allowed to be certified, though I was unable to find the result of the outcome that day. Next day I received a telegram, "Certified milk is cow's milk." I called the inspector and the man at the milk distribution plant and asked them if they could help me in any way.

"It's political," they said, "and unless you have a lot of money you can't fight it."

So we were through and broke, far too broke to fight it. A few years later they rescinded the law, but in the meantime certified dairies made a killing. It was a big swindle but it finished me before I got started. When I wired my father what had happened I received a letter from which I inferred that it was my fault and to all practical purposes he disowned me. He canceled the check that I had to buy goats with and also a small check for expenses. After all that effort and money spent, I was broke and in debt. I heard later that the town of Tiburon's summation was that I didn't have what it takes. I wondered too. I wondered about the *Princess*. Surely I was not to blame for the tuberculosis. And the *Sonoma*—I couldn't help what happened there. And in this goat ranch, I had not wasted a nickel and made every physical effort possible. Still I was beginning to wonder if I were a jinx.

A jinx—an unlucky man. I went up to my Sugarloaf place, but left it at once. I hadn't time to figure it out. I had to get the wherewithal for living. Food was first. We had ten goats, seven of whom I sold at once. There was a quarter ton of concentrated goat feed and seven hundred pounds of wheat, and a little hand-cranked coffee mill so we could grind the wheat into flour. We had plenty of goat milk and we could slaughter a kid every other month for a while, and we had a calf that was weaned and growing and there was a fair amount of game around us, mostly ducks but also quail and rabbit and rarely a deer. We cleared a small ten-by-ten patch of ground by the house and sowed it with turnips and always we ground away at our wheat, making coarse flour for our bread, hotcakes and pot pies. I scoured the country for work, uselessly. I found that in two months I would be eligible to work four days on the roads at four dollars a day. I would get that every other month.

Before the goat ranch failed, I bought an old Ford pickup in downtown San Francisco. The sign on it said seventy-five and no one-hundreds. I tried it out, looked it over and paid for it. As I looked out the window of the dealer's little office, I saw one of the dealer's men erasing the "no" on the sign and putting a "dn" or down on the sign. Then I noticed my bill of sale now said three hundred and seventy-five dollars. I told him to give me my money back. He refused, smiling. He shouldn't have smiled. I tickled his belly with my knife. "Tear that up and give me one marked paid!" He did, though it was difficult the way I had him. "Now," I said, "you call a crooked cop on this and when I get out I'll look you up." I drove away and nothing came of it.

I had joined the California Goat Milk Association. I read everything there was on the subject and very much respected the writing of an elderly lady who lived near Salinas. When I found that I could buy an advanced registry Nubian buck and a doe and a kid very reasonable near Aptos, I decided to go by way of Salinas and see her. I left with sandwiches, a little tool kit, canvas and rope, and four hundred dollars.

It was raining as I eased down along the country. The rain stopped as I was starting up long San Juan Hill. A fellow appeared by the side of the road and raised his thumb. I picked him up and told him to get in back, another came running out of the brush and got in with him, then a third jumped in with me.

"Get in back," I said.

"To hell with you," he said, "I'm calling the turns here. You get this rig moving." I looked at him. Viciousness was on his face. Again I had use for my hidden knife. I shoved the knife against his side.

"Jump or in she goes," I said. He turned on me a diabolical glare such as I hadn't seen since the Greek monster. He leaped out and his partners and he were down in the brush while I got that rickety little Ford going uphill and at last down into Salinas where I phoned the goat lady. She welcomed me but asked me to come about seven in the evening. I had a couple of hours to waste. I wandered around town bored stiff. I passed the offices of the Chamber of Commerce, then I went back and in and said I was looking at some farming land over on the coast and thought I might inquire on the fertility of the Salinas Valley. What information on it did they have? They phoned a man and in five minutes a Colonel Horton appeared. He gave the appearance, his face at least, of a scalded hog and I could not but wonder if the rest of him under his clothes looked like the carcasses we see hung in butcher shops — overplump, pink and hairless. He asked me to sit down and did the same and let fly a barrage of deep black soil, ground water, nice healthy girls, bumper crops and it seemed that turnips hereabouts were without parallel. Then he took a deep breath and away he went again. Words like "figs" and "warm nights" and "cauliflower" whizzed by my ear and how the World War should have been fought and about how the Salinas Valley was a better place to raise chickens than Petaluma, and so on and so on. Worn out, I thanked him and left.

I had dinner in a very small Chinese restaurant, more a counter. The cook, a slender Chinese, worked with such a dearth of motion —cutting up the greens and meat, cooking it over a gas flame in a wok—it seemed a slow and beautiful dance in which everything happened too quickly for the tempo. He seemed less a cook and more a magician.

I arrived at the goat lady's barn at dusk. We talked for maybe an hour about breeding, feed problems, on many aspects of goat raising. We were out in a shed with one light overhead, leaning on goat pen sides and fondling velvety goat ears as we talked. I left charmed with her and her knowledge. After that visit the other goat people I was acquainted with grew extremely reserved in my presence. About six years later a member visiting me told me why. She had said of my interview that I raped her. All believed it of me, until she died and it came out that she was insane on the subject and her husband, a lawyer in San Francisco, kept her off by herself with the goats. No wonder people were so suddenly chill with me.

With my notebook full of feeding regimes and the like I went happily on my way, driving through Salinas and on into the night toward Aptos, singing along when suddenly, with a grinding roar, the truck stopped. A survey revealed the magneto, a large contraption, had slipped a disc and was dead. I walked back the six miles into Salinas and not once did I burst into song.

At a large all-night garage I told my woe to a mechanic who drove me out in a Dodge and towed me back. Then he went to work on my rig, took it all apart to get at the magneto, when another mechanic slipped him a bottle. Other bottles were passed by other mechanics. It was the night before Thanksgiving and they were putting on a rehearsal of their activities on the feast day. Soon all were too drunk to work. I stood in the complete disarray of my transportation. Not wanting to waste money on a hotel, I went to a flophouse nearby, paid fifty cents, and went to my cot with a chicken wire enclosure around it. I was taking off my shoes when the vicious looking man and his two pals came in, looked me over and took adjoining chickenwire cells. They knew me, but said nothing. Maybe they'd think from the way I acted I had a sum of money on me. What to do? The place was lit all night. I got out my knife and tried to sleep with it in my hand, but in sleep I move about and I might slash myself, so I put it under the pillow and put my hand beside it and fell asleep. When I awoke in the morning they were gone. I ate my breakfast and dinner with the Chinaman and somehow got through the day and night. With terrible hangovers, the crew came back and finished my Ford next day but ran down the battery, so they started me out with a push. I was on my way to Aptos again.

After a moonlit drive the moon suddenly disappeared and in a few minutes it began to rain. I stopped on a hill where a sign said "Aptos three miles." The garageman had warned me to stop on a very steep hill to roll down in starting. I parked beside, but off the highway, and put up the side curtains. The rain came down in cloudbursts all night. I sat in the center of the seat with a small pillow on each side of me. As they became soaked I wrung them out on the floor. By morning the seat of my pants was sopping wet. As dawn approached the rain went elsewhere and I catnapped until a truck passed and woke me. I got out to relieve myself and wring out the cushions, then stared in consternation at the ground beside the road. It had been washed away under the car and all the way to the bottom of the hill. The highway was a foot higher than the shoulder. I got out a lucky claw hammer in my kit and pulled the staples that held the barbed wire to the posts of the fence beside the road, worked the posts out of the ground, made a ramp of them onto the highway farther down the road, got the Ford rolling and rolled up the ramp onto the road, left it there and rebuilt the fence, then got the car started and entered Aptos in great style and drove up the hill to the goat people's house.

They gave me a fine big breakfast and sold me the goats. We put the buck with his great horns and the doe and the half-grown kid in some hay on the floor of the pickup and tied the canvas down over them so they couldn't stand up and I left those hearty people on a ninety-mile trip to Tiburon. All went well. I drove carefully, for if the engine stopped I was quite sure it wouldn't start unless we happened to be on a hill. Eventually we neared San Francisco, for traffic began to get thicker, and then before I was aware of how deeply I was into the city I came up to a stop sign at Sutter and Van Ness and stalled the engine. I got out and cranked and cranked, as the streetcar came behind and dinged, dinged, dinged its bell at me. More cranking, uselessly. I went back to the street-car and told one and all that I was green at starting Fords and if they wanted to get going, someone in there who knew Fords would have to start it.

They laughed good-heartedly. I'll never forget it. Half a dozen burly men stepped out into the street to do the job. It was at this moment that the buck stood up, thrust his horns through the canvas, swung his head, and tore a great rip in it. At once he and the doe and the kid jumped out into the street and scattered about in the intersection. Immediately more men emerged from the streetcar and chased down the goats, as the people on the side-walks cheered them on. They caught the three and hog-tied them and heaved them into the truck and tied down the canvas with great good humor and one of them spun that reluctant engine till it showed life. As I crossed Sutter, the men who helped, redolent with the billy goat's odor, cheered. I swear it on the gentleness of my mother. I chugged up Van Ness and down onto the ferry.

At that time, even with the Depression hampering its style, San Francisco was capable of such camaraderie. Across the Bay a deckhand got the Model T started and soon I was at the goat ranch with three excellent animals and a tale to tell of goats rampant at Sutter and Van Ness.

Back when I had been a deckhand on the *Marin*, somebody from Belvedere discovered that I whistled classics, though out of tune, and: "Well, what business has a deckhand with the classics?" and: "I always say, Clara, give me a workman, square and true, who knows his place or one of our own, but these people in between! They're bad for business and for the country too. Radicals and ruffians, they infuriate me. I'm broad-minded, very broad-minded, you'll have to admit it, Clara. I know they have a right to life, but symphonies were written for the nobles and the rich. That man Mozart proved it. I read a book about him, Clara, a family man, really. Children at his knee while he jotted down his concertos, but this deckhand! It's unwarranted arrogance, that's what it is and I know it."

On another occasion, as I was going to Sausalito on the *Marin*, I was reading Anatole France's *Penguin Island* when I felt a breath on my neck and turned to find an old fuddy-duddy peering over my shoulder.

"Do you understand what you're reading, young man?"

"Quite," I answered.

"I don't believe you," he said.

I burst out laughing at him. "Why the presumption?" I asked. He grew red in the face and hurried into the women's cabin.

There were dozens of occasions like that. Once it got around that I was an oddball, interested in literature and the arts and amused at their belief of superiority, they disliked me. It was a very slight thing. By and large they were as unaware of me as I could wish, but it was there.

Now as I tried to ferret out a job—and a ferret would have been hard pressed—I found that there was a combined community effort by Tiburon and Belvedere to help those who had lost their means of livelihood. I came to them looking for work. They had a lot of projects going: repairing the seawall, draining swampy places, ditching the roads and doing work offered by the people on the hill. The head of this work center was the son-in-law of Mrs. Bland. He knew me as Nordi's husband and "that deckhand." Now he, and they, would put me in my place. He got me a job pulling dead ivy out of some dead and rotten oaks on a cliff above the Bay. Neither gardener of the estate would chance it. I did. I got all the ivy out and trucked it away. I received a phone call from Mrs. Bland's son-in-law—I'll call him Wesley.

Me: "Hello."

Wesley: "Well, Clyde, hello, hello! Say, Clyde, I heard you finished that job for the Crocktens. Mrs. Crockten was pleased. Fine woman there, Mrs. Crockten. You'll get all the work you can handle now. Several people up there heard about that job. They'll keep you busy, I can tell you. They've known you by sight for years. There is a slight problem, though. You know, Mrs. Crockten still keeps her butler and all, but she's strapped for cash. They all are up there. She can pay most of what she owes you, but she wonders if you'll take the other half of a ham they had for dinner the other night as part payment. She can wangle the rest. What do you say to it? It's difficult times now, my boy." A long wait on the telephone.

"Okay," I said at last, "Okay."

Wesley: "She'll pay you tomorrow, then. I've got a week for you at the Pankles'—you know, the editor of the *Chronicle*. See me Monday."

Next day I went over to the Crockten's. She met me smiling extravagantly. She gave me fourteen dollars and then a maid beside her handed me a platter with half a baked ham on it. "You've stripped me of cash," said the lady, "but will the ham cover the difference?"

"Yes, that's fine," I said, took the ham and drove away. I hadn't been home more than an hour when Wesley phoned.

"Clyde, I've just talked to two other people who want you to work for them," he said. "Of course the Pankles come first. Did Mrs. Crockten pay you?"

Me: "Yes, she did."

Wesley: "All cash?"

Me: "No, fourteen dollars cash and half a ham."

Wesley: "They're very clean with their cooking. By the way how was the ham?"

Me: "Excellent."

Wesley: "How did your wife like it?"

Me: "She didn't eat it."

Wesley: "Well of all things. Why not? They have a wonderful cook."

Me: "If you're really interested in that ham, go down behind the pen in the yards where they sometimes load cattle. There's a bum down there eating it and he told me it was a damn fine ham."

Monday my job with the Pankles was canceled, nor was there work for me on the seawall or the roads, but I was still my own man.

I sold six kids to be roasted at a religious picnic. After the party they scattered and I couldn't tag anybody with the bill.

I decided to be crooked. I went to Sam, the bootlegger, who had many famous people as his clients. Errol Flynn had been up the week before on his schooner *Zaca*. I heard his bill with Sam was seven hundred and fifty bucks. Some such people are drawn to having seasonal things out of season: strawberries in February, fish on Thursday, sex with a lady flagpole sitter, at noon on location. I wanted Sam to sell my old goats as venison, with a few hairs from an old deer hide sprinkled over it. Deer hairs are hollow. Everyone knows it. A glass would prove it. And venison out of season should get five dollars a pound, if the purveying of it is done in hoarse whispers with gutterals every few words to provide the necessary macho effect. Sam wouldn't go for it, not at all.

"Clyde," he said, "I've always looked up to you and your stupid honesty. Now you let me down." He stopped sending my free gallon of whiskey.

Nordi and Bunky needed shoes. Jesus! I should have sold that ham to the bum. Fifteen or twenty cents looked big to me now and a quarter looked downright meaty. They even felt thicker than dimes, pennies or nickels. What to do! It was becoming hard to laugh when misfortune kicked me in the face.

One morning, walking down the beach below Paradise Cove, I found three acetylene tanks the tide had brought in. They were lashed together but I got them apart. I sold them to Sam Mc-Donough for seven dollars apiece. That paid for the shoes and a few groceries. My God, I thought, you're not only living hand to mouth, but you're thinking hand to mouth. You've lost your horizon.

I had trouble with game wardens. In the annual dipping of herring my dipnet was two inches wider than the legal one. A change of law had narrowed the opening. I couldn't afford a new dipnet and I needed the herring badly. Olddag, an immensely fat German, reported me to the game wardens and boasted he did. I decided to stay and see what would happen. It was winter and the floats at the ends of the wharves in Tiburon had been towed away into the lagoon, but the gangways that led from wharf to float were still outstretched, held up by their blocks and tackles of rope. I went out on one. I took the rope end of the tackle that held up the gangway out to the outer end with me and tied it. That way no one could lower me into the water. There were fishermen with nets all around, jeering at Olddag, for my infraction was very slight and each man knew how we needed to salt down fish in these dreary times. Eventually a warden showed up, heard my plea for leniency,

considering the times and the fact that I had only one keg in which
to preserve my fish.

"No," he said, "the law is the law. I arrest you. Come off that
gangway and I'll take you to jail."

I stayed out on the other end of the gangway. "Officer, you're
supposed to make the arrest," I said. "Come out and take me."

He could get out a couple of feet when I'd shake the gangway
and cheer him on. "Come out and make your arrest."

He tried to come out but he knew I'd try to pitch him overboard
if he did. After an hour of making a laughingstock of himself, he
left and I heard no more about it. I still remember his tall shiny
boots. I salted the fish down and we ate the pickled herring all that
winter.

When I got in the real bind after the milk law debacle, I hunted
out of season. I think it's the only thing that I had ever done that
was blatantly against the law. A roly-poly warden was sent out to
catch me. I saw him several times and talked to him. He hung
around too much, so I lined him up between me and a crow and
shot the crow, the bullet passing several feet over his head. I went
over and picked up the crow. I did it twice, but he continued to dog
me.

I met him in a deep shady place in a ravine and while we passed
the time of day, I said, "Say, mister, you've got fat arms," and
while he looked on indecisively I rolled up his sleeve. "Meaty and
fat," I said very seriously. "You know there's a great meat short-
age for some of us poor. Sending a plump fellow like you out here
was a careless thing for your bosses to do. If I were you I'd get
changed to an area where there weren't so many hungry people." I
lowered his sleeve, buttoned it and left. I didn't smile. I was dead
serious. I made myself out to be much more crazed than I was.
Anyway, after that I had no more trouble with wardens.

The buck that I bought in Aptos was a registered Nubian and a
very fine animal. As he was of oriental blood we named him Suisan
Bey. We changed the *a* to *e* in "Bay." There was of course a
Suisan Bay in the upper reaches of San Francisco Bay. He had
long curved horns and, deciding he was very tame, I came within a
quarter of an inch of being disemboweled by those needle-sharp
horns. After waiting for a long time he finally swung his head

fiendishly quick and with all his power, spinning his horns sideways. This he did as I was close, fixing his collar. He ripped through my coat and shirt and undershirt as if they were paper, but I have extremely fast reactions too and he missed my stomach. He broke free and, running, hid in the groves and brush adjacent. I ran him down and beat him. I had to help him home. His front legs wouldn't bear his weight. Two weeks later he tried it again, so I cut off an inch from each horn and blunted them.

A big buck sheep charges with head down and can deliver a knee-joint-snapping blow. All the billy goats I've seen rear up on their hind legs and then come crashing down at you or slash at you sideways—both easy to avoid. Goats are smart, very smart. They've been with us for five thousand years or more. They know us like an old shoe—like a well-read book they know us—and they are not impressed. In fact, I believe these cynical animals are thoroughly bored with us. They have their manners and customs too. If I came into the barn where a group of does lay chewing their cuds all would get up in their places and urinate—their way of saying hello. They had formalized ways of dealing with other things too. Tanner's Newfoundland dog killed the half-grown kid I got at Aptos; Sukey was a great pet but the dog got her cornered and killed her. I would have loved to shoot the brute, but I didn't want trouble with my weekend neighbor.

To see what would happen I caught the dog and tied him with a six-foot rope to a stake in the middle of the doe's covered resting place. About twelve does were up on the hill. I don't know how they knew but no sooner had I tied him up than down they came. Silently they entered the area, one by one, and they arranged themselves all around him within a minute. They stood there alert and silent, then they moved a step in, and after another interval, another step in. Now they were a tight circle and they moved another step in. They stood immobile. The dog, who wasn't afraid of goats, grew apprehensive at each step. That way they terrorized him. Finally he tried to free himself of the stake and rope. Immediately a doe drove at his hind end, knocking him sideways. He started to snap at her but from the opposite side of the circle a doe butted him in the kidneys. He swung on her, but opposite her a doe got him in the back, then they all started to work him over.

Not once was he able to retaliate. This was not a casual attack. It seemed to me to be craftsmanship of high order—the terrorizing, the closing of the circle, and then striking each time he turned on his last opponent. I let it go on for a minute and then drove them away and picked the limp dog up and carried him away and, when he could stand, turned him over to Crescentia Majoris, Tanner's keeper of the park. The does made a good dog of him. Was all that display of knowhow and precision and group effort pure instinct? I'm told so, but I can't help feeling that goats are very sagacious people.

If you're running a goat dairy you have to have a steady supply of milk. Now as does give birth, they increase their flow of milk by four times or more. Fine! Does come in heat periodically, eager to be bred, but the lordly buck, the most sexual of animals, has periods when he will not breed, thus hindering the even flow of milk. What to do!

A buck is not allowed to run with the does—he would annoy them with ceaseless overtures and is terribly smelly. The smell would adhere to the does and eventually get into the milk. You are fighting goat odor in every way you can, therefore the buck lives a solitary life and for want of anything else to do makes love to his water bucket. He longs for company, but when company comes he rears up on his hind legs and butts down at his visitor. It's his way of saying hello and playing with you. I visited Suisan Bey every day to change his staked place, to feed and water him and to be company for the lonely animal. We became friends and then I got an idea and started an experiment. I would take his empty water bucket away from him and shove him in the face and then I would make love to his water bucket. It was a certain way he cuffed it with his forefeet, while making a gibbering sound. They were courtship moves he made before he mounted a doe. I'd let him get a lot out of this tussle. I was the opponent buck stealing his lady. It brought action into his life. Finally, in his abstinent season, I brought a doe who was in heat to him and then shoved him in the face and banged the doe around with my arms and made the gibbering sound and shoved him in the face again and more of the same and then knelt as if to tie my shoelace. He saw the chance and in a flash mounted her and impregnated her. I had solved the problem of an even flow of milk in a goat dairy. The Doctors Kilgore, the owners of the place, got a laugh out of my inducing Suisan Bey to breed in his off season.

In time, under his effort and mine, we got so we celebrated our fondness for each other with goatish antics when I came bringing him his food and water. If I came into view, he'd rear up his six-foot-six of hairy-bearded, heavily-horned self and dance around bleating. After the grain was consumed and the water drunk, I'd move him to fresh grass and tie his chain and then I'd tease him. He didn't want love — he wanted a friendly adversary. His endless fascination with his penis — a thing of cartilage (the gods were good to goats there — no wonder old men are jealous of goats) — his fascination with his penis demeaned him, at least pictorially for me, but what else had he except to nibble for burrs or maybe fleas in his fur?

I tried to get the goats to eat the green seaweed that came onto the beach on each tide. It was green and salty and they liked salt. It might also be nutritious, but goats are an ancient race and have settled ways.

One day, Bunky said, "Look, Da'," pointing up the hill to the road, down which came Carl, Keith and Dodd, and several women. Between them they carried a hamper as wide and long as a card-table. It was full of cracked ice, bottles of gin, whiskey and Dodd's excellent stout. It took four to carry it. Then there was laughter and carefree joy at the goat ranch. We had a great pot of beans on the stove and in the barn hung a kid slaughtered the evening before. They would have none of it. Out came the steaks. We ate and drank and played on the beach and swam in the chilly water. One of Keith's women, a just slightly overripe brunette who was fiercely hanging onto his hand and always glaring at the other women, dunked herself before swimming. She came up like a sick rainbow with her makeup of pink and red and blue and black running down her face and neck and flowing into the bodice of her bathing suit, much to the amusement of her rival, who was ash blonde and couldn't slap much on. They all had jobs, these people — no wonder they were happy — and Nordi and I began laughing as if we too had jobs. Ah, it was good!

They left before dawn, calling their good wishes down to us as they climbed the hill. Wrapped up in a blanket, Nordi and I sat on the beach and watched the sun come up before we milked and ground the grain for breakfast. After they left it struck me most acutely what a dull life I'd gotten for Nordi, for we were far from everybody now and only the rare appearance of friends lightened her heart. Still, as the saying goes, "bed is the poor man's opera," and on top of that she said, "Our love is greater than sex by far." And there was such an accord, such a sweetness just to be near one another, impossible to explain, that mitigated our condition.

At last the day came when I could work on the county road. Indeed, four whole days I'd be employed as a laborer and for each day I'd receive four dollars—four dollars for yeast cakes and socks, for soap and aspirin (for toothache dogged my days and nights now). I reported at a small quarry, for we unlucky ones loaded trucks with the crumbly rock we blasted from time to time from a bank of it. I reported to the foreman. Our eyes met in a flash of recognition. I had fired him for laziness when I ran the repair crew.

"Mr. Reesa," he said, "you fire me once. Now I boss."

We worked as two crews. You could work on either crew. By noon, the men, about a dozen of us, had sorted ourselves out as the workers and the lazy. Four of us filled five trucks, while seven lazies filled three. The foreman kept berating me, but I worked on. Finally he began insulting my mother. Still I worked on. When something he said about her—the tone, the sound, maybe only the end of the word—dislodged me from my resolution to consider the unworthy source, I tried to climb the cliffs, shovel in hand, to get at him. By the time I got up there he was gone. He was back the next day with venom in his eyes but a damn civil tongue in his head.

Sixteen dollars and in another two months another sixteen dollars brought a sense of rhythm in an ongoing world to my dulled and groping mind.

What I wanted and needed was a big horse, for I had an idea of hauling stone from the backbone of the Peninsula to sell in San Francisco.

One morning I came down a steep bank of the road with two gray squirrels in my game pocket. I almost collided with a car that came around a bend. The car stopped. It was Mr. Graton, an acquaintance of mine. Several years before he was about to buy a waterfront lot near ours. It was a lot that, sitting on slanting serpentine, was slowly moving into the Bay. I had put a little stake on solid land and one on the slipping piece and in three years the slipping land had moved well over a foot. He was a big blocky man, the overweight kind that makes a ceremony of sitting down. He'd do the shuffling around of the feet, then the bending, a grunting lowering of his massive posterior, and he'd come down way too close to you—a big man jammed against you—then he'd turn his head and, breathing down into your ear, would postulate that the weather was such and so and then gradually he would get around to what he was trying to find out. When I told him of my findings on the lot, he thanked me.

Now he got out of his car and passed the time of day with me. He said of the gray squirrels, whose tails stuck out of my pocket, that the shells of the 25-35 deer rifle were worth more than the meat they brought down. I told him it was all I had now. As he turned to leave he asked me if I could be at the same place same time tomorrow.

When we met the next day he handed me a new single-shot .22 caliber rifle and three cases of boxes of shells—that's fifteen hundred shells and a case of shorts.

"All you need for squirrels," he said of the shorts. "Don't thank me, Rice. You saved me three thousand dollars on that lot. Now save your deer rifle for deer." He got in his car and drove away. That gun was a boon to me. Now I could bring in much more meat and, as it was a gift, at no cost. I sold two milk goats to a poor family—the little girls looked so peaked. The father would pay me, "next paycheck," he said. I doubted but another look at the underfed kids made me forget pay. Three days later they moved God knows where with my goats. I had only three goats left and a few kids.

It was odd that I, who could not filch paint or whatever when it was offered me in lieu of earned wages, could break the game laws without misgivings. I can't remember with what quirk of the mind I did it. Probably one of the times I've bent my morals to fit the occasion.

The good people who owned the place did not ask me to pay

rent when the milk laws changed. I did little things around. I planted many trees and protected them from my goats. I found some wire grass, three clumps growing on their property above the road. I dug in there and about six feet down found dampness, while all around was bone dry. I dug until I hit bedrock. The rock was damp. I asked the owners to bring me dynamite and fuses and a star drill and a ten-pound sledge hammer. Their property was devoid of water. Their water was piped from a spring on the adjoining property and they paid for it in a manner that irked them.

I cleared away the clay from the bedrock. Here the surface of the bedrock slanted down to quite an angle and, pounding incessantly on the star drill that poor Nordi held and turned with each blow, we penetrated that rock and found the dampness. Slowly, laboriously, we made holes in that rock, put dynamite in them, covered all with mud and blasted. In a month we had blasted a tunnel into that basalt rock for thirty-five feet, following the tiny water vein. It flowed only eighty gallons in twenty-four hours, but the owners were ecstatic. I capped the source back there in the rock and led a copper pipe to the outside. The copper pipe was sheathed with glazed tile and when all was done we sealed the tunnel. That was hard-earned water. A short time later, Tanner, the man who owned the place next door, was up at his spring with me. He was complaining about the water we drew from his pipes, in return for which he used the extra house on the doctors' property. North of his spring and within three feet from the line between the two places was a lone clump of wire grass, while about the spring it grew in abundance. He was still grumbling about providing us with water. All at once, looking at the clump of wire grass, I knew there was a flow of water right under it. That psychic, that certain feeling, had come to me. The ground was dry all around, except at Tanner's fine spring.

"Mr. Tanner," I said, "if I developed a spring right under that clump of grass would you give it to the doctors as theirs and end the squabbling?"

"Sure," he said.

"On your word?" I asked.

He turned on me—a sly, at times, but essentially bombastic

man, a big rich fellow who pressured people. Hot eyes on me, he said, "I've tricked a lot of people in my time. Every man for himself, I say, but my word, Rice, I'm proud of it. It's good as gold. You make water run out of that clump and she's yours and the damn doctors too."

He handed me a shovel he was carrying. "Let's see you dig."

I knew exactly what I'd see. I removed one deep shovelful of dirt from under the wire grass and up welled water from a hole about the size of your thumb in a jut of bedrock that came up just below the turf. I removed debris from the hole and it came out fifteen hundred gallons a day, as a later measurement proved. Tanner was flabbergasted.

"How did you know," he asked, looking me over as if I were an alien species.

"I didn't," I said. "Wire grass signals dampness."

We looked over the shovel of dirt I dug and found I'd removed a rotten rock plug from the hole with the first shovel. Tanner stood by his word and, laying pipes to two tanks I'd picked up, we at last had water for everything, including irrigation. How did I know so certainly? I haven't the slightest idea.

Once, years later, I was driving down the highway when I slammed on the brake. My wife said, "Whatever is wrong, Clyde?"

"In a moment a farmer will drive out from a side road and stall his car on the highway crossing." Just then he did. I don't know anything about these sometimes awarenesses, except to ignore the people who deny such occurrences because it upsets some cute little scheme of things they want to believe in.

I gave two kids to a well-to-do dairyman across the county from me. He said he would pay me later and from all reports on him he would.

I made a determined search for work, but now without the ferry-boats I didn't have a trade to offer. In eight months I brought in two hundred forty-five dollars and twenty cents. Some of that went for gas and two second-hand tires. Then there was ten bucks for taking a bit of steel out of my eye. I laid up the old Buick. The Ford fell to pieces shortly after the Aptos trip—a seventy-five-dollar loss, so I had two hundred and ten dollars for eight months' food, clothes, soap and kerosene for my lamps. Of course it wouldn't cover and we became shabbier: sheets wore thin, socks finally gave up the ghost and kerosene ran low. I must have been ineffectual in some way in asking for work.

All I had to do was to go to the county and join the relief, join the dole, and say, "take care of me." Millions did, and food and clothing and job preference would be mine. But I was proud. I was proud of my father, I was proud of his pride, as he was an upright man. I was an essentially upright man: we were, in comparison to our contemporaries, much more honest and dependable. As my father said, if you lean enough fenceposts together they can all stand up. The way we saw it, one could help others but must never accept help. We believed that if twenty percent of the citizenry were honest, though it paid to be dishonest, the fabric of society built on trust and plain honesty would stand. The trouble with being honest was it held you back in politics and worldly goods. But if certain men were not stalwart enough to accept the losses incurred by straight dealing, the whole government and interpersonal relationships would tumble. We accepted the burden because somebody had to be a tent pole, to hold the tent up, and, as in Plato's scheme, we were paid in esteem and self-esteem. And we were proud—not overweening pride—but a sense of an ill-paid job well-done. That being the case, I had to go on as I had been going.

Things went from bad to worse. I went to get work on the road, as was due me. At the office of the county roads in San Rafael I talked to a big Irish politician who headed the road office. He was also on the state parole board at San Quentin. He told me that he had no work for me, that I'd frightened Manuel Pinto, so that he came all the way from the quarry on hilltops fearing to use the roads.

"Look," I said, "I used to hire and fire for the ferries. He was lazy and useless. I had to fire him, and where do most useless people end up—why in government jobs. So he's a foreman here. He cursed me and made remarks about my mother. I don't allow that. He got off easy. Now I've got a right to that work and I need it."

"No," he said.

"Wait a minute. Are you by your stand saying you approve of

what he said about my mother?"

"No. But we can't have our foremen threatened. No work for you."

I looked out the window. Across the street I saw a man walking. I said, "What would you do if I went over and clubbed that man on the head?"

"We'd put you in jail."

"What would you do with my wife and son?"

"We would have to take care of them if there was no evident means of support."

I stood up and picked up the chair I was sitting on. "You want to take off that excellent Stetson before I save steps and bash you instead of that innocent across the street?"

He wrote out my right for four days on the road and for some unfathomable reason did not call the police. A month later he was in the penitentiary for bribery of some sort on the parole board. I don't know how bad he was, but at least he didn't call the cops after I put the chair down.

I was making a shallow ditch alongside the road, where the road came over the hill at Alta Station. It was raining and I dug the ditch a very long way to protect the road from flooding. Because of my belligerent act on my first time on the road work, I was sent off alone like the half-crazed dog that I was gradually becoming in those times. I knew this, but in spite of it I dug the ditch joyfully. The rain would be heavy for a time, then suddenly there would be a few drops and then none and in a moment the sunshine that had been pent up by the clouds would find a way through and dazzle the dripping countryside with refracted light from ten thousand droplets that clung to the grass and the leaves of the trees around. My shovel sliced into the wet ground so easily. I'm good with a shovel. I was hired to do this job and I was doing a very good one. I was doing what three men would normally do. Steam arose from the ground, mist formed and dispersed, and once in a while all would clear. Down in the valley light glanced from wet roofs and far out on the horizon was a streak of light that was the Bay. That was the last road work I got. The foreman I had run up into the woods had made such claims to the new superintendent that he had a police officer with him when I applied two months later.

"You'll not get any more county road work and you get out of line with me and I'll have you jailed. Have you got anything to say?"

"Only to compliment you on your forethought and bravery."

The last couple of weeks we had really leaned on that sixteen dollars I was going to make. It was a bright thing up ahead there. Now, without it, and God knows we needed it, we became a bit frantic. Broke, I couldn't drive to look for work. I walked, and walking I learned every turn and twist of the road for twenty miles around. I was out with the bums asking for work at whatever wage, but there must have been something about me in those days that turned whoever looked at me against me. Maybe my fury and despair showed. I was now subject to terrible toothaches. Fury and despair and exquisite pain that never ended raged within me. Nordi was short with me, for our condition was bitter to her. The wheat and the milk and the game I shot kept us alive; hope was gone.

One night I went to bed, an ulcerated tooth lancing incessant pain through my guilt and despair. I held back the groans that would ease me but, try as I might, a whimper escaped my lips. I bit down on it, but Nordi left the bed—in disgust, I believe—and slept with Bunky. In the morning as I ground the grain for breakfast, she apologized. I acted as if I didn't understand. I must have been dreaming, I said.

It was at the end of one of those unlucky runs of things that I decided to look for a horse. I had heard that south of Livermore somewhere on the edge of the Diablo Mountains there was a horse slaughterhouse. The bones went to sugar refineries. Surely I could arrange to get an old horse to haul rocks on the sledge for me. I expected to trade my deer rifle, but I wouldn't take the gun—I'd look first and then make arrangements—so off I went with a few dollars for ferries and trains. First I went to Livermore, then walked southeast toward a little wheat ranch I had once visited with friends. It was at the end of a long wandering road into the mountain region, but I missed my way somehow and finally gave up—though I thought the farmer could direct me to a horse in the district. I slept in hay in an open shed where there was not a house for miles. I was still ranging around for the wheat grower next day when I found his farm abandoned, the building burnt to the ground, and I spent the rest of the day looking for the horse-butchering place. Again I hunkered down in hay and ate the last skimpy meal that I brought with me. Early in the morning in a narrow arroyo I came upon the penned horses. There must have been two or three hundred standing in knee-deep mud, no blade of grass was near. Completely barren hills held the miniature valley all around. Horses lay down in the mud and couldn't get up. They would raise their heads on their long necks above the mud till their strength gave out and dropped them back into the mud, only to raise them again now massed with mud, then to drop them again until, after hours of torment, they strangled in it. When the dim light first showed me the terrible scene, four horses in different places in the vast corral were dying so. There were racks of hay and great troughs of water, but few seemed interested in them, the mud so deep that moving about could throw a weak horse.

I hurried down to the slaughterhouse. Already the crew was working. A great dappled Belgian mare was dragging those that had fallen over in the mud to the slaughterhouse where, if they were still alive, they'd be shot and bled, then a powerful jet from a hose would wash them off. In a moment they would be skinned and disemboweled and the meat, quivering and jerking, would be slashed from their bones and loaded, in crates, into trucks that left the place for a dog food establishment. Other trucks hauled the bones away to the sugar factory. The poor Belgian mare quivered too and shook, as she dragged in the near-dead over the mud. She was terror-stricken, as she worked in the midst of that carnage, and the fellow who rode her beat her constantly as she shuddered at her task.

I went to the house of the owners and told them of the dying horses up in the corral. How they laughed at me! Then they ordered two wrinkled bloodhounds that were there to screw. It was revolting. On and on the male humped, as I tried to barter my absent rifle for one of the farm horses among the usual cayuses.

"For a gun? Hell, kid, we've got a hundred guns. You got eighty bucks on ya, we'll turn you out a plow horse. You got it?"

"Well, no," I said shamefully.

"Okay, kid, we gave you your chance. Now git! You're in the

way here. Git off the place or we'll sick the dogs on ya!"

I saw several brindle mastiffs chained in a pen and I left as one of the men added, "Hit the road pronto, kiddo, or you're gonna git chawed!" Out on the road the horror of the place stayed with me.

I was hungry when I came upon an olive tree. I picked some of them and ate them. They were very bitter, but oily and I needed that oil. The road skirted a vast estate fenced with strong woven wire on steel posts set in concrete. The fence must have been seven feet high and as I slogged along I saw elegant wall-less pavillions where the blooded horses that wandered there could avoid rain storms. The road was lined with big black walnut trees whose fallen nuts I cracked for their meager meat. Olives and those stingy-meated nuts, what was I doing here? Even if I'd brought my beloved rifle it wouldn't have gotten me a horse—a horse? my weary mind asked. I sat down and figured it slowly. A horse to draw a sledge to get fancy rocks to sell back home—back home? So weary and disorganized was I that I couldn't believe that I'd ever get back. I was ready to drop, to sink in the earth, my mind completely blasted of the idea that I was or ever had been a thing of worth.

In the evening I reached a town. I now had fifteen cents and my fare back on the trains and ferries. A small, well-lit restaurant stood before me. I went in. No other customers were about. The waiter said, "Evening. What can I do for you?"

He looked as dense as I felt, a small guy but very well set up and not cocky about it.

"Give me a slice of pie and coffee," I said.

"I got apple and custard and punkin."

"Give me the pumpkin," I said. I ate it slowly, absolutely in love with the leathery crust. Surely it will stick with me. "You own the place?" I asked.

He nodded, modest pride in his dark face. "Here, have another mocha," he said, as he filled my cup again. "Where you from?"

I sipped that hot coffee, luxuriating in the heat, the sweetness, and the flavor—God!

"Tiburon," I said.

"No kidding," he smiled, brightening up. "You know, I know Tiburon. Where did you live?"

"East of town, near Waterspout Point," I answered.

"Yeah," he said with that inflection that asked for more salubrious information. "A fellow built a little place there, oh, say six years ago. It was about three hundred feet west of the Point. You know him?"

"Middling well," I answered, "he's me."

"No kidding," he grinned. "I watched you lots of times—I had these glasses you know, magnify thirty times. I was in the army on Angel Island. Spent a lot of time over in Quarantine Cove right across from you. How's that blonde wife of yours and the kid? Could tell he was a boy the way he walked."

How sweet it was. We talked as if we were old friends. He asked me what I was doing and I told him.

"Jeez," he said, "it sounds rough. On your way home, huh?"

"Yeah, it was a fool stunt coming over here," I said. "But I need a horse bad. Thought maybe I could work for one. Hire out until it was paid for, but not there, not in that hell."

"Way I'd feel about it," he answered. "Say, how about a hamburger?"

"I can't," I said. "I just got the fare to get back."

"No, I mean for free on account we was like neighbors once."

"Thanks," I said, "I appreciate it, but if I start taking things for free, I'll end up figuring I got a right to what isn't mine."

"Yeah, I guess you're right," he said. "How about one more cup of coffee for old times sake. If we don't drink it, I'll have to throw it out."

"Well, okay," I agreed.

We each had a cup. We were sipping slowly when the door opened and the town cop came in and had a cup too. My friend took the cop out back. Pretty soon they returned. The cop sat down next to me.

"Say, Ernie's been telling me about you," he said. "Some bad breaks, huh? Well, where you gonna sleep tonight?"

"In some hay wherever I find it."

"Well, Ernie wants me to bed you down in our new jail. It's never been used, fresh sheets and blankets, you understand, and we'd have to lock you up, but I'd be down in the morning to let you out. We're worried about you sleeping in some barn. You might get shot."

"Thanks," I said, "but I've got to get along. I wouldn't go for being locked up. I'm still a free man, whatever that means." We three sat there drinking our coffee and, when the cup was empty, I said "thanks again" and left.

There was no moon, but the night was so clear that starshine let me see the road and, after my eyes grew accustomed to the dark, fences and gates, while on some eminence to the north an aero beacon cast its searching light over me and the country about, coming and going with a regularity I wasn't finding in things at the moment. I came upon a barn near a house and very quietly slipped in and lay in the hay. I heard breathing of other sleepers moving about and two more blotted the light of starshine as they came in. Soon I felt crowded and, as I stayed on, more crowded, so as silently as I'd come, I slipped past the house and walked along the road under the stars. A tooth came to life in my jaw and the pain became insistent and demanding.

There was really no reason for it. It was little things piling up that did it, but I believe that I almost became stark raving mad that night. That revolving beacon light became a heartless cyclops, the long straight road seemed intent on denying time and distance. I was walking nowhere with my guilt about how I kept Nordi and my failures for company. The *Princess* surged through lively water away from me. Dogs came rushing from the farmhouses I passed to bark and sniff at my legs. On I walked on my hopeless dark treadmill of a road. I tried to concentrate on Ernie and his restaurant and the friendly cop. They seemed like cameos in a display case, like something I had dreamed, but not something that had happened on this very night. There was a hole in my pocket of treasures and I'd lost everything along with their gem of kindness. I mourned it, though I couldn't believe it as I trod through a surrealist world, trying not to see in my mind's eye the dying horses, the horror-filled area, the copulating bloodhounds in slow disgusting motion. I was tottering on a brink; I couldn't pull myself together. Wearily, I said, "You've had some bad breaks. So what? Get a hold of yourself." I tried. It was like trying to truss up the wind. I was gone. I don't know what would have happened but a picture came before my eyes of Bunky and the sturdy way he walked. Oh, I hung onto that image as if everything depended on it. And I'm afraid it did. After a time his sturdiness became mine and I walked on as if I was my own man and before dawn I was over it. I think the loss of the goat dairy along with the loss of the *Princess* and the tuberculosis and the loss of the *Sonoma* undermined my self-respect far back in my essential being and somehow I was unable to balance out the juxtaposition of that day's kindness and horror.

In the morning a fellow picked me up and carried me for a few miles—a brash young fellow in a new pickup—and from his talk I saw that for some the Depression had produced no trauma. The job was the same, they worked for less, but with the cheap price of goods they were doing very well, thank you. If twenty percent of the men in the nation were without work, then eighty percent had jobs and the men that had jobs cherished them, so there was no turnover, no openings, seemingly. Of course there were, but I couldn't find one. When a job opening did come up it was filled by someone eminently qualified for the job.

When I got home Nordi gave me soup and then plump roast duck and then rubbed my back until I slept. I never told her of that strange trip nor how for some obscure reason it tore me down and then put me together a somewhat different fellow.

Next morning I took some of my better books and left for Mill Valley. I had heard that there was a dentist there who was not expensive. When I got to see him, I explained that my teeth were driving me mad, that I had no money. I offered the books as payment to stop the pain. He was a small, shrunken man with a quizzical smile. I could guess that he was quite interested in things in general. The main thing that flowed from him, however, was kindness. He fingered through several volumes and, not looking at me, said, "How did you know that books fascinate me?"

After he deadened the nerve on the tooth he went into his office with me and sat down. "Mr. Rice," he said, "I'd like to relieve you of all your pain, but I have to make a living so I can help people like you. No, don't tell me what happened. It's written on you. I've known you by sight for years, on the ferries. Over three quarters of my time is taken by people who can't pay me except in books and rings. I'm glad I can help but I have to pay bills, so, because my schedule is so loaded, I cannot deaden another nerve for you until the same day next month. I'm glad to get that book on archery. Do you know anything about yew wood?"

"Yes," I said, "quite a bit."

"Great," he said. "Tell me about it next time. Good-bye."

Free of the pain I could think a little bit. As I walked home I thought of the Tiburon Peninsula—a rocky spine, an ancient up-heaval along whose crest small springs seeped through fissures of quartz. Spring water passed from the High Sierras under the Sacramento and the San Joaquin Valley, to flow out of the top of the Tiburon ridge. Time had covered the rocky base with soils of several kinds on which the sloping meadows grew grasses. And in the ravines oaks and bay gripped this soil and on the eastern side was brush, penetrated here and there by a solitary oak. There were small cliffs and innumerable outcroppings of stone and quartz and scattered over one half of its surface were rocks of every size and often of remarkable color, as if colored granular sugar had been troweled on the surface, and on all these stones, whether color-encrusted or not, grew gray and green and lavender lichen, so tight to it as to seem part of the rock. I had read that they were extraor-dinarily old. I felt there ought to be some way to sell the stone. I had sold those that were flat to neighbors in Tiburon for stepping stones, and of course had my own pile for that house of the future. I wondered what I could do with them if I could buy them from the heirs to the rancho, but that was too far away from immediate necessity, so I put the idea on a back burner and let it cook a little more.

There didn't seem to be any game at all or fish. I brooded about those rich people over on Belvedere who liked my work and had work to be done, but wouldn't hire me unless I took their leavings, unless I symbolized somehow their superiority—the bastards! I'd like to see any of them in my position—oh, they'd whine, how they'd whine! Well, I won't. I'll win through somehow.

I butchered our last kid and hung it in our cool storeroom, for now we lived in the old house where Tanner had spent his week-ends before the spring deal. We got four leg roasts from it, then I didn't shut the door tight enough and Tanner's dog got in and tore the carcass down and what he couldn't eat he chewed. Oh, what stupidity! We used it for bait for crabs, but the rotten rope broke and we lost our crab ring too.

Grinding grain on the little mill gave me cramps when I ground enough flour for bread baking. I planned to make a windmill to grind the grain when I got enough time, but now I couldn't even look for a job. I had to keep hunting game. Then the idea that had been cooking in me—about the stones—came to a boil. The area where the best stones were was the northern half of the Peninsula. This was owned by Miss Reed. Her grandfather or great-grandfather had established the rancho in 1834. She lived in a great house on the west side of the Peninsula. I went to her, an aging recluse, and received the right to take what stones I wanted for so much a ton. I then went to San Francisco to the California Landscaping Association offices. In my shabby clothing I was ushered into a pleasant-appearing man's office and given a seat.

I said, "I want to sell you stone, but let me explain myself. When you use stone on an estate or in walls about a townhouse the stone in essence implies old stability. Maybe the family's wealth is only forty years old, or twenty or five, but the use of stone, outside of its intrinsic beauty, is a status factor. In these times your people's clients are rich, for no one else can afford your work. Am I in any way right?"

"Well, Mr. Rice," he said smiling at me, "you're in no way wrong."

"Thank you," I said. "Now people that buy stonework are rich enough not to quibble about the cost of materials and if you could make the stone look like it had been there for a century instead of two years, wouldn't they gladly pay for that? Of course, they would. And that's where I come in. I have the stone and in many colors, some very rare, some weathered gray stone, but all have lichens growing on them—different kinds of lichens, some large splattery ones of subtle grays and lavenders. I'm reminded of Marie Lorenson's painting as I look at some of the rock and lichen combinations. I have a great amount of weathered stone so enhanced, only it has to be brought out on mule or burro back, its surface lichens protected by monk's cloth and burlap over that.

These stones of all shapes and sizes are the very essence of age that stone itself implies."

"You have a good point and I am interested," he said. "How do you know about Marie Lorenson?"

"I haven't seen originals but quite a few color copies of her paintings."

"Are you an artist?"

"I went to art school. They thought I was good. I knew I wasn't good enough ever to call myself an artist."

"You've had it rough?"

"Yes, as you see."

"You say they have to be hauled out on muleback?"

"Yes, it would be easier. Some I can haul on a horsedrawn sled but not many. There's one set—would have to be used where money was of no moment—a great shell of a rock, like the shell back of Botticelli's Venus, and some surrounding rocks that would make complete some superb landscaping. I have a contract control over the area," I said, and ceased talking.

"You have put forth several good ideas," he said, "and for an outsider a nice summation of the use of stone. A month from next Tuesday our organization holds our annual meeting." He gave me a program with the time and place and some of the topics to be discussed.

"If you come in the morning ready to stay all day, somewhere I'll squeeze you in and, if you'll tell the group what you've told me, I'm sure I can drum up some business for you and more to follow. Until then, good luck!"

I went back to Tiburon unable to believe that the chance had come when all was so hopeless. Nordi, however, refused to believe the news or that anything would ever come of it. She had lost faith in me completely. Good news, but our tiny garden had dried up from some blight. Bunky looked thin—we knew he was getting all he needed to nourish him. What was wrong? The owner-doctors said it was adenoids and they operated and didn't charge us, still happy over the water I'd brought to the place. But there were little expenses and I had a nickel. I walked six miles for a yeast cake, carrying the nickel, only to find the hole in my pocket. The clerk offered me one free, but I couldn't take it. Half way home I broke down. I didn't know one thing from another, just dullness. I laid there all night. I was frightened, very frightened. I began to believe someone would come and take Nordi and Bunky away from me, because I couldn't provide. I hid out in the woods all next day, afraid to go home. In the evening I got myself together, talked myself into a wholeness once more and went down to the house.

"Clyde, whatever happened?" she asked me.

I told her I lost the nickel. She tried to keep exasperation from her face. She handed me ten pennies. "Get the yeast tomorrow," she said. She made a porridge of coarse wheat and goat's milk. We ate it and went to bed. Another tooth started to ache, still somehow I got some sleep. We had breakfast from the same milk and cracked wheat. "Go get the yeast," she said, "and Clyde, see if you can't find some work—anything."

That afternoon I brought her the yeast. Among other things I'd tried to get on with the chicken farmer. I was so persistent. "I'd work for next to nothing," I said, "if only you'll use me."

Finally, no end annoyed, he yelled, "Get out or I'm going to call the police."

Oh, I'd been there before—I'd been everywhere before. Pride? What was it? Why didn't I go on relief? What was it that made me askew of everything? "Go ask for help before you go nuts!" I howled. Next day I walked over to San Rafael and tried to go in the office where they handed it out—food, clothing, even money! I tried and I tried—I just couldn't do it. Think of Nordi and Bunky and do it! I can't, I can't. I won't let them become second-class citizens. I walked away. If I can't find anything by the end of the month, I'll knuckle, but it won't be me anymore. And Bunky and Nordi, they'll be different. We'll be other people.

No duck! No deer! No meat! No work! Toothache to make me bang my head against the wall for the easement of other pain.

For several weeks I stayed out every other night sleeping in barns or in the brush while I combed Santa Rosa and Petaluma for work. I was three days around Vallejo. It was no use. Back in Santa Rosa I became sick. My diet of cooked and then dried ground grain that I carried in a sack suddenly was going against me. I realized I'd better head for home or I'd be in trouble. I inquired in the railroad yard when a freight would pull out south and was told in fifteen minutes. I went to the train crew. They recognized me. I asked them to go slow, very slow, at Reed's Station. "I'm sick," I said, "so slow down." I got on a flatcar of machinery. I was chilled through when we got to Reed Station. They slowed for me, but I was weak and took a tumble, but not under the wheels.

Somehow I got over the hills from Miss Reed's and after dark stumbled my way down to our house. Hot wheat gruel and milk warmed me. For several days a high fever held me uncaring, out of my head part of the time, Nordi said. She shot three big wood-peckers—flickers—and made a broth and finally I could sit up. It was then that she told me that the annual meeting of the landscape architects had been held the day before. I took it. I was getting too tired to roll with the punches, I just took it.

"Part of the pattern," I told her, but really down deep I was, with this loss, barely me anymore. Couldn't she see there was nothing left?

When I got out of bed, Nordi steadied me. "I'm weak too," she said, "but Bunky has all he can eat. Thank God for our goats." She brought me gruel and milk. Later I heard two shots and much later she came in with two ducks.

"I had to strip and swim for them," she said. "The wind was blowing them away from shore."

She had found two cups of dried beans and a handful of prunes in the back of the cupboard at our other house. We had a meal, spartan, but marvelous, of bean soup, roast duck and a big pudding she had concocted from our coarse flour and the prunes. It strengthened us both so that next day I was out banging away at the windmill for grinding our flour. Nordi was still talking about her luck in finding the flickers and the ducks, where no game had been for months. I got all the materials together—an old casting from the dismantled Ford, a plank and four slender pieces fifteen feet long. The propeller would be four-bladed with the cloth stretched as blades on the slender pieces, turning a shaft that turned our coffeemill to grind the grain. I sank a large timber upright about five feet into the ground and on top of it I drilled deeply and drove in a one-inch diameter rod leaving six inches of it sticking up. The machine also had a tail to steady it, so the blades always faced the wind. It was a thing of toggle joints and fittings from the Ford, of pipes and rod, cloth and plank, a well-planned project. With it grain could be ground on any windy day, so we would not be slaves to that tiny mill again. That night we ate the rest of the bean soup and the duck and went to bed early to be ready to mount our windmill on the high post in the morning.

Our rope was old and rotten, as was the rot-weakened ladder— it was all we had. With blocks and tackle we hauled our rig up eight feet above the ground to finish the fourth wing of propeller blade of muslin on slender, outstretching support. We got it done, when Nordi let go the blade for a second and away the blades went, whirling their fourteen-foot span in a good breeze. We tried everything to stop it. We could not lower it—it would dash the blades on the ground. Straining at it started the tooth pain and tension in me. Still, with infinite patience I started raising the whole thing up to fit it over the peg of steel at the top. We used strap and wire and more old rope and everything to get that whirling contraption over the peg. We added a jury piece to the post to hang other blocks to. All day we labored to get that whirling devil over the peg, but the ropes and ladder, everything we had, weren't equal to the task. The whirling vibrated it and all the while the little grind mill ground away on nothing.

At dusk, with my body wrapped around the post just under the peg and Nordi holding a long board pressed up against my hind end to keep me from slipping, I heaved that vibrating machine over the peg and slid slowly down the post, the pillar of our machine, and lay on the ground too exhausted to stand up.

There was no food in the house and now no way to grind our grain. Nordi put a batch of wheat to soak. We three were hungry and for Bunky there was nothing to eat but milk. I went out and climbed the ladder with hands that would barely grasp anything and poured some grain in the small mill's hopper. At once flour blew down the wind behind the mill. The blades never slowed. It worked. I climbed down and got a small sack and lashed it to the flour outlet and poured a cup of grain into the hopper. The sack started filling with flour when a bent spike in part of a toggle next to the mill caught the sack as it flung about in the wind, wound it up and tore it to shreds, like some remorseless monster. Three times, ever weakening, I climbed with fresh sacks and grain. It was always the same. I was too weak to hold on for another try. Worn stupid, barely able to stand, I hadn't the strength to turn the whole affair broadside to the wind to stop it. Numbly I crawled into bed. The tooth at last had no power over me. I slept.

The light of morning disclosed the wreck of my machine. In the night the casting from the Ford, where the whole apparatus had turned on the steel peg, had broken and all was destroyed, except the little coffee mill, which Nordi took in the house to grind flour for our breakfast. But not for me. I was going to die this day. It had been three years since I was fired from my job on the *Sonoma*. For over a year I had kept my family in poverty, barely ahead of starvation. No one wanted me unless I turned suck-ass. "So I can't work without knuckling, huh? Hierarchy, huh?" Statements of Marx flitted through my mind, bits of the Constitution. I seethed. The people of Belvedere I saw through a twisted mirror. I knew it, but with this pain and my uselessness I let myself be inflamed. I hungered to fight, to smash, to destroy. Oh, to die and have done with failure and useless striving! To lie gripping the sod until at last the travail ebbed away! Nordi would soon be married to Art or some other guy with a job. Oh, I wish there were a God to lean on! Can't you lean on beauty and meaning, you fool? Shee-it! Shit! Shit! There's no hammock for me. Obscenities flew from my mouth like bitter gall. I was a jinx! I'd been a jinx all along. I was through all along, but I couldn't see it. Now I saw it. Okay, okay!

I took both my guns and my knives and plenty of ammunition. I had Nordi pour some boiling water over some wheat and I took the wheat and left.

I didn't say goodbye. I didn't look at her. I just plodded up the hill, took the cut-across on my way to Belvedere. In the woods I saw two silver-gray squirrels in a tree, the first in many months. I shot them and put them in my game pocket and headed on. Near the old redwood company's dock a mile south of our place I shot at a duck and missed it. A man on the dock waved me over. He was Boyle, the outside superintendent for Robbling Wire Company, the famous company that made the wire for all the great bridges. They had bought the dock. I came up to him on it. A big, hard-faced man whom I knew to speak to, he had caught an enormous eel, the greatest delicacy in fish hereabouts.

"You want it?" he asked. "If it was catfish I'd take it home, but I shore couldn't eat this thing."

I took it and put it in my game pocket with the squirrels. "If it was catfish I couldn't eat it," I said.

"Yeah," Boyle said, "I guess it's where you were raised that counts. Home vittels, that's the story. Say, Rice," he said, "I've heard a bit about your recent history, about the milk ranch. You've had a bitch of a time. Well, it's all over now. In two weeks from now you'll have a job here with me and for the next three years, beginning at four dollars a day—really until the bridge is finished. All the wire from those cables will be shipped by steamer here first and then barged over to the site. How's that?"

In my walled-in place I heard and thanked him and turned to head for Belvedere. "Too late," I said to myself, "I hope Art gets on here." I left the road again secure at last in my fate capsule. I saw some big pink leaves in a pink-leafed poison oak bush, threw a rock in and out bounded a big jackrabbit. I shot at it at the third jump and put it in my game pocket and headed down the slope to Tiburon.

As I passed the American Express office, Fred Taglerini hailed me. "Got a bicycle for you." There was a letter attached. It said:

"Clyde, after that goat fiasco I suppose you lost everything else. Now I've got no money to send after lost causes, but I don't want a son of mine walking the streets on thinning soles. Here's a bike on your thirtieth birthday to keep you up off the street.— J.M.R."

"The stinking son of a bitch," I said, but of course he was right. We were in full agreement now and I was going to fix that problem. I took the bike out of the crate, lashed my guns to the handlebars and headed through town toward Belvedere. As I passed Randle's place, he called me in. We'd been friends when I ran the *Sonoma*.

"Look," he said. "Last night I won two rabbits at a raffle and Lou's fallen in love with them. I got to get some rabbit wire and make a pen for them. You're up on such stuff. Where can I get some?"

"Well, I have several rolls of it at the goat ranch."

"I'll give you five dollars for a roll of it," he said.

So I left my guns with him and peddled out to the ranch, left my squirrels and eel and rabbit, grabbed a roll of rabbit wire, lashed it to the handle bars and peddled back. All this was happening to another guy; the real me was useless to people, a jinx, and he was through. Back I went, scooting along the road. He gave me five dollars and my guns. I left his place heading for Belvedere, now only a quarter of a mile away, when he called out to me, and again louder. Okay, I thought, I've got lots of time—time, I snorted at it —so I came back.

"Clyde, I don't know how to put it together," he said. "I'll give you five dollars to build a little hutch for me." As I looked disinterested he said, "Will you do it for a friend?"

Well, I would. We had a drink, a double snort of whiskey, and then I started on the hutch. He tried to help me and we had another snort—me secure in my capsule where nothing mattered anyhow. We hammered away and we had another and maybe another. That's all I remember. I woke up with an awful headache and I was in no capsule. Lou gave me an eggnog with a bit of whiskey in it before I ate a big breakfast with them.

"You were going to kill them up there until they got you, weren't you?" said Randle.

"Uh huh," I answered.

"What I figgered," he said. "If I hadn't seen you passing I believe you'd got ten of the bastards before they got you. Here, have some more ham. Lou, we're out of toast."

What drove me to such mad extent? Of course what I'd been through, but more deep down in me, unknown to me, the underdog's unthinking fury at hierarchy, blind to seeing hierarchy as an eternal fact.

I can't tell you how it was to sit with friends in their home— friends who somehow had an inkling of what I'd been through, friends who actually cherished me. I saw it in their faces, then I thought of Nordi and Bunky out at that forlorn goat ranch. I told them and they said, get going, and Lou, who'd once been a whore and had ten books on bridge construction, one of her hobbies, kissed my cheek and looking most seriously into my eyes, said, "Your luck has changed, Clyde. Go tell Nordi."

Away I went on the bike to tell her. I bought bread, potatoes, onions, mayonnaise, six oranges and candy with some of my ten dollars and hung it in a gunny sack on the bicycle and pumped my way home. I hadn't told her of the job when I came home last night for the wire, because I didn't expect to be alive to work at it. I came down the hill, braking to go slowly, and swung by the house. I handed her the oranges and showed her the other food. I told her about the job. It was as if we were talking about miracles. We were laughing again, and the stimulus was not Keith's booze, but the near future — *our* future — and beyond.

X

In Which I Find
Salvation Isn't What It's Cracked Up To Be,
We Acquire A Horse And Wagon,
and
Nordi Leaves Me

◇   1932   ◇

Experience, if it has taught me anything, has taught me that it's the tough go that one remembers and treasures, not the easy living. Of course, that's in retrospect. One could say that the fates tried me with a lengthy but simple travail and I broke. Henceforth I would live with my broken integrity, making the best of it, as do most men anyway. The Galahads I've met along the way have lacked dimension. Without humility, hard-earned, a man is a pretty but unfinished thing.

That same day after I'd eaten and shaved I cycled over to the dentist and paid to have two teeth deadened. Wow! I wouldn't do that again, one at a time was all I could take. But then it was the gesture I needed, for I'm allergic to Novocaine.

When I got home, Tony Betancourt, the dairyman, was there unloading a team of horses from a trailer behind his truck. Betancourt, a plump Latin with smooth features and sleepy eyes that belied his great vigor, said, "Rice, I'm paying back for the two kids you gave me — you know, for church stuff — but also because Tim O'Dell, the milk inspector, told me you made those certified milk crooks sweat before they gave you the axe. Anyway, here's a team to do what spring plowing you have and I left a veal with your missus. I'll come back next week for the team. They don't kick and they're gentle. Say, I've gotta be milking in half an hour — so long!"

After he left I put the team in the barn and all the harness he'd left under cover. Admiring the shiny plow and harrow I realized I didn't know fiddlesticks about how to harness or handle a team, and the only person around who did was a broken, oldish man who got around on two canes.

If you happen to have access to the photographs of the 1880s or thereabouts you'll see him — maybe in a group picture of the silver coronet band of any western town. There he stands, a slight, woebegone figure, big, sad, hound-dog eyes above a great droopy mustache, the growth and upkeep of which apparently has taken most of his energy; it's not so, though. He was a thing of tendons and sinew and know-how and his woebegone expression was the style at the time. Men of his kind usually had a late brother named Alf who was "took with consumption" and he would tell of Alf's last days as the family sat around the fire after "the dishes was done" and Hortense's kid brother kept playing a muted but annoying mouth organ in a corner.

I had been over to see our crippled neighbor, Mr. Carter, several times before and I had gotten the impression that he had worked with horses at one time. Now I went over again and he tried to explain how to harness the team using words like "hames" and "tugs" and "thoroughbraces" and "cheekpieces" and "collars" and many other things. I got it all mixed up and the upshot of my blundering was that he would come over in the morning and instruct me. This he did and, very awkwardly, I got the harness on the patient animals and attached the plow. But when I tried to plow the half acre in front of the barn, even the horses sensed my lack of know-how and faltered. This the cripple watched in disgust until, as I passed him on an inept turn, he yelled, "Whoa!" most authoritatively. He came stumbling over on his canes, glaring at me with great distaste, grasped the plow handles, put the reins around his waist and roared commands at the horses, who at once settled down to work. Dragging himself as he clung to the plow handles, he turned a beautiful furrow two times around the little field and, exhausted, halted the team before me and called for his canes, glowering in exasperation at me. Somehow after that I caught on and plowed and harrowed that and two other small patches, giving us over an acre to garden. We planted it to every kind of seed— potato, beet, corn, squash, celery, bean, tomato, cabbage, and a great beet called mangel for the animals, and there were melons, parsnips, kale and peas; there were seven different kinds of squash and three of beans and two of tomatoes. The three gardens were on an old Indian burial mound full of shell on top of which hundreds of pigs had been raised, making a foot of well-rotted manure on rich sandy subsoil—all under irrigation. I've never seen such a garden. It grew quickly and luxuriantly. We had no more than got it planted when it was time for me to go to work on that miraculous thing—a job.

There were seven of us there under the foreman, Bill Watson. First a steelworker from the East; then a local over-muscled, well-balanced fellow; a fine old man; Proudfoot, half Indian; and two brothers who did their work and agreed with everything anybody said. Bill was a former night watchman on the Redwood Company's Wharf and their steamer. The company had gone bankrupt, the place sold, and he rather came with the place.

The Robbling Company would bring their big spools of wire from the East by ship, unload at the Redwood Wharf and barge it as needed to the bridge. The wharf had two traveling cranes. It was a perfect arrangement for Robbling, though they needed more space and we were to dig out the cliff behind the wharf and use the diggings to fill in under the wharf and make a bigger area of solid land. The cliff was crumbly rock that made excellent fill. With picks and shovels and wheelbarrows we went at it and Bill saw to it that we ran with the wheelbarrows. I didn't mind, but some of the others crabbed about it.

A job! I had a job! I tied into it with exultation. They took some of the men away to do other things: the nimble, muscular man was experienced with cranes and the steelworker worked with some steel construction. Four of us continued clearing away at the cliff. After a while I noticed that the old man seemed to be faltering. "Sick?" I asked him.

"No," he answered, "I can't hack it, but oh, God, how me and the missus need this money."

I began to help him. I kept the wheelbarrow loads moving out to dump in rotation with the other two by helping him. We hacked down our rock, loaded it in our wheelbarrows, ran with it about a hundred and fifty feet, and dumped it down a chute. Each in his turn did so. I hacked down rock for both of us and helped him fill his wheelbarrow full and heaping. I was very tired when the whistle blew each night, but the old man still had his job.

One day Bill came to me. He said, "Clyde, I hate to say this, but you're not cutting the mustard!"

"I'm putting out as many wheelbarrows as the others," I answered, "and they're always heaping."

"No, you're slacking. You've got to do better or I'll have to fire you."

There it was, but why? It didn't make sense. Bill and I were sort of halfway friends. Why? Next day was the same. I'd have to do better. "Why are you loafing?" he asked.

"You know better than that, Bill, or else you haven't been watching."

"I'm afraid I'll have to let you go," he said.

"If I won't do the work or can't do the work you can fire me, but if I will and do, you fire me, Bill, and I'll put you in the hospital. I won't kill you, but they'll have to take you out of here on a stretcher. Bill, I never miss a load in this lineup and I can prove it."

Bill went away. That afternoon he came back with the muscular crane man. They stood around for a while. Then Bill said, "Nelson here thinks he don't like you threatening me, and I say you're not doing your work."

I knocked the pick off the pick handle. "Bill, did you ever notice how big and roomy ambulances are? There'll be room for Nelson too."

An hour or so later he came back with Nelson and the steelworker. "Look," I said, as I knocked the pick off its handle, spat on my hands and hefted the club it made, "this is a put on. I'm doing more than these other guys and by now you've got to know it or you're not handling your job. Let's quit acting like little girls. If you're going to jump me, jump me! Otherwise I've got work to do."

Writing about it now, it seems incredible. Why me? On I went. One day the old man didn't turn up. Later I learned he had died. I was sorry. Something about him appealed to me.

One morning when I came to work Bill gave me another job. I was to shovel down the rubble they wheeled to me where it stuck on the slanting planks of the sluice. I was away from my pick handle. The big coal shovel that I worked with had no heft as a weapon, but I was philosophical about it. "I'll just put more force in the blows." That decided, I tied into the work. From where I stood I could see the office door and out of it, after an hour or so, came Superintendent Boyle with a check and a yellow slip attached to the end of it. At once I thought of Lindstrom and his check and slip. I'd heard from the others that Bill had complained to Boyle that I wouldn't let him fire me, and Boyle, outside superintendent of Robbling, had fired thousands.

He came slowly over to where I was working below the wharf floor and stood over me. I said to myself, I'll do as well as I can with the shovel. I've been without work too long, suffered too much to let anyone bamboozle me out of my job. I kept shoveling. Out of the corners of my eyes I could see his feet over me and once in a while the tip of that yellow slip, but I worked on. He was trying to sweat me into speaking to him, then he'd fire me. *Okay, mister, I* thought, *I wonder if I can put you into the ambulance with this big thin shovel.* I swayed into my work and wouldn't cave in to his trick.

After a while he went to the office and came back with a chair and sat down above me and dangled the check and the slip lower. *You can't wear me down,* I thought. *Why don't you make the move that brings me out of here and on to you?* I kept to the thought as I shoveled the rubble down the chute. I swayed into the work rhythmically, hypnotically. I was at peace, for there was no doubt: I'd fight for my job. And another peace helped me, the one that comes with the rhythm of work and the good feeling dexterity in work gives to you. I was keeping the planks clean of pileups, but no more rock came and after some time the whistle blew. It was noon. I looked around. Boyle was gone, and over past the lunch shack the rest of the crew were going up the zigzag trail to the road. In the lunchroom stood Bill.

"Why don't they come to eat?" I asked him.

"Boyle fired them," he said, "and if I don't give you a share of the loot I got off the Redwood Company's lumber schooner, I get fired too. But you are to stay on. Come up after work and I'll show you what I got."

That's all I know about it. I went to his cache that evening and received a lot of cordage and implements—some of them I still have.

A cofferdam went out and stopped the construction of the bridge's support on the Frisco side. Bill was fired because he couldn't keep up with me in the work so I had it all to myself and still there are those who claim that accident or luck are not factors in each of our lives.

The third week I worked for Robbling Wire I got my horse. I must tell you, though, that although we had a phone line out our side of the Peninsula the electric lines ended two miles away. Light and power were lamps and horses. There was not a tractor on the Peninsula.

The phone rang one night. A fellow introduced himself as the former groundskeeper of the Belvedere Golf Club. He said that at last the club was bankrupt and did I want to buy a horse, cheap. Next evening I pedaled over and met him at the barn on the club grounds. He showed me an enormous horse, a dappled gray Belgian named Frank, standing in his stall. His hooves had grown while he stood there, so each hoof looked like he was standing on a big platter of extended hoof material. A shameful thing to show. We dickered, because all of it had to go at once: a new Studebaker wagon with low bed, two plows, a harrow, an almost-new one-horse hayrake, harness, and a lantern—all for thirty-five dollars. The wagon was lacquered green and had gold striping all around. It was a beauty. I had the caretaker put the horse in the paddock so he could move around. The boy that had been caring for him did that, and they promised to give him extra grain.

It was dark when I came next night but with a brilliant full moon. The horse, a patient animal, loomed large out in the paddock. I stood him so I could see his hooves in the moonlight and then with a sharp hatchet chopped down alongside each hoof and removed the great spreading pancake of uncared-for hoof: A chop an eighth of an inch off might have ruined the horse but luck was with me and in a half an hour with every blow true he was free to gallop around the corral in exuberance. Then I harnessed him to the wagon, put the plows and harrows in it, tied the hayrake behind and rigged a narrow board so that the lantern could hang over the inboard wheel of the hayrake. I then set out to pass through Tiburon and on to our crooked five-mile road to the goat ranch. We reached home, having encountered no one on the road, and pulled into the barn after midnight. I gave Frank, who was very tired, a rub-down, water, and a feed of oats.

Next morning I worked happily, proud in my status as a horse owner. Frank loved us after that terribly lonely life in the barn. He reveled in his new life as much as an old horse could. He obviously liked the company of the goats and, when Suisan Bey tried to consummate his affection for Frank by trying to have sex with the horse's left hind leg, he knew he was accepted in his new home. Every morning before I went to work we would open a large window of the kitchen and Frank would carefully push his great head through and lap up a washbasin of long-boiled tea leaves, sticking his tongue far out as the hot tea warmed it.

The wagon and equipment we cleaned and polished like family heirlooms. That thirty-five dollars was about all we spent of my wages, for now the garden began to produce and, though not the right season for them, Nordi got at least one duck before breakfast each morning and had learned to remove all fishiness or wild taste from them as they hung.

I had found a customer for my stones. He used them in an extensive rock garden and on two Saturdays I took a wagonload of fine ones to him, and at no paltry price. A friend of his, enamored of the lichen, bought two wagonloads, so we bought a quart of beer and felt sinfully wasteful. Still, we continued to save every cent possible, living on the vegetables of our garden and what our hunting brought us, though we now bought flour.

By now, I was only chipping rust on the job. The cofferdam setback had put the bridge schedule back a year and in the end I was let go.

From the job and sale of rock we now had six hundred and seventy-six dollars. We spent a hundred dollars on shoes and extra food and, after that happy activity, we salted down a deer. It didn't make an appealing meat, but it was food and we consumed it. So we had five hundred and seventy-six dollars and two goats and a kid about to become a doe and our buck and horse and two hundred pounds of wheat and plenty of ammunition, plus good shoes and a renewal of spirits, for again we had levers to pry with. Before we were seemingly without them, and man shorn of his levers is only an animal. Through the other two rock gardeners I had found a third who, envious of what they had done with lichened rock, must have at least as much himself.

The kind of rock he needed I got in a very difficult way. I went with Frank and the sled, or stoneboat as they are called. First I carried the rocks out of a copse of oaks that seemed actually to be choked with stone piled on stone. I carried my loads stepping from high-perched stone to high-perched stone, all too big for me to lift, and put mine in the stoneboat. When I had seven or eight in it, Frank, under my guidance, would haul them up an obstacle course, up to the foot of a steep place, too steep for a horse, in fact a bit steeper than an ordinary flight of stairs. Here I would unload the stones one by one and carry them up the incline—oh, about a hundred and fifty feet. When I got those big rough brutes up there I would give myself a quarter of an hour rest, then take Frank to a place where the horse could get the stoneboat up on top. We'd go back then to the stones, where we would reload them and travel for about a mile, till, going down, we came to the road where I'd load them in the wagon to take to my customers in Mill Valley. I charged a good price, for the labor on them was terrific. Most of the stones I sold weighed between fifty and a hundred pounds and were extremely awkward to carry. Old Frank would watch all this.

Then one day, when we came to that steep incline, he broke away from me and tried to climb it, stoneboat and all. It was a very rocky incline and he stumbled over some rolling ones as big as my head and fell near the top. I ran up to him and held his head and let him know in no uncertain terms that he was a hero and how I loved him. Then I took off his harness and got the stoneboat unloaded and away and then said quietly, "She's all yours, Frank, go to it!" He understood, for he reared up on his forelegs, spun on his haunches and ran down the incline, dislodging many rocks that bounced after him. At the bottom he waited trembling for me, rock-cut meanly in several places and shaking, but so proud. How else could I interpret it, except that he knew the score and was trying to help me, because I loved him, because we all loved him. I still see that heroic horse charging the incline, steep as stairs, for me. No wonder the does would sleep under him as he stood. I came upon him once, and two does lay beneath him chewing their cuds and he was holding one leg up, his hoof above them, fearing he might step on them if he put it down. Nor will I ever forget how he said good-bye to me when we finally parted. I subsequently found that in his prime he had been a dray horse, one of a magnificent team, that hauled big loads from the ships to the factories along the cobbled Embarcadero.

With the money hid away, we went back to living off the land. The fruition—the harvest of our gardens—was a thing to behold. We had grown sugar beets to feed to the goats, but each big seed in the package held seven seeds and they all came up, so we continued to thin and thin the rows of beets to give room to the dominant ones, and the thinnings were delicious greens with their marble-sized beets. And our sown turnips were sweet and we ate them as apples, so tender and crisp. Then came radishes and peas and chard.

Game pot pies and all manner of fresh vegetables and rich milk, pickled herring, and always our erstwhile calf that we got for fifty cents and raised on goat milk, who got bigger and more solemn among our more capricious goats. The neighbors came and loaded their cars with our produce and took it to their friends. I heard of people of Belvedere in semi-starvation. I borrowed a small truck and gave piles of our produce away in Tiburon and Belvedere. We had corn enough put away for ourselves and for our friends and to carry to two families in Belvedere. We had over-planted everything. We had bought seed and had seed given us and received government seed, and we had a place for all of it. We put it in the ground and watered and weeded and then we distributed our explosion of vegetables gladly. Not a cent did we ask for it. For us, at least temporarily, it was a beautiful time. With the peas and the beans dried, and the sauerkraut made, we sowed fall turnips, brought in firewood, and netted our herring later in the winter. How good it was after all the travail.

One day a man from the bank appeared while I was out. When I returned Nordi told me the man had said we were far behind in our payments on our house in Tiburon. He'd said, "In the shape you're in I'd advise you to sell before we foreclose." I went in and asked him if he had a buyer. Yes, he did. So I sold to a lawyer whose dribbling payments were six months apart. He stood me off, through one trick or another, till his death the following year. I sold my interest to a doctor and that was stalled until over three years later. It was no use to me now. In those years property sold for less than half its value.

There had been a slide on the road adjacent to my property and Bessie Drake, now living in her house again and dependent on the road to get to a pinchpenny job, gave my marvelous collection of rocks to the county to fill in the slide place. One should not look back too thoroughly.

At last I found a job as a carpenter's helper—and in Belvedere at that. A man, new to the community, was putting up a mansion. I heard of it from a feedstore owner in Petaluma where I was looking for work. "I got a brother's a carpenter down there. Tell him I sent you," he said.

His brother, a gaunt working machine, looked me over and said, "What does that brother of mine think I am—a hiring hall?" Still, he spoke to the boss and, as two men hadn't shown up for work that morning, he hired me.

There was quite an article in the *San Francisco Examiner* about the mansion. The "joe" who was building it was an importer and manufacturer of art objects. He had a big building of four or five stories jammed with them in San Francisco. There was a photo of a great fireplace mantel of carved marble he was bringing over from Italy. It was for the main room. I thought I'd seen that mantel in books of Italian sculpture, so I went to the library in Frisco one evening with the photo from the paper and found that I was right. That very fine and famous carving was going to top the fireplace I looked at as I passed back and forth in my chores! At first I was merely fascinated. Then concern began to haunt me: it would pass through my hands. What would it weigh? Again I looked at the photo and at the place where it would be ensconced. It would weigh at least six hundred pounds I estimated as I rushed materials to five carpenters. I got one of the other helpers to agree to tell me when the marble came, for by now I felt that its safety was my personal responsibility.

I was going about my usual chores when the guy came saying, "It's here." With great anticipation, I went with him to unload it. It was in a box a little bigger than I expected and seven hundred and fifty pounds was written on the box. Four of us, including two shifty-eyed bums, took it from the truck and began walking up the broad sidewalk with it. Christ! I knew one of those sons of bitches was going to squawk, just like they did in anchor drill with our seven hundred pound anchors on the ferries. We got halfway when it happened—the weight got a little too much for one hungover bum and he yelled "look out!" and jumped clear, as did the others.

"No," said some part of me, and I grabbed the whole thing. God, it tore at me! But I carried it a yard or so and slipped it down over my thighs to the lawn. The foreman had seen and came out with a yell and fired the guy who chickened, and that was all of the incident.

I didn't act for the builders or the owner of the mantel. I acted for *Art*! For once I was able to serve *Art*. It was a great satisfaction. That evening when I bathed I noticed two swellings at my groin. I had ruptured myself on both sides in saving the mantel. Next morning I told the boss. He fired me at once. He and the straw-boss ordered me off the job.

I went to the then-equivalent of our worker's compensation office in San Francisco. A doctor stuck a thumb into each of my new contours, emitted the vile odor of ancient chewed cigars, but no word, and left. I sat there on a little stool until two smooth, somewhat elderly gentlemen of the minister or lawyer variety came, oh so thoughtfully, so compassionately before me. Their hands rustled together—both of them were doing it—and then one spoke to me reproachfully:

"Young man, we are here to protect your interest, but you have lied and tried to fool us. You were born with those ruptures. The state will do nothing for you, but if you wish them operated on I have a friend in private practice who would do the job—that is if you have savings. What do you say?"

"I say," I replied, "that if either of you had the intelligence or wits to see yourself as I do, you'd run screaming to the street and cut your throats."

Closing my ears to them I dressed and left, despising those sanctimonious tools of the insurance company that handled the state insurance. The ruptures didn't bother me, but I wisely withheld from such heavy lifting after that. What I'll never understand is how my rather small hands held that mantel as I walked the several steps.

All along through these difficult times two animals were growing upon the goat ranch—one was a Guernsey calf of advanced registry. She was all the pay I got for four days' work on a dairy in hay time. We raised her on goat milk, goat feed, and wheat we cracked in the coffeemill and cooked in a weak gruel. She grew upon that fare as a small, beautiful cow of tan and white color. The other was Scheherezade, whom we called Zadee. When I could get a purebred goat for thirty dollars, I bought Zadee's dying mother for eighty dollars. She was very sick besides being pregnant, but her bloodlines were impeccable. Had the goat ranch prospered I would have built an excellent flock on Suisan Bey's and this one's progeny. I brought her in and kept her in the house. She was too feeble to be left out with the others.

One winter night she staggered up from her place by the stove and went to the door. We let her out. She went to the barn and laid in deep bedding of straw. We rigged carpets and canvas around her, for the place she chose was drafty. About one o'clock that stormy night she gave birth to one kid of great size and died. We fed the kid goat milk from our two remaining goats when we needed it ourselves and she grew in time to be a big doe, much smarter than the other goats. Because we fed her by hand, she decided, I believe, that she was a person. When the calf and kid were weaned they had the run of the place. They became inseparable and never associated with the buck, does, and Frank.

While still a carpenter's helper, I got a job on Saturday nights, running the generator that produced electricity for the ballroom at the park next to us. It was an open-air affair purported to be the biggest one in California. I got the job for three dollars a night. The generator was in a little cupola-covered house that had seen better days as a ticket booth at San Francisco's World Fair of 1912. Its soiled ornateness was distressing. The ancient equipment it housed had, by accumulating all the dust and grease it could, disguised itself as a sleeping maiden in a very dirty gown. It ran, however, like a top if you knew its ways, and from my *Sonoma* experience I did. I had to stand by to oil and grease the machine every fifteen minutes, so I stayed close and watched the dancers.

Tanner had a small excursion boat—a kind of crude *Marin* that would hold about a hundred people. They would arrive about eleven a.m., spend the day, and were rounded up at eleven p.m. and taken back to the city. There were many different kinds of groups who came on these large picnics—lodges, religious organizations, neighborhood and ethnic groups, and they all danced their own special dances. The worst were the straight Americans whose dance at that time was a pitiful limp walk, while a picnic of Swedes dancing schottisches and polkas would liven up a dull orchestra.

These Saturday night dances affected me. I began to awaken. For several years bitter irony was my only humor; now I had moments of carefree laughter. I began to look forward to my bouts with the antique electrical system. One night a group was there much different from all the others. They were Americans all right and had come in cars bringing their own liquor. Tanner's bar sold no beer that night. The men were hard, older men—many were in evening clothes. The women, in semi-evening dress, were very young and rather hard too, and faultless in their dancing. Something about them affected me strangely. I trembled to the sound of the music and the sibilance of dancing feet. They danced marvelous tangos and polkas. It was the time in certain circles of a rather moving and intricate waltz—a more complicated hesitation waltz really. I was in oiling the thumping engine and came out and looked down to see a young, painted, exceedingly beautiful girl dancing with an ape-like, acrobatic, bald-headed old man. Something of nymph and satyr was about them, something of cultivated and enjoyable sin. They passed by pausing at one place, only to sweep on in long graceful curves to other pauses. He dominated her artfully and she was pliant in his arms. I watched them, wrought up for adventure—sexual adventure. Once it started in me, it kept recurring.

I tried to blast it with extra hard work and I did bury it. All through this time I had sneered at beauty and—though once in a while I'd be caught off guard—in the main, I was so filled with rage at the shortcomings of our system of government that I was blind to its values. The hope of the world seemed to be communism—of a primitive, utopian sort—but communism flew in the face of one of the great facts of life, both animal and vegetable, the fact of hierarchy, of stratification, of the domination of some by others. It is true that the vagaries of Christianity, Islam, and Buddhism have not destroyed the governments that allowed or espoused them, but to start not only a religion but a government in the twentieth century by denying a fact and basic principle of living things could only be done by fanatics or cynics. From a realistic study of history it was patent to me that, with the proper twisting of logic, emotional appeal and faith carried to idiotic extremes, a large segment of humanity could be induced to live and die for, say, Bismarck's wife's epileptic sister and the divine symbol of a certain wooden spoon. Properly handled, such a civilization could last two thousand years. Knowing this, I had contempt for the whole damn human race and for myself as a member. I was somehow unable in those bleak years to see our race's grandeurs.

I felt that if people, a small group, lived as a community, getting their food and fuel and homes from the land and sea, selling fish or handiwork on the outside for certain necessities, that the people in the main would be more content. I didn't have the messiah complex, so prevalent in that time. As proof, I had no sandals, nor had I ever dressed myself in a sheet, nor worked at a holier-than-thou expression, but my thinking was affected by Thoreau and Rousseau and Jefferson and their followers. Nordi and I drew up bylaws for such a colony, made drawings of the houses and barns. We found many people frightened by the Depression, eager to band together to live such a life. I had made a trip up the coast of Oregon, looking for such a place, when I was running the *Sonoma*. My interest was in Winchester Bay at the mouth of the Umpqua Estuary, but land there—at least in places suitable—was ridiculously high. I went on to Portland and looked into some cut-over parcels of land offered at very low prices. I found one near Molalla—an eighty-acre plot with two streams, a spring, and a large, deep pond—a stump ranch where only one acre had been cleared. The owners, a logging company, wanted four hundred dollars for it. Had such a place been on an inlet or bay at the coast, it would have been ideal. I came back home by the coast route and tried again at Coos Bay and Florence, but uselessly. Still, the dream persisted.

When I hadn't work and things were going good at home I made trips farther from home on my bicycle. An old man named Bingo I knew in Petaluma told me of a chicken-breeding farm there where I could buy fine birds of champion laying stock worth seventy-five dollars apiece for fifty cents, if I slaughtered them for food. I got ten hens and two roosters of prize-winning stock. They were only two years old but had passed their prime as breeders. We didn't eat them as we were supposed to.

With six big cardboard boxes lashed to my bicycle I pedaled down the thirty miles from Petaluma and installed my marvelous flock in the old chickenhouse. From then on we had eggs to eat and sold some in Tiburon, for the hens laid most every day. They soon finished our wheat, so we invested in four sacks of chicken feed, feeling somehow prosperous in doing so.

In my ceaseless wanderings, looking for anything that would make a penny, I got a job cleaning up the old Grippencurl house where Lynwood and Madeline had once lived. The new tenant was a lady from the East named Varnice, who, with her adopted daughter, was spending the summer by the Bay. A violinist, she hoped to finish a sonata she was composing while there. Somewhere in the East was a husband from whom she was presently separated. The place had been vacant for several years and the shrubbery was climbing in the windows. There was also some broken plumbing and several leaks in the roof. I put in a week making the beautiful building livable.

As I worked, Varnice's little daughter followed me around and she, Varnice, kept making small sandwiches of different kinds that we ate at the various coffee breaks she called. Her facial contours, the set of her eyes and her manner of holding her head tilted as she listened to things only the birds could hear—these were the attributes of my mother. I was drawn to her from far below conscious thought. The Depression hadn't laid its heavy hand on her. I marveled at her innocent laughter, untrammeled by irony, her spritely movements. We talked of Brahms on my last day there and she hummed some phrases from his first piano concerto—that humming caught me, barely emerging as it did from within. I came close and sat beside her. Innocence claimed me and I was back in childhood. Finally her humming ceased. She sprang to her feet and turned on the lights. It was getting dark.

"You'll be late for your supper," she said.

I gathered my tools. The job was done; she paid me, then she caught my eyes. "You are more than welcome here," she said. "Come whenever you wish, but no sex, Clyde. That would spoil it."

I was on my bike, my sack of tools on a strap over my shoulder. Twilight was past and in the first dark I pedaled toward home. Soon I was free of lighted houses and sped into the darker dark under the oaks that covered the road. I wanted to walk. I hid my bike and tools back in the brush and moved on. It made my step light. Maybe, I thought, we'll pass through this Depression thing; maybe we'll act as she does when things open up. Perhaps she's a harbinger, a dove with a leafy twig. Giddy hope tried to push aside the facts—I did let it in beside them—as I sauntered along; a guy who'd found something he'd thought he'd lost.

I was late, but not too late for supper. Nordi noticed that my mood was light, though I'm sure I gave no evidence of change. Finally she said, "Tell me what happened, Clyde."

As I spoke I saw a grim expression change her lips, her eyes. When I was through she laughed. It was a bitter laugh and contemptuous of me.

"Had she been married to you these years, she'd have no sparkle. Now that you've killed it in me, you trot around seeking it in others."

I looked at her in amazement and disbelief and in that moment I saw she had lost her great joy in living and all because of me. Not only that, she had aged. Worry and lack of social life had had their effect. I realized that it had been a tough row to hoe for the best model in San Francisco, with her adoring husband and her baby and with her faithful lover, along with the open admiration she had received from many others. She had hidden the loss of that side of her life from me, for it seemed I could do nothing about our situation. Now the fester and poison had broken out. She was trembling violently.

"And don't say you're sorry," she said. "You're a weakling and lazy."

I had made a mess of things. That was true, but weak and lazy—

no! I was strong and hard-working. These, it seemed, were all I really was. If she took that from me I couldn't go on. "You take that back," I yelled, coming at her.

"A weakling and lazy," she screamed.

I grabbed her and threw her against the wall. She fell beside it crying and spat at me when I tried to help her up.

"I'm all right—weakling!" she said, "go out and sleep with the goats."

We all try, at least most of us try—try hard! I knew I had tried desperately hard, too hard. People must have seen the desperation in my face and didn't want me around—that and with one thing and another, I hadn't anything left to deal with—no nickels or dimes, no levers, no way to pry a dollar out of another guy, no way until now. Didn't she see we had reached the bottom before I got the job at Robblings? She knew we had over six hundred dollars buried in a fruit jar under the house. We had levers now—a hand-to-mouth existence, sure! But not without resources. We had wanted to live simply, to be working with the basics directly. That had been her dream as well as mine, but we were askew the culture of the time, where getting away from the basics of growing and harvesting for our primal needs was prized.

In the morning when I came in breakfast was ready. She evaded me when I sought to embrace her. She would not talk nor let me apologize. She limped as she moved about and there was an ugly bruise on her upper arm.

"Nordi, I don't know what got into me. You know I've never acted like that before."

She turned and stared at me, then walked past me and out of the house. Up the hill she went and I didn't follow. In the afternoon she came back. I saw her coming down the hill from where I was repairing our sledge. I'd trimmed Frank's hooves and greased the wagon—small chores. I'd spent most of the day on them, as I tried to understand what had happened. I knew she was leaving me, taking Bunky. I had lost her. I had had my chance and muffed it. I admitted to a lot of stupid moves, like my pride not letting me go back to the landscape association because I'd flubbed a chance to talk business at their convention. I would have had to explain I was sick that day—excuses. How I hated excuses! But that was a flub

I'd never forget and the rest—oh, hell, have done with thinking! I did. I left. I went a mile, but something drew me back. We were silent at supper, even Bunky was withdrawn from me. Why in hell this jagged tear in us when we were over the hump or I thought we were over the hump. But they would not look at me.

Again I slept in the hay. Next morning I saw that she was packing. "Is there anything I can do?" I asked. She shook her head. What was happening to us? With tremendous effort I wondered about it, but a dullness had come over me. It hampered me.

I heard a sly, triumphant voice: "Mr. Jinx," it said, "Mr. Jinx, you're getting licked once again. Step up, Mr. Jinx, and see her go, see her leave. I'm the law of averages, Mr. Jinx, no offense! Some guys are lucky, some just so, and then there's guys like you, Mr. Jinx. Guys like you."

I left. I wandered, not on roads but on ridges. I came down from them for water or food or to get to another ridge. I went on toward the coast. A few days later I turned back still incapable of understanding the suddenness of our separation. "She's gone," I thought, "but maybe she left a dress or a shawl." A small volition stirred in me. I tramped along all the next day and in the evening reached home. All the animals were turned out in the meadow, chickens and all. The water trough was getting low. I filled it and fed grain to them.

At last I ventured into the house, hope bursting in me as I searched for some bit of her clothing. She'd left me nothing. I took off my shoes—for each step I made sounded hollow and empty. I still had some of what Varnice paid me in my pocket.

"How about a drink?" I said aloud—no answer, so I said, "Yeah, how about it?"

I got on the bike and soon I was at Sam's among the others and ordered a double bourbon and downed it and asked for another when Sam caught my eye and waggled his head toward the back room. His eyes looked like gimlets back of his heavy lenses.

"Clyde," he said, "I like you. Forget about that goat meat. I—oh, forget about it. Now Art was in here a couple of days ago and had a few. Then he said he was taking your wife north with him."

"Yeah, I know," I said.

"Anyway he was out there in the bar and told all of us that he had your wife and he hauled out an automatic—looked like a forty-five—and said, 'tell Rice when you see him—I'll put all five shots from Lulu here into his guts if I ever hear he's come north of Vallejo.'" He examined me carefully with those thick glasses of his as he said it. I thought a moment, then grinned.

"Thanks, Sam," I said. "Where can I rent a car? Mine's busted."

XI

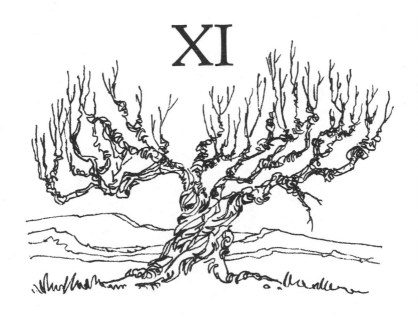

In Which
I Decide To Bring Nordi Back,
Avoid Violence Through Strange Counsel,
and
Plan For A New Life

◇ 1933 ◇

Several hours later I was in an old borrowed Buick, heading north. I went through Vallejo because he had mentioned it and on through Sacramento. I drove toward the place in the mountains he often mentioned—Ballard's Bar on the North Yuba River. There were mining operations around there, and a fellow I borrowed a light from said, "Sure, young Coulter was through here several days ago, trying to sell a claim he's got near West Hill."

Remembering names he had named helped me. I found two other places he'd been through lately, trying to sell claims that he or his father had held.

Way up in Feather River Canyon I found his mine tunnel and his shack, but no Art. I talked to several people who knew him and about me. They grinned, but wouldn't say yes or no. They were secretly derisive.

I went back to where I climbed in and climbed out. It was a broad path and steep as stairs. It must have been a quarter of a mile up to get out of the canyon. I clambered up panting and stood at the top. I wondered how much money I had left. I felt in my pocket—it was gone! I'd lost it somewhere on the climb, for I'd had it at the bottom. I searched and searched the length of that winding path, but it was useless. It was autumn, the leaves of the maple, the hazel and the oak lay on the ground, many the color of greenbacks. As I stirred in the leaves along that upward path, I saw it was no use—a one in a million chance. I put a little sign at the top telling of my loss and offering a reward. I knew those derisive bastards would hunt for days and weeks. I felt I had the last laugh.

In Chico I traded a watch of my grandfather's that my grandmother had sent me the month before for eighteen dollars. There in Chico I got a clue. In a service station posing as Art's uncle I found that Art was in Redding with his father and would be coming down to Chico in a day or two. I listened well to the man's voice, then I called Art's father in Redding, said I was the man at the

Avalon Station in Chico and asked when Art was coming down. He said Art would leave Redding for Chico in about an hour.

As the chase led me from the locale of my defeats, the excitement of the hunt cleansed me of I know not what. I was no longer swathed with trouble, but nakedly myself. I drove out of town on the road to Redding. Eighty-eight miles to Redding, the sign said.

When I was clear of the town I looked for a place to wait. Several miles on I saw a row of eucalyptus beside the road. I drove to them and parked under their shade. The only thing I thought about was to take no chances on a deflecting bullet hitting Nordi or Bunky. I injected a shell in my 25-35 and laid it handy on the seat beside me. The hour would soon be up and then they'd be coming toward me. I lit a cigarette but threw it away. My mouth was dry. After all the days of searching the quarry was coming my way. I wouldn't look at the foolish reasons of why I was here. This was north of Vallejo and Bunky and Nordi who had not left me a shred to sustain me would soon again be near. I stared at the road and then started the motor again and backed into a vague lane among the eucalyptus, then waited and again would not let myself think, shifting about restlessly in the seat. The country about seemed almost deserted but across the highway was a grove of young acacias and beyond it a house. I got out to relieve myself and from there could see through the grove that there was a sign by the gate of the house, which said, "Cider for sale." I stared at the road ahead. "More than an hour to wait," I muttered to myself, and walked over to a small square house. It was up high off the ground on, I suppose, a musty cellar. The front door was blocked by shrubbery and hanging plants, so I went around to the back door and knocked. From there I could see the road where it crossed the ridge into the rolling uplands.

The door was opened by a fat Italian woman with keen eyes and a mustache. I stood over her in the doorway. "I'm thirsty," I said.

"Cider is good," said the woman with an unbelieving inflection.

"Without wine I must take cider," I suggested.

"We will let the next customer take the cider," said the fat woman. Her appraising glance had a willing camaraderie about it. I could conceive of a roistering wench of other years, forced now by conditions of the flesh to stately gestures. "For you I have some zinfandel, dry only as alum, and yet I put no alum in it."

"But sometimes you do," I said grinning.

"Yes, sometimes. It is not to improve nature, but to improve the trade. They buy that dry flavor, yet pounds of alum cannot cure most from being loose-mouthed."

I smiled. "Would you have a glass with me?"

"Ah," she examined my eyes, probing, it seemed, from different angles through their surfaces and color, to some place back of them which she touched this way and that with many touchings and all in the briefest of moments. Then she agreed and told me to sit on the bench by the back door while she got a bottle and glasses.

I was pleased, for from the bench I could see that long length of highway even better than I could under the trees.

She handed me my glass and then sat down beside me with hers. She spread her knees, put a hand on each one, and, leaning forward, stared intently up the long highway for a moment. Then she leaned back against the wall of the house at ease, took a sip of her wine and accepted the cigarette I offered her.

"A fine paisano you are, and new here and worried," she said with affable conviction as I fumbled for the matches. "Was I not right about the wine?"

"I like it and it's dry," I said, "though I'll never know if this is the one you spoke of or the one it's usual to improve with the alum."

"Oh well, my friend," she replied with a sidelong glance, "there is a little alum in it, but what do you care? You'll be gone soon."

I gulped what was left in my glass and she poured me another from the long black bottle. When I raised it to my lips, she said, "Sip this glass, worried one. You have more than enough time and, sipping, one does not notice how it is doctored." She stared into her glass for a moment. "I use a few cherry pits and broken peach pits and that is all about the wine I'll tell you."

I looked at her. I'd seen many odd creatures, but at first glance I'd been fond of this one. All I thought, though, was she's about forty-seven, but she caught the thought and said, "Sometimes on the surface not much shows, eh, paisano? Like you now, much is hid beneath the surface. And look at me, under all this great surface I too hide some nuggets."

"But no alum?" I asked.

"Life is wry enough," said the fat woman. "In living there is no need for alum."

"How about sugar?" I asked.

"Anyone who puts frosting on the black bread that is life and calls it cake has a burro's cabissa."

I kept silent.

"And yet at times," said the fat woman, smacking her lips over her wine, "life sometimes is so?" The tone was searching and she made a little gesture with her fat hand that started in one way and came back gracefully, as if she were indicating an arrow with an undulating shaft and only one barb. It was absurd, yet I knew from it a sense of delicacy, of exquisiteness, of subtle poignancy. I was oddly moved.

We sat sipping our wine, watching the road running straight up and over the first ridge. Around us was a house garden—a commingling of flowers and vegetables—peppers, eggplants, cactus and vines. It was like birth: as full of untidy remnants and as full of riches.

"You wouldn't believe a lot of people come here, would you, paisano? It is true sometimes I wait a week and no one comes in my gate, then sometimes there'll be several in a day. Some I bring to the garden. The old men I take into my house. My best profit is there. Some I cut bouquets for. It pays me a quarter. And some I deal with over the gate, selling them cider but letting them come no farther. Ah, the tricks I have with the cider. Good apples, mind you, no worms, but the tricks to keep it from turning—to keep it always sweet, a permanently sweet cider. The thought sickens me. I never drink it myself. I put saltpeter in it and benzoate of soda and several other stuffs that kill it but keep it sweet. A lot of things are like that, aren't they, paisano?"

I sipped my wine and was conscious that, under the strange influence of this dominant-voiced woman, I was relaxing a bit, that the muscles and nerves were coming unknotted and a certain vicious hogging of the scene was gone from my scanning.

"You come pretty far, bambino."

"Sure, and I'm not your bambino."

"No, you are not, you are my paisano. The thing I wanted most was a bambino, but I never had one. Some trick of the belly wouldn't allow a bambino. Now this road," said the woman, "we watch it, yes! Why do you think I look at the road going up and over the ridge to Redding and back along its ribbon to Willows? Today I do not care for customers." As she talked she picked a flower from a plant that grew beside her. The flower was astonishingly beautiful, a thing of pinks and lavenders. It had a meatiness about it, and as I looked, it suddenly reminded me of certain portions of the entrails of a chicken. Yes, they were very much alike. Why did I never see that beauty in a chicken's guts? Oh, I miss so much, I thought with sadness, and listened again to the woman, who was saying, "I do not think you'll like it if I tell you I know why you watch the road."

I said nothing.

"Still, I will tell you. In the car over there under the trees is a Winchester and with you now you have a long heavy knife that is sharp to follow your whim. Right there it is hid," she said and touched lightly where the scabbard was beneath my trousers at my groin.

"Yes," I admitted. "That is a knife."

"But you doubt I have read it at all, don't you, paisano? Guess work, you say inside. Well, a gray car is coming with a man and a woman. Is that guess work, paisano? Is it guess work that in the right hand glove compartment of the gray car there is an automatic and the man said he would kill you if you interfered? No, do not answer. I do not want an answer. Sip the wine slowly, mixed one, while I think."

We sat there quietly in the afternoon sun. How can she know? I asked myself and told myself no answer.

Why was I here? Well! There were many reasons, known and unknown. A conundrum of half-understood values—it's too late to think here, far from my Sugarloaf. Soundlessly, I mumbled a familiar phrase—"I'll play it by ear"—and I rested in the cliché as in a hammock, just like the Joneses. I thought of Bunky—God how I missed him! He's coming nearer, I thought. Then completely without reason a picture was suddenly in my mind of Madeline's expression as she drove by me, carrying dying Lynwood to the ferry.

"I'm going to have another glass," said the fat woman, "but I'm not going to pour one for you. You must be very clearheaded. These two people of yours keep coming closer."

"I know," I said. "I found out that he would be leaving Redding at two o'clock and be coming this way."

"Why do you do it, mixed one? These people are not your enemies. The letting of blood should be avoided. You may be killed! Have you any bambinos?"

I held up one finger. "One," I said, "he's with them."

"Oh," she mused. "I wasn't sure. Do you have to do it because of the manner in which other people look at you?" She stated, rather than asked. I nodded, though now it was very much more than that. "Ah, it is coming clearer," she murmured and then the thoughtful look was replaced by a certain piquancy about the eyes and lips, almost sauciness. Once more she looked deeply into my eyes and said brightly, "You like the treeck, the cleaver treeck? You like to do the slick theeng?"

I turned a sad face to her. "I'm wooden there," I said, "but I will try."

"I see," she said, looking me over fondly, yet dispassionately, as a mother does her doltish son. "You must take the woman back for face—is that it?"

"No, I wronged her," I said. "I want another chance."

"You'll probably wrong her again. It's the way of things," she answered. "You must be stupid to only be able to end this with bloodshed. I suppose a fat old woman can tell you nothing."

"I've listened to you this far," I replied. "I'd be a fool to not hear you out."

"Then," said the woman, "let them pass when they come. Do not let them see you. Follow and they will park in front of the Safeway store in Chico. To the right of them will be an empty parking place. Drive into it, step from your car and reach into the open window of theirs and take the pistol out of the open glove compartment. Direct them, then, east of town by the creek where there is an old quarry. There let them have a small time to make their parting, keep the bambino with you. Let them know you'll fire with the carbine if they try to avoid you. Are you a good shot?" she asked archly.

"They say so," I answered.

"Will you do as I say?" asked the woman.

"Yes, I will," I said. "I'll give them five minutes to make their parting, and?"

"And?" asked the woman, drawing my thoughts from me.

"I'll tell him I don't hate him but couldn't avoid the challenge."

She beamed, her hands warm on my shoulder. "The treeck is more better than to be the brave burro."

"And I'll take her back forced. I think she won't hate it too much." I grinned. "I'll tie her up."

"Bind her with wire! I have some bailing wire here handy," chortled the fat woman. "Tie her tight so she cannot move around much and treat her roughly. And how will you leave this man?" she asked, beginning to quiver with pleasure as she concocted color around the scenes we saw together.

"I'll leave with dead seriousness, but with a note of respect and with such care and caution as to give him food for his pride."

"Ah, God!" exclaimed the Italian woman, "I'd give a year—my house even—to be for a week this woman of yours. Remain to her grim for a week. Do not approach her for ten days. Only then take her in your arms. But hurry now. The gray car will come over the ridge in a moment. Get ready for the end of your hunting and, ah, paisano, if ever you come back this way, knock on my door and we'll share my best bottle!"

I kissed her cheek and ran, and it happened as she foretold. With his automatic in my hand I stared at them in consternation (how many people is a man, anyway?). I stared wordlessly at their frozen startled faces.

Bunky's voice broke our silence: "Hello, Da'!"

"Don't touch that starter, Art," I said. "Don't move." We three continued our still wariness, then I spoke. "I had to, Art," I muttered. "Nobody tells me where I can and can't go. And you, Nordi," I went on with the same air of grievance, "you could have left an old dress or a slipper— something a guy could hold onto in hell. Both of you let me down."

"What are you going to do?" asked Nordi through still lips.

"You're coming back with me, you and Bunky. For better or worse—remember? And, Art—I've got your gun and I'll use it if I have to, and my 25-35 is with me. This old Buick will beat that car of yours. Now head for that quarry east of town. Drive in there and make your parting, then send her out, Art, and don't follow. I'll shoot." I stared at my friend's face. "God, man, I'm sorry. Luck!"

We drove to the quarry, Bunky with me. Amazingly, he seemed to be taking all this in stride. The old Buick had a windshield you could leave half down and it was down with my rifle leaning on it, but there wasn't anything Art could do and he knew it. She came out all right, but ran bawling down the road. I got turned around and drove after her until, well away from the quarry, she turned off into the brush. It was there that I caught her. Biting and scratching, but soundlessly, she fought as I tied her with the bailing wire, then I heaved her up on my shoulder and carried her to the car and dumped her in. Watching my rear view mirror and using back roads, I headed south.

With her bound in wire, but in the front seat, and with sweet Bunky in between us, we drove through the warm night and he leaned against me as he slept. Before midnight we were home, where I removed the wire that chafed her wrists and ankles, heated some buns and sausages, and brought in her duffle. The goats were milked as usual, for when I was away Mr. Carter had taken on that chore. So I told them I was back before wrapping my blanket around me in the hay. We were back in the same scene with the same problems and a new one—Bunky was six years old and must start school. Next morning, I dug up our savings and found that Nordi had not taken one jot when she left me, though half was hers. I spoke to her. We did not look at each other as I handed her a hundred dollars.

"Bunky needs school clothes and so do you. I'll take you to the ferry and meet you when you come back."

When I picked her up that evening they were both loaded with packages. As we drove out home we were very formal, but I had a feeling that under it, Nordi was beginning to enjoy herself again.

After supper they put on their new clothes and acted as if they weren't parading before me, but they were. One value of the times was the amount of things you could get for one hundred dollars. She had outdone herself in shopping. I was pleased and she was pleased and our formal attitudes were hard to hold. One more week and Bunky would be a school boy. We were on a very winding road four-and-a-half miles from school. That bike my father had given me along with insult was now our transportation, as I had returned the Buick. I could ride Bunky to school on the handlebars each morning, but he would have to walk the four-and-a-half miles back every evening, as I had to be out on odd jobs or rock work, or just looking for work the rest of the day.

He was a strong and resolute child and, I would say, rather woods-wise for his age. We had trained him to be independent and to figure things out for himself. It would be hardship, but we hoped it wouldn't fatigue him overly much. I had walked two miles each way to school as a boy, but four miles all alone at the end of the day, that was something else. It would have been simpler to go over the top of Sugarloaf and down, but now there were often bulls loose up there, so that was out of the question. He'd just have to try it and if it didn't work we'd have to teach him at home. Only then he'd lose the companionship of kids his own age that he needed so badly.

One night when I went to my bed in the barn no blanket lay on the hay, so I came back to the house and took my place by Nordi. Of course the usual things took place and that was splendid, but we spent the rest of the night coming closer in all ways, for we felt that the overall conditions I'd gotten into had ravaged the happy care-free quality of our marriage. We swore that from now on we would be gay in our relationship.

At last the morning came when, freshly dressed in his school clothes, Bunky kissed his mother good-bye and came with me as I pushed the bicycle up the hill. On his back was a small flat pack that carried his lunch and books. When we got up on the hard gravel road I held the bike while he got on the handlebars, then away we went on the endless curves. Most of the way it was level, but at two places there were long inclines where we swooped along. One was just before I let him off—a block or so from school. I'd have the bike going at a great rate and then I'd brake and stop and he'd get off. That was the moment! Excitement would be in his eyes as he turned and kissed me. "Bye, Da'," he'd say and start for school.

Sometimes if we'd really been rambling along on the way he would say, "That was a good one, Da'."

Then I'd spin slowly in a tight circle on the road and, standing on the pedals, pump my way back up the hill and on to Nordi. We would have a bit of time together, some coffee usually. Once when I came back she had the paints out and was doing a lovely wood scene over in Tanner's park-like grounds next door—a small red building (the women's toilet, really) against the many leafless limbs of autumn. It was good, no doubt about it. She had great facility, but was uninterested in pushing it as far as it would go. Anyway, we would have these few intimate moments together when we sought to know each other better, then I'd get on with what I was doing.

In the afternoon I came home early from worming some flat rocks out of an overburden of the wrong kind. It was about four-fifteen and Bunky should have been home, but he wasn't. Four-thirty, five, five-thirty, and six passed. At six-thirty he appeared in the dusk—a tired little boy. We hugged him and finally got out of him that he'd played on the school grounds for an hour after school was out.

"Was it a long walk, darling?"

"Yes."

"Do you like school?"

"Yes."

Our solemn little boy ate his supper and went to bed. Next day was the same. In the morning we sped down to school. "Hurry home," I called after him as he left me and he flashed me his smile from where he turned on the road to the school. But it was late dusk when he pushed open the kitchen door. Oh, we felt guilty that evening after he kissed us good night.

"I'm no good out there working, looking for work, if it's going to be like this, I said, after I came back from taking him to school the following morning.

"I know, Clyde," she said. "Be patient. Wait till Saturday. It's his first chance to play with a whole schoolyard of kids. You could go meet him at dusk, though."

"No, I don't want to interfere," I admitted. "Though I'd gladly quit things early and bring him back each evening."

"You can't do that with a living as precarious as ours," she answered. "Let's give it a week and if it doesn't work out I'll keep him home and teach him myself."

So we fuddled along till Saturday. Saturday he wanted a lunch—the same as if he was going to school, he said. Wondering, she made him one and he disappeared. He often played with the goats or made sand castles on the beach or spent time with Mr. Carter.

We were busy working up a winter garden spot for turnips, carrots and cabbages. We both went at it at a great rate, boarding it up, mixing lots of goat manure into the rich ground. It started to rain but we kept on until we were soaking and the job in the main was done. We ran for the house and changed. No Bunky! It was three-thirty. I hurried over to Mr. Carter's, who said he had not seen him today. I rushed around looking everywhere for him. Nordi was worried.

"I think he walked in to play with the Longo kids," I said. "He must have got acquainted with them at school. I'll wait until dusk. If he found someone to play with I don't want to interfere." The old business of worrying and reassuring myself. At dusk I sped down to the Longo place—a mile up our road from Tiburon.

"No!" They hadn't seen Bunky that day, but Longo, a genial Swiss-Italian whose corded throat vibrated every time he spoke, said he thought he'd seen my boy walking along the road with a big grubbing hoe that morning. A grubbing hoe is sort of a pickaxe, but the blades are as wide as the palm of your hand and heavy. That was this morning. Jesus! We were so damn eager for him to play with other kids that we'd lost him. Maybe he lay injured somewhere in the dark, and now I thought he'd been out in that rain too instead of holed up with playmates.

I pedaled into town. Nobody who had kids had seen him. I went back along the road, stopping every hundred yards or so to call for him uselessly and arrived home wild with worry. There he sat, eating his supper. His explanation of the day didn't make much sense, though he said he would show us next morning.

And he did. He had made a cut-across trail that cut a mile at least off that twisting road and in the banks and washes he'd traversed he had dug out stairs and footholds. All day he had worked at it, using that clumsy grub-hoe, and stayed until he finished—four miles of it. A six-year-old boy assuming a project like that so he could stay longer with his companions after school! I was so ashamed that I was unable to carry him both ways and so proud of his initiative I could only dance a jig around him and Nordi and hurrah.

The next few days I came home early and went toward school and picked him up, but then I had an offer of four days' work on a chicken farm in Petaluma and had to leave. I made three dollars a day, so I came home with twelve and with the last rocks sold we were somewhat secure for the winter, when there was very little work of my sort to be found.

I thought often of Art as I cycled back from carrying Bunky to school, ashamed that I had to deprive him of our lady. That was an odd way to look at things, but in a way it was true. It was obvious that having two men so eager for her companionship that they came close to killing each other brought Nordi's fresh beauty back, and stranger still that she could bloom so or wither so. She was a creature of the airs of the time, more than of the architecture.

Finally, I opened the door of the landscape association offices again. A new man was there who had no time for me. I did get to chat with his secretary, who was there on my first visit. I explained myself so she understood what kept me away from the convention. She was friendly, so I asked her if she knew of a large estate that was being built in the area. She mentioned Hearst's extravaganza below Monterey and one being built for a financier from the East at Burlingame. I went there by bus and got the names of the landscape architect and the owner. I wrote the architect, and in time he came to Tiburon and looked at my stones and fell in love with my favorite group, marveling at its dramatic arrangement of masses. He stared at the base and the great shell rising up to a knife-like edge eleven feet above the base and to the large stones on either side of the shell, balancing the tableau. It seemed impossible that some great artist hadn't had a hand in the placing of those masses and the arrangement of lines to be found there, but there it stood, a one-in-a-billion marvel of nature in an improper setting. He finally turned it down. The expense of moving it would be more than the owner would accept.

"People," he said, "who can amass that amount of money in less than a lifetime are very seldom people of taste. Perception with them has been consolidated in one direction."

When he left he shook hands with me and he held on a little longer than is usual, not as homosexuals do, but more than that—because he was not a talker, the pressure of his hand would have to tell me of his joy in sharing with me the tableau of stones on the old widow's property.

We settled down with more than enough to carry us through the winter and early spring. We had time now to consider schemes that would get us to Oregon. The country still was in the grip of the Depression. President Roosevelt strove mightily to alleviate the situation, but signs of real recovery would only come as we sold supplies to the Allies, just before we ourselves became involved in World War II. Still, people in general were walking with a little more elasticity and there were fewer zombies.

On a blustery evening I looked up the hill to the west. Clouds came hurtling over the high horizon and shouldered their way east. The low sun cut through whenever it could and gleamed on the wet trunks of trees and rain came—one heavy shower after another. I looked out from the kitchen door on all this and closed it—more than ready to give sovereignty of the farmstead, for the night at least, to wind and rain. Under cover the goats and cow and Frank chewed contentedly on their hay while the barn above them creaked occasionally from the wild west winds that, crossing the coasts, were racing inland on whatever adventure.

In the warm kitchen the lamps' glow left darkness in the corners, but immediately under them, one at each lamp, sat my self-sufficient son and that person highly-skilled in all the arts of her sex, Nordi. Trouble was, outside of being a darling, she was a better shot, could hike farther, swim faster and handle a boat in rough water better than most men. Who was I, then, coming in now, forcing myself on such excellent people? Yet they swept toward me from their seats and embraced me high and low, and the freshly broken cherry of her lips were placed on mine. For a moment before I had beaten both of them—three games of penny guessing—and had been shoved out the door to see the last of daylight while they considered a prize for me. Now Bunky gave me two of his pretty agates from a collection of hundreds and Nordi said she could give me a prize before midnight.

Supper was ready. She was about to put it on the table when someone knocked at the door. Then it opened and our friend Carl stepped in and forced it closed against the storm. His overcoat shone with its wetness. In fact all his clothes were saturated with water from four miles of downpour. "Hello," he said quietly, dispiritedly. "I thought I'd come out."

Well, we got him out of his waterlogged clothing and into a bathrobe and slippers and the fine stew she served was more than enough to stuff the four of us. After we'd eaten, Nordi made cigarettes from Granger, a burley pipe tobacco we bought two pounds of at a time. She had a little machine that rolled the cigarettes in great fashion. It and the small crystal radio sets were the symbols of the time. We puffed away. Carl was coming back from a trip around the world, he said. He'd signed on as a navigation officer and had taught himself navigation on the way and had made an exhaustive study of the slide rule and had read everything he could find on Trotsky. In New York he had his teeth pulled and his false teeth were giving him much trouble. He seemed acutely embarrassed when wearing them.

Carl, a radical and an idealist with a weird sense of humor, was Nordi's cousin, who had visited us before. A brilliant, erratic man, he'd been a streetcar conductor in Oakland, where he had met Martin Keene, a motorman. Martin had been in the Irish Rebellion. When he came over to this country after the Rebellion, he had joined Capone's gang in Chicago, but was forced to leave it because of his roughness with people. "Bad publicity," they said, and he ended up as a streetcar motorman in Oakland, who loved and could quote vast splendor from the plays of Shakespeare. He also liked, Carl said, to run over people with his streetcar. Carl had been a seaman of sorts and had made one trip around the world on the *Stanley Dollar* before he became a streetcar conductor in Oakland. As a boy he had spent a year in a college run by Seventh Day Adventists. One thing it was possible to learn there was elocution, which he despised, but at which he became very good. The streetcars and ferries of Oakland, Berkeley, and Alameda were run by a company which called itself the Key System and once a year they gave a vast banquet for their motormen and conductors—and others too, I suppose. The men had to appear in evening clothes and, I believe, pay fifty percent of the cost of the banquet. How they didn't love it, but appearance there was mandatory. To these horrors the company invited speakers and solicited speeches made by their employees. They also had a school for their employees offering classes in oratory, weaving and correct posture. Carl took oratory. He saw to it that he was most awful at first, but he strove and his orations began to lose their roughness. The instructor singled him out. "A vast improvement there, Carlson," he said.

"Do you think so, sir?" said Carl, acting timid and hopeful, and though a sallow fellow, trying vainly to blush.

"Didn't you have public speaking in grammar school?" the teacher inquired.

"Oh, no sir. My family was real religious, sir. We was taught that oratory is blasphemy."

More lessons and more marked improvement and Carl was brought to the notice of the management: the possibility of becoming a fair-haired boy. He struggled on each Wednesday night with his oration; then suddenly he was so impressive that the instructor got a raise. He was to be a speaker at the banquet that would be broadcast over the Bay region. The subject was to be the company's teaching of courtesy to their employees.

Then came the night of the great renting of tuxedos. At an immensely long table sat company officials and conductors and motormen who, if caught drinking on the job, were summarily fired; so someone always opened the banquet with a toast to water —the perfect drink. Then the whole damn bunch rose and toasted water, whatever their inclinations, and felt solid with the company.

Carl arrived—yes, now it can be told—with liquor on his breath and, when the festivities were at last declared open, stood unsteadily on his feet and intoned, "Gentlemen, I offer a toast to whiskey."

And, not knowing what else to do, they all got to their feet and toasted whiskey and sat down, but Keene was on his feet then with a "Gentlemen, let us toast gin, a splendid invention of the Dutch," and gin was acclaimed by the multitude.

Then Carl arose for his speech, but fell backwards into his chair, hauling the mike down with him, and proceeded to castigate the company who, by claiming they taught employees courtesy, were taking credit for what every man got at his mother's knee. (I'll not attempt to do it justice; the material was slight, but in Carl's use of it, it made the company look small and mean.) For three or four minutes he held the Key System to ridicule, before they awoke with shock and cut him off the air. Oh, how the Bay area loved it! Carl, of course, was fired, but immediately used his notoriety to engage fellow ex-conductors and motormen in talks that led to the unionizing of the Key System's motormen and conductors. Then, pleased with his life, Carl took ship as able seaman on one of the Dollar Line's freighters and sailed once more around the world. Adios.

As you see, he had a great deal in common with Pushells — oh, a great deal. Now, out at the goat ranch sitting in our kitchen, he turned to us from a sardonic staring into a corner, as if at his past. "I'm through with the sea," he said. "Sick of the goddamned cities. I've heard you talk of moving to the Northwest and perhaps starting a little colony somewhere up there. I'd like to join you. I've taken an awful beating in every way lately. If you'll keep me for the next six months, on the first of the seventh month, I will receive a six hundred dollar army bonus. I will turn it over to you if, when you go to Oregon, you will take me along. When we get there we could get a stump ranch somewhere, clear some land and start a little farm and from there we could start figuring on a colony on the coast. As I see it, it can't be done in one jump."

Stump ranches have their beginnings on cut-over land — land from which the timber has been shorn, leaving a maze of stumps and debris. You stacked the debris of limbs and the poles of lesser trees around the stumps and then burned it, then you farmed in and around the stumps while you burned them and their roots out — an endless, backbreaking job. Seventy-five percent of all the land in America was won for farming in that manner.

After much thought we agreed that it would be necessary to reach our goal in two steps. "If we had a base to work from up there—farming and working out, we could acquire the cash and equipment and the right people to move on to land on the coast," said Carl. "How many families are you figuring on?" he asked.

"Four or five," we replied.

"Well, I'm for it," he said. "I'm broke, but if you got the dinero to keep me until that army veteran bonus time, then six hundred dollars goes into our joint effort. What do you think of it?"

Nordi and I looked at each other. Ever since the milk law change that broke me, and all through the travail that followed, there had been a distant star in my sky, and I saw that star rise now in Nordi's eyes. It was Oregon. After all these years—in fact during all these years—we had been homesick for Oregon. In short, Nordi and I agreed. We were going home.

XII

*In Which
We Begin The Long Journey Home,
Lose Our Brakes On The Way,
and
Arrive With Less Than We Began With*

◇   1934   ◇

Next day I wrote to the timber company about the stump ranch near Molalla. They answered it was available, so I sent the one hundred dollar down payment and relaxed.

With Carl around, we shared the chore of wheeling Bunky to and from school. One afternoon, Carl took a spill in bringing Bunky home and sustained a mean rock cut on his hand. Bunky showed me where it happened the next morning. "He don't know the road like you do, Da'," he confided.

Carl's accident occurred where a groove in the road led you into it one way and out the other—a place of slippery rocks. I knew the place in a most personal way. Yeah! A sneer of fury, of self-loathing, struck me. Why attuned to rocks and not money, I snorted! I'd never let the feel of money come, with its indirection, between me and the oar and the plow handles—between me and the heft of my froe and the sound of my maul. I say *never*. Really, I'd fought a losing battle with the metal and paper of currency trying to stay too close to what is basic, while the culture of my time became once removed and twice removed from the source.

We tore into the place to escape boredom as we waited. Soon it looked like Dutch people lived there. We made a new bathroom in the house we lived in, paved it with stones of many colors and built a big sunken tub into it.

It was while we were working on the tub that Keith Guiness and his friends came once again. This time he had a new fellow along— the husband of one of his girl friends, the one that went in for heavy war paint. His name was Curt Ordwell, the manager of a big salmon cannery in southeastern Alaska. He spent six or seven months of the year as master of a town of two or three hundred, set up on pilings in the far reach of an inlet where the grouse in early spring made such a drumming in the timber about that the whole inlet throbbed as a great heart and a fellow knew a vibrancy of life completely absent in the other half of his existence down in the

States. In the course of the evening, we put our dreams of a colony to him. He listened, smiling thoughtfully.

"Yes, I understand," he said. "It's been tried many times and very seldom works for long. There's a colony on Malcolm Island, alongside the upper end of Vancouver Island, that works. I mean, really works. Financially, it's a marvel, and yet with success all around them—with all a man or family could want—their young people leave. Sometimes it seems to me they've achieved a life too certain, too secure. Still, fishing on the high seas as they do, and logging, it should have produced enough excitement. It must be something else."

Woefully, I had to admit that my grandmother had told me that between 1850 and 1900 there had been nine socialist colonies, some of them free love colonies, between Portland and Salem on the Willamette River and none of them had survived. And most of the islands in the San Juan group above Seattle had at one time or another boasted a colony. There were none now.

Carl wondered if the colonies were units too small to offer variety enough to keep the offspring home. "Could the movement to cities be the result of a broader interest in everything?"

"Stop it!" exclaimed the cannery man's wife. "Stop this silly thinking, Curt. You brought your fiddle, play it! I want to feel gay!" She looked longingly at Guiness, from whom she had had to disengage herself until spring sent her husband north again. Though deep of bosom and rich of body, she had, it seemed, a head of confetti. Dutifully, he got out his instrument. He played it well—"Swanee River," "The Prisoner's Song," "Camptown Races." We sang along with him.

Carl asked him to play "Humoresque" and he played it—lamely, but he played it. Carl loved music, as Nordi and I did, passionately. He wanted the cannery man to play "Valse Viennese," the one that Fritz Kreisler made immortal. We had consumed a lot of booze by then, for it must have been around three in the morning.

We were a big kitchen full of people and tobacco smoke that the two kerosene lamps tried hard to enlighten. The effect was dramatic in the way of the old masters—a group scene of night activity. Chin dug down on the curve of the violin's frail loveliness, as if to crush it, with fingers at random and the bow poking up here and there in the dim smoky light, he played. The scene was splendid, but the sound from this great chiaroscuro happening came weak and faltering, vaguely resembling that heartfelt melody. Carl's muddled brain could not accept the facts against marvelous fictions and his hunger for music. He tore the violin from Curt's hand, nestled it between chin and shoulder, and at one with beauty and guided by the gods and trusting them, drew an unearthly squaw-aw-k!—a sneer and a scream—from his bowing of the violin before it fell from his horrified hands into the hands of its owner. I saw the look of disbelief, of utter disenchantment, of Promethean pain that was his and I couldn't laugh—oh, I did, but inside me I hated all those negligent gods. I would have loved to be up on Mount Olympus and piss in their ambrosia.

Then everything quieted down. We sat there in the dark before dawn, staring at one another through the smoke. Finally, Guiness' sidekick, Dodd, mumbled, "I guess we better get along."

With much handshaking and patting of backs, they left—lurching up the hill followed by their long shadows of a late full moon's design.

The six months Carl spoke of turned out to be nine. With Carl boarding, as it were, with us, we had to provide food that he would eat. He despised goat milk. In fact, he changed our frugal, healthy way of living on what we raised and hunted, and the cost of living tripled. We had to give him pocket money for, say, a pair of pants, that always turned out to be a pair of pints. Our money dwindled. Still, his companionship was very welcome to us both.

At last the time arrived for Carl to go to Oakland and get his money. By now we were grievously low on food, and the can under the house where we kept our money was empty. Carl knew this. One moment he was there and the next he was gone—he had sneaked away.

We waited three days and then called Keith's aunt, whom Keith lived with—a big Irish girl with great physical power and a sort of energy over people. She knew of our arrangement with Carl and was outraged. She told us that, on receipt of the bonus money, Carl had hired the ballroom of the Hotel Oakland and staged a big party for all his friends, intellectual and ape. The disimilar mix soon polarized and, in the battle that followed, they did everything but pull down the drapes before they were evicted. A stately scholar received a cherished black eye, and a cleaning lady rescued Carl's false teeth from the base of a potted plant.

Keith and his aunt corraled Carl and asked him of his commitment to us. He said, "that was out," and that he would have to stay in the city where he could keep his "finger on the pulse of the people." Funny, he usually said "masses." Anyway, they bundled him up and brought him to us, and Keith said, "If you don't live up to your arrangement with Clyde and Nordi, I'll hunt you up and beat you till your guts hang out." And from Keith, that was a certain, if hideous, ultimatum. So Carl decided to come with us—a man with strengths, but with debilitating weaknesses, and the shorthand of it written on his face.

One of my favorite people—an old man named Bingo, the guy who had told me about the chicken-breeding farm—came by one day with a truck, wanting to buy Frank. He offered thirty dollars; I was pleased. "Take good care of him," I said. "I'm an old horse myself," he replied. "Frank and I are going to live out the rest of our lives together." He backed his truck against the low bank and I led Frank onto it and tied him. Then Bingo brought his truck around and was ready to leave. Frank knew the score. How much, I don't know; quite a bit, I surmise. As the truck moved past me, he stood as a show horse and, with great arched neck, looked down. "Good-bye, Frank," I said. He raised his fine head and bugled—it was more than a loud neigh. It was a salute to a friendly place and a friend he was leaving. I took it deep in me to remember always.

The two milk goats we had kept through all the trouble were sold, and only Heidi and Scheherezade were left, and they stayed close to us, afraid they might—like slaves—be sold too.

From another neighbor I had bought a truck commensurate with our means—an old Model T with a Rucksell axle. The truck had come with the promise of two new rear wheels, and now, as our departure time neared, I rode over to my neighbor's house and questioned him about the wheels. He was worried but sincere. "Clyde," he said, "when you are ready to leave the new back wheels will be on—even if I have to steal them."

Even with the old wheels, the truck could climb our steep hill with a small load, so we began bringing up things to a shed up on top and sorted them endlessly. Finally we had so much of our belongings in the shed that Carl spent his nights up there guarding it.

When the day of departure arrived, Carl helped us arrange the final set of things in the truck. Looking at what we had to leave in the shed, Nordi wailed aloud. I had terrible misgivings about what we were doing, but I knew there was no turning back now.

That night, splendid back wheels with tires of eight-ply—and with tread galore—were placed on the truck's rear axles (years later I found that they were stolen from a country road grader that same night), and the final rushing around for trifles began. Up and down the steep hill we went, carrying out the leaving of our home where gladness and despair and some rewards had been ours. All day we cut the strands we were loathe to sever, until we brought up our cow, Heidi, and Scheherezade, our goat. They were greeted by the chickens, cozy in their cage atop the trailer. Cow and goat alike were now heavy in their pregnancies. We would have to handle them gently. The poor things were to be hauled away from their home. They balked, they fought, nothing would induce them to step up into the trailer. An hour later, furious, we beat on the rumps of those "sons of bitches." We pinched them. We lit matches against their hides. But they only pulled back from where we had them tied. The torture would do no good. It was getting dark, and we were ready to fly at one another, when I got out a block and tackle from my stores in the truck, and slowly, with its power, I drew Heidi into the entrance. Then suddenly she stepped in, and the goat rushed in beside her. We closed the gate of the trailer. The older doctor came over to me, put a ten spot in my hand and said, "Luck, Clyde," and turned away with delicacy.

Nordi and Bunky got up on top of the load, where lay two mattresses with a wall around to screen them from being seen in their undignified perch unless they sat up. Carl and I got in the cab. I stepped on the starter and we pulled out on the road. I turned on the lights and, slowly, guardedly, I drove north. Not thinking of our goal, but of how to cover the next mile with an old, overloaded truck and trailer. All night I drove as a different and dedicated person, every ounce of me concentrating on moving forward another mile. We all have strengths we never use, or use perhaps a dozen times in our lives. Once before I had used this strength that was mine now. It was when I brought the *Princess* up from Saint Martin's Isle with a two-inch rudder. It had taken constant concentration for twenty-three hours, and now that strength had come to me again, a total involvement in the truck and the road. Its steering gear was beyond description. It sought, it seemed, to dump us over each bank or cliff. Every moment under way my steering was the countering of another attempt at mayhem with a trick of my own that got us around curves and down straightaways. My life now was the thwarting of that steering gear's attempts at murder, and gaining miles in spite of it.

Dawn came. Morning came. And slowly, our equipage moved up the highway. Every hour or so we stopped and fed the animals grass we plucked at the roadside while our tires cooled. For, with eighty pounds of pressure in them, they still looked almost flat on the road, and built up dangerous heat.

In the late afternoon, a few miles below Hopland, Nordi became hysterical. I saw a grove surrounded by brush with a vague opening in it and carefully drove into it. No house was about. I got her down and on a blanket. She seemed to have a fever. Carl removed the bicycle from the trailer and wheeled down to a town to get beer and some store food that might relax her. "It's too much," she kept saying, "too much."

I knew what she meant, but I was locked into gaining another mile, and the not-to-be-thought-of-now dream of Oregon. I heard the faint lisp of running water and, investigating, found, just outside the grove but in the brush that surrounded it, a stream we had in better days often picnicked on. I got her by the hand and, reluctantly, she came. Tentatively, she dipped in with her hand, then she walked in—dress, shoes and all, and dowsed herself. Then she tossed her shoes ashore and lay in it. After a while, she smiled. When Carl came back, she was quite herself, and we ate pickled herring and Danishes and sausages and drank our beer. She laughed when we called her "Queen Gelda, restored." Bunky combed her hair, and even Carl forgot his classic despair for the evening.

Queen Gelda came from a country we invented in those long

winter evenings now behind us. There was a sentimental love story called "Graurstark" at the time, set in an imaginary country in the Balkans. It was a comic opera affair but many editions were printed. It had a sequel and a villain named the Black Duke. Our mythical country was between author McCutcheon's Graurstark and Dalmatia—we named it Birfnig. It was ruled by Queen Gelda, a blue-eyed, golden-haired, rather plump lady who loved the local beer. And there was a villain—the Blacker Duke. We made maps of the country and wrote its history. We sang its national anthem with fervor and wrote its folk songs, its poetry, and a nationalistic jargon taught in its schools. We painted portraits of the Queen and her late husband, the bow-legged King Fnurph III. All this in a wet, cold fortnight. Now the mention of it helped—Nordi relaxed. We lay out on blankets and slept in the grass, as did Heidi and Zadee. In the morning, ready once more for the stress of voyaging in our ancient equipage, we struggled out on the highway and rolled a mile under us and another. It was level country, so we were soon past Ukiah and heading for a place known to the truckers as the Willits Hump, a steep grade up and down a small mountain.

We approached with sweaty hands. At the bottom of the grade I got out and hiked up, looking it over. I decided that, if Nordi, Bunky, Carl, Heidi and the goat walked up, I might make it. Then I decided I would need Carl to put the blocks under the wheels if we stalled and started to roll back. Those wheel blocks were made of four-by-four redwood. They were about two feet long, handle and all, and hung, handy by each back wheel, ready to be laid under the wheels if we had to stop quickly, for the emergency brake had ceased to work and the foot brake was fast losing authority. We got the animals out and put lead ropes on them for Nordi and Bunky to lead them and made a run at the hill. We just made it to the top and stopped there when the truck shook. We got out and saw the cow and the goat standing in the trailer, while far down the hill Nordi and son brought up the rear. When the animals saw their traveling home leaving them in strange country, they pulled away from their herders and tore up the hill after us and bolted into the trailer. They wanted none of this country. So after a laugh—considering our difficulty in getting them to accept the trailer at first—we started on again. And then the engine set up a fearful knocking, so we pulled over and stopped.

Neither Carl nor I knew anything about engines, but I'd seen some of it done. We took the hood from over the engine and laid it on the ground beside us. Then we got out all the tools concerning engines: pliers, screwdrivers, odd wrenches of many sorts and some rusty socket wrenches I'd found in the old Buick when I bought her. We laid all this on the hood, then I rolled up my sleeves and said, "Scalpel." And it wasn't funny. I stood there for some minutes and then crawled under and called for tools till I got the right one to fit the plug. Then I drained the oil from the crankcase and dumbly took that tightly bolted receptacle down and passed it to Carl. Rattling and feeling around, I at last found that one bearing on the crankshaft to the connecting rod was gone. We found glints of metal in the oil when we strained it. Well, now we knew the score, but what to do? We stared stupidly at one another and were bereft of puns. A car came past, stopped and backed up. Two men got out and, with a "having trouble?" came over.

"Bearing on the crankshaft," I said so authoritatively they must have thought I could handle it.

"Gee, too bad," said one, but as they walked to their car, I heard one say, "I've heard you could put shoe leather in a bearing and, driving slowly, reach the next town."

Before I could react they were gone. After much useless discussion, we did just that—with the top of a high-top shoe. Then we put the pan back on, poured in the strained oil, and, though the truck thumped badly, got down the mountain and into Willits, where a car junkyard guy said he could fix it in another two hours (he had to fix something else first) for fifteen dollars.

Leaving Bunky to guard our all from the top of the load, we three wandered up the main street of the town. Soon Carl saw a bar across the street and invited us in for a glass of beer. The bar was not what we expected. Four stolid men stood at a rather high bar in a room with no seating arrangement. Behind the bar stood a doleful-eyed Italian. Carl asked for beers and was told quietly, "no beer." "Three glasses of wine then," said Carl. The man sat them on the bar. I don't think a woman had ever been served there before. It was a workingman's bar. The four customers left, obviously embarrassed by Nordi's presence. We sipped the wine. In San Francisco, Italian establishments usually have somewhere about a calendar offered by steamship companies with a great liner with its massive flaring bow almost bursting into the room. On the wall here there were several in full color. One calendar spoke of Genoa as the home of its many-decked monster. Carl was staring at it.

"It was in port once when I was in Genoa. It's quite a ship," he said.

"You say Genoa?" spoke up the man behind the bar.

"Yes," said Carl. "I like Genoa."

The man didn't believe him. He said, "you know _____ Street in Genoa I believe you."

"Yes," said Carl, smiling at the glass of harsh wine before him. "I have some very good friends on _____ Street. I stay with them whenever I'm there. Gino Victrola and his wife and daughters are excellent people."

The proprietor's eyes flew wide open. He grabbed Nordi's and Carl's glasses from the bar, mine from my hand, dumped them and filled three beautiful glasses with select wine, sat them on the bar before us and shuddered as if hexed. "She my sister," he said.

"You mean Mrs. Victrola?"

"Yes, Maria Victrola, my sister. Tell me," he pleaded, "how them bambinas look when you see them?"

"It was last year," said Carl. "Rosa and Carlotta are no longer children. In a year or two they'll have beaus. Carlotta takes after her mother."

"How my sister?"

"Well, not exactly skinny," answered Carl, at which the man behind the bar laughed as if at a family joke in which he included Carl.

"My name," said our host, "is Bernardo Colti. How you come here?"

"Passing through," said Carl, and introduced us. "We're going to Oregon."

"Time to eat," said Colti. "You like to eat here?"

"That would be fine," spoke up Nordi. "I'm starved. My son guards our truck and belongings. Could we have a tray for him?"

"Yes," he answered. "Forty-five minutes you eat. My wife cook like Maria." He grinned at Carl and said, "Call me Ben."

"We're in luck," said Carl, as Ben showed us into a back room where three or four tables were surrounded by chairs, a probable meeting place for local Italians.

I went back to see how Bunky was making out. He sat up in the loaded truck and around below him were several boys about his age with whom he was in deep conversation. When I came he leaped down and scurried off with the boys to get nearby grass to feed to our animals. They chatted and jousted with each other as if they'd known each other for years. As they fed the animals I told Bunky to stay atop the load after I left and soon we would bring him dinner. The mechanic said he was about to work on our engine.

Back at the restaurant and bar I sat down with them as we waited. Ben's daughter played childishly at the piano. Ben had closed the bar and went to hurry the women, for now his wife's aunt was also cooking. Eventually the door of the kitchen opened and Mrs. Colti, a short, plump woman, approached us bearing brimming bowls of soup and heaved a great sigh of relief when she placed them before us without spilling. She glanced at us with pride because of this accomplishment, then back behind the door she went to reappear in a moment with grated cheese for the soup. Then she was gone again. But the aunt opened the door a bit and gave us a long and thorough consideration. We sipped our wine once more as the soup cooled and then we tasted it—oh, it was a most memorable soup!

The girl played her school's marching song as the first course appeared. God, what marvelous food! Many of the herbs and seasonings I couldn't place. Spinach in our cook's hands became a dream. A salad so small and so incredibly piquant that I had to restrain myself from rushing to the kitchen and demanding a great bowl of it, but other courses came—intriguing tastes and textures made the last—the one that you wanted to hold onto, to suck a tooth about and consider—only a fond memory. Coffee came at last—dark in little cups and tasting of chicory and yet giving off a great fragrance of the grinding of toasted coffee beans. Then all was gone and we sat in front of mellow goat cheese and some wizened apples. The meal was over. Midway in this banquet I received a tray of like foods that I took to Bunky. Now we pushed back in our chairs and smoked cigarettes as the oldish aunt, apron a bit askew, was dextrous with a toothpick as she scrutinized us from head to foot and one at a time. Carl paid. It was a fair price. He left a good tip, and after much shaking of hands and murmuring nothings about the Victrolas of Genoa, we disengaged ourselves and left.

The man under the truck said, "Fifty minutes."

Nordi had not returned with me, but was sauntering with Carl along the main street. Just before the mechanic filled the crankcase with new oil they came back, looking sheepish and a bit ashamed. In their stroll, they said, they were passing the big windows of a spic and span dairy lunch. Exhibited in the window were two wedges of cherry pie. Carl grinned at Nordi. "I'm overful," he said, "we both are, but maybe we could wedge it down with those and be above it all." So they went in and were sitting by the window eating the cherry pie when Mr. Colti with his wife on one arm and her aunt on the other strolled by taking the evening air and saw them. They stared at the scene with mouths agape then turned bewildered and retraced their steps, while Carl and Nordi laid their forks on their plates and slunk away from those half-consumed slices.

Well, we paid the mechanic and dragged our load down the street and out of town and, once more on the highway, Nordi and Carl, crammed in with me in the cab, burst out from time to time in fits of guilty laughter.

Reared up ahead of us, but still seventy-five miles away, was the Ben Bow Grade. We expected to drive all night and get over it somehow next morning, but sometime in the night, rumbling and rattling along with that tiny, weary old engine drawing two unwieldy masses behind it, the lights went out. We drew to the side of the road, nearly going over an embankment we didn't see until next morning, and went to sleep.

Next morning at Laytonville a mechanic took one look at our wiring and said, "Forget it! I can't see how any of it works. You'll kill yourselves with that steering gear and the weight you carry. When you get to Oregon it will crumple on some sharp-banked turn. They bank turns like a racetrack up there."

I began to realize what a dangerous juggernaut I had for our transportation and that I'd probably sacrifice my wife and son and Carl too. All this because I didn't want to wear a collar and talk and think and live "bi'ness." I was appalled by my selfishness. "I've got to keep going," I told him.

"Yeah, I know," he said wiping his hands on a soiled rag. "I got up here and got this job by the skin of my teeth." He walked away, a youngish guy in dirty coveralls, then he turned and came back to me. "Look," he said. "I been up there a coupla times myself and, on the outside of them sharp curves, they always got a little shallow ditch. If you could get your outside wheels in the ditch coming around the curve, that would take the strain off that rod running between the wheels and you just might make it. It's only an idea," he said, walking away.

He didn't know it, but he'd taken hope away from me and then given half of it back. That was good. He gave me facts, and a romantic often operates with too few.

In the early afternoon we stopped under the shade of a tree—a weariness held us all. Back several hundred feet from the road sat a well-kept cottage and, as we stared at it, we saw the door open and a slight, gray woman come up the path toward us. She carried a tray of gleaming things. She brought it to Nordi, a tray with a shining silver tea service, cups and all. Folded in a napkin were scones and a pot of jam.

"We were just going to have tea," she said, "but you all looked so tuckered! I was born while my folks crossed the plains, so you and me are kindred," she smiled. We received her smile and thanked her. "Have your little boy put the tray and things on the porch when you're through," she said, and went back to her house.

Rested, we drove on, but nothing could allay the dread I knew. I looked back in spite of myself at the goat ranch as a haven lost forever.

In the evening we reached the Ben Bow Grade. Work was being done on it and its tilted surface was covered with rocks bigger than baseballs. It was only about a quarter of a mile long and without turns, but very much steeper than anything we had met with yet. Still we had planned for it. We unloaded half of our goods from the truck at once, and stored them beside the road. Then, unhooking the trailer, we were able to take the truck to the top. There we found an indistinct, short side lane, shielded from the road, where we unloaded all that was left in the truck. Back we went and put the rest aboard and went to the top and unloaded it. It was getting dark. We had made a nest for Bunky beside the road, wrapped him in a blanket and told him to snooze until we could get him. Then we hooked up the trailer and brought our animals to our hideaway. While we were unloading them, I heard a scream. I grabbed our handaxe and tore down the slope—as scream after scream urged me on. I got to him where he was hung up in the barbwire of a fence alongside the road. He pointed in through the brush behind him and, sheathknife in one hand and axe in the other, I charged. But whatever it was was crashing away from me, so I turned back and unhooked him from the barbwire.

"What happened?"

"It was sneaking up on me and when I could hear its breathing I just couldn't stand it, Da'. Guess I screamed like a girl."

"You did just right," I said, hugging him.

"What was it?" he asked.

"No hoof marks," I said after I had looked again. "No cow, no pig, I think it was a bear." We got his blanket and walked up to our camp. It was completely dark now.

"Da'," he said, "I love you."

Nordi had made a big campfire. Hugging Bunky, she glared across it at me. "I put the blame on you, Clyde Rice," she said, and scowling into her pots and pans she cooked our supper.

I kept busy reloading the truck. Farther on in a cul-de-sac at the end of the lane our animals and chickens all drank from a spring before they grazed on the clover thick about. Carl sat to one side in snarling distaste and, when I wasn't noticing, took the bike and disappeared. Nordi and I ate soberly, a great freight of discontent working on us, except for Bunky who tried, as children will, to heal the wounds that poverty was gouging in us. We sat staring moodily into the fire not communicating. She murmured to herself from time to time. Once I was sure I heard her say, "lower than gypsies." Poverty was hidden at the farm. Now we were displaying it to two states and she was shocked by it, taken aback, as the many fine cars sped past us while she sat atop the load. Ah, my heart grieved (the phrase is unbelievably accurate), but there was nothing I could do.

Carl didn't come back. We slept apart in our blankets on the grass. In the night I came to her and combed her hair and kissed her as she wept. In a frenzy she needed me, shaking and trembling all over, as despair drove in needles everywhere, then I came upon her and we gave and took of each other—gave and received fiercely, and after the fierceness left us, we slept, awakening in the morning once more belonging to each other.

Below us the railroad wound up and over a small pass. Along the railroad tracks where ties had been replaced were piles of old ones that had been set burning. Close beside one fire we found Carl fast asleep—so close had he been to the fire as he slept off his binge that his face on one side was brown and slightly blistered and a new Stetson that he had bought in the town up ahead of us was heavily singed on one side and ruined.

Nordi proclaimed that we should rest that day. She heated water and we all bathed in a washtub we carried. She washed clothes and dried them on the bushes and the chickens and animals enjoyed the clover and none strayed. We decided to jettison the two spare back wheels with tires and we separated from the rest about a thousand pounds of heavy stuff that we were going to leave off at the next town for shipping to Portland, for we realized now that we could not go on as we were. We rolled the two wheels down a steep incline for maybe a quarter of a mile where they would cross a small meadow that hugged cliffs on the other side. There were no fences or habitation, but still it was foolish, though thrilling to watch. They bounded high as they descended, then leaped across the meadows to crash among the boulders of the cliff. How can such a thing pick your heart up? But it did.

We left and, at Garberville, sacked our half ton of heavy equipment in five big coal sacks to be forwarded to my father's place of business in Portland. Still we drove without lights or starter and with only the tiniest hint of brakes. To add to this the radiator began seeping water from innumerable tiny leaks and I knew I must hurry before the whole set-up foundered. That day we crammed the trailer full of grass and chicken feed, watered the animals well, and only stopped to fill the radiator every two hours. We passed Eureka and Arcata, not daring to look east at the mountains of my prospecting, watching the road with mad concentration. A few miles out of Arcata we pulled off the road and got a fire going and did the usual chores.

With an early start the next morning we hoped for a longer run, but a big landslide had swept the road away and, while bulldozers worked to make a temporary one on the hillside, traffic was held up for hours. I put in three new lampwicking bands in the clutch—a thing peculiar to the Model T. One of the cars held up with us was a Model T Ford and the owner came over and watched and advised me as I did it. It wasn't a very good job but it was no worse than before and would last longer.

Late in the afternoon we were passing through great redwood groves when we saw a place where we could get our truck off from the road to a level area where the trees towered all about and there was little undergrowth. We all left the truck to explore and were pleased with what we found. We trooped back to our ailing transportation to find a car stopped behind it. It was Lenore—Bessie's sister-in-law—the one who stayed in the Drake house when Annie Marge was with us. Laughing and hugging each of us in turn she said, "I knew it could only be you, Clyde. That spotted steer hide over the top of the chicken coop gave you away." She had her mother and father and her young son with her. They too were going to Oregon, so we camped together in a clear space in the grove. They set up a tent across from our truck and trailer with the campfire spot in between. We let our chickens and animals out as usual, but first we made a little cooking fire. We had a steel plate—a long narrow one—and we made a narrow fire under it, so we could have several pots and a frying pan cooking in a row. Nordi had greased her frying pan and left it heating at one end of the plate. Heidi, always curious about our ways, was making slow, dumb observations. A pet with no fear of humans, she wandered in between the truck and tent and, as we watched, stared at the frying pan and then leaning nearer stuck her big flat nose into the hot grease, and with her slow reactions, held it there a moment while it sizzled then leaped into delayed reaction and went charging away, tail high in the air and her udders swinging wildly about, till at

some distance she turned and gave us a glance full of distrust and
hurt. Nordi salved her nose and everybody patted her and made
over her till it seemed to me that her expression was that of a
spoiled child—bovine of course.

There were little harmless, pink centipedes about by the thousands and our chickens rushed about grabbing up the succulent
morsels till dark. Zadee sneaked around camp hoping she could
grab a loaf of bread and make a break for it. We were ten around
the fire, counting our important-feeling animals. By now they
seemed to enjoy the evening fire as much as we. After eating,
Nordi cooked our next day's lunch and set it to cool—but high,
where Zadee could not get it. We laid aside the cooking plate and
let the fire's light shimmer and flicker on our encampment—all our
ten faces staring into the flames. Carl uttered sort of an inner
snicker and told a story about his childhood and the story was just
right for the moment. Though our animals probably didn't get the
point of it, they liked the talking of people and moved a step closer.
Nordi made some laughing remark about his tale and he told
another about a strange mate he had had on shipboard. I found I
was leaning my back against one of Heidi's forelegs and Nordi's
hand was smoothing Zadee's long velvet ears, as Lenore told of a
boyfriend—a Swede—who became enamored of a tribe of Indians
in Round Valley and joined them and was locally famous for his
loud tribal yells when drinking. Lenore's parents were rather silent
people but good listeners—they didn't interrupt you with a tale of
their own.

Encouraged, I began a funny story, one that Nordi and Carl
had heard me tell again and again. Most off-color stories start out
very pure and lose the pallor of innocence as they move toward the
raffish end. This one ran the opposite way: it started out at an
explicitly described orgy and ended up with the girl of the story
being refused a berth in a convent as being too angelic and pure.
"Cover that marvelous ass of yours," said the abbess, "and uncov-
er the beauty of your saint-like face, and, walking among sinners,
lead them to the light."

But trying to tell it differently—hoping to spare Nordi and Carl
the oft-heard phrases—I got mixed up, forgot the punch line and,

avoiding the word "shit," said "dung," which had the timbre of a very dull bell and certainly no shit-like meaning. I tried to liven up the story and to remember the punch line, but Nordi and Carl began talking loudly about Gortel Dwalmanson and his sister Dwalma Gortelson. This was an in-joke, the aforesaid siblings being hypothetical friends I had invented to gossip about when I had been skipper of the *Sonoma*. They were over-large Norwegians, who seemed always to adapt to how we expected them to act. For Norwegians, they were extremely malleable.

Now Carl began talking of Gortel and of a big brick chimney he had laid in a day. Nordi said, "I bet Dwalma helped him."

"No," he replied, "she was back in Norway trying to win the Nobel Prize for physics. She took her track shoes with her, not being sure just how the event went."

"That's right," said Nordi. "Now I remember. And she also took a bale of chittum bark along—to show them how it's done in Oregon. Don't they make a physic out of chittum bark?"

"Of course," said Carl. "She thought maybe showing them she knew the source of physics might help her win the Prize."

By now Lenore's mother's smile no longer glimmered with the dew of anticipation—or even of comprehension. Abandoning my already scuttled story, I joined in.

"Well, Gortel's no slouch either," I said. "When I think of the wonderful feats of strength he's done—like leading choir at church. I tell you, the mellow golden tones in his voice had half the women there bawling."

"Good old Gortel," Carl broke in. "I tried wrestling with him once, but couldn't even budge him. Why the fellow's made of *iron*."

"Yeah, Carl, I know," I said. "Knuckle? Not him. He'll brazen it out with that steely look of his."

"And the gals running after him the way they do," said Nordi. "He's got lead in his pencil all right."

"Oh, I don't know," said Carl. "He's not much to look at with that heavy acne on his face and neck."

"Not any more," I said. "After going to skin doctors for years, he finally went to an old sea captain who turned the trick. The old skipper took Gortel down to the drydock, where they chipped him and gave him a coat of redlead. That stopped it, and it's never come back."

Lenore's father got up suddenly and stepped into their tent, that awful corn getting to him at last. Then he reached out and grabbed his wife and pulled her in behind the flap too. Lenore's eyes danced in spite of the extreme silliness of it, for she was pleased to see her father show emotion. Her parents were very staid people and vivid Lenore was not.

Our two roosters kept fussing around outside the perimeter of firelight. I went out to them. At once they started to lead the way into the darkness. I went back and counted the hens roosting in the cage atop the trailer. There were only eight, two were missing. We lit our lanterns and Nordi and Carl and Lenore and Bunky and I all followed the roosters through the woods to where vine maples writhed out among the redwoods. There they stopped and looked up, so we did too. Vaguely in the lantern light we saw the two hens roosting high above us. Bunky shinnied up and threw them down and the roosters set after them and gave them an awful pecking and drove them to camp and into the cage, whose door we closed. Then we sought our beds in the top of the truck.

In the morning we fed our stock as our friends pulled down their tent. We were ready to go, but watched them leave in their new shiny car, watched them go down the long straightaway, dwindling and then gone. The joy and the release from tension went with them and our faces fell, as we turned to our shabby transportation. I removed the spotted steer hide and stowed it under the mattresses of our beds. That day we passed Crescent City and, several hours later, crossed the border into Oregon. On we went, always filling our milk cans with water for the leaky radiator. We found that the sharp curves were heavily banked and, coming into one, as the mechanic had said, our weight on the steering gear— not made for such forces—tried to drag us across the road and down into the ravine. It was a wonder I was able to bring it out of it —pure luck, really. It taught me to watch as I had never watched before, but they were very few here and we moved along until, on a long downgrade, I lost control. The brake band no longer gripped.

There was no way to slow down or stop. All I could do was steer and hope. Nordi was crowded into the cab with us. We were fairly rocking along now, when we came around a turn almost on two wheels and saw a long, straight, level road before us. Far out on it we stopped and we all got out. I was frantic, angry at myself that I was endangering them so, but Carl was pleasant. They all said, "sink or swim." They were with me. We are trying to get to a new life, they said. Carl said, "Fine, forget it, let's go."

So I opened up the plate that covered the bands and fiddled around until I got the brakeband tightened and the other two a bit better adjusted and on we went, crossing the Rogue River on a long bridge, rolling slowly along until we passed Port Orford. Coming down a hill into town the brakebands held this time. We ate cold food that evening and I sent them to bed and, lashing a coal oil lantern to the back of the trailer and another to the front fender, went on moving in the light of a full moon. Most of it was long straight runs. At fifteen miles an hour I could handle it. I made twenty-seven miles—not once did I see another car on the road. Finally I pulled over, fed and watered the stock that Nordi had tended earlier and, climbing up, slept with them on the top of the load.

We were now going to Toledo, a big lumber town a few miles back from the port of Newport, way up the coast ahead of us. Carl's parents lived there. Carl for some obscure reason hated his father as much as he loved his mother. Why, he never divulged. He snorted and sighed, as he thought of his meeting with them. He would not go on with us as we'd planned, for he was in as depressed a state of mind as when he came to us that winter's night. He had never driven an automobile, but now he pestered me to drive and continued pestering me. I finally showed him how to work the foot pedals and such, and eventually let him drive.

After he had driven for about an hour, he saw ahead of us a gas station perched on a bit of flat land on a cliff above the sea. He drove across the highway and into it to get gas. I saw what he was doing in time and as we came abreast of the pump I jerked the wheel from his hands and spun it. In a very tight turn we stayed within the cliff's boundaries as we made a complete circle and were once more heading north on the highway. I wish I could have seen that top-heavy load and the trailer with the cow and goat spinning around on the edge of the cliff.

Carl was furious, but I made him get out and change places with me. Finally I made him see that using the handbrake with the weight we had would not stop it, and at the speed he had entered the station, we would all be dead at the foot of the cliff if I had not acted. This incident made him more sullen than ever. He might brighten up a bit at times, but in a few hours self-hatred would take over and a cynical look would half hide his despair. Both Carl and Pushells were gifted in many ways, quick and clever. It was strange that they got involved in political movements that, in their own way, were as half-cocked as capitalism. Neither of them were much interested in women and each in time found his shield of irony good for the glancing blows of most adversaries, but useless in fending away the knives of introspection.

We came down an area of sharp turns and through a small city, crossed Coos Bay by ferry that same night, and headed on. We found a place to exercise our animals and chickens and Nordi cooked, then we went on. And later in moonlight while they slept, I proceeded as I had the night before. In the morning by ferry we crossed the Umpqua and, as we made a brief camp, I slept.

That day it seemed our truck was about to give up. We crawled along over hills. We were three hours getting up over Cape Perpetua. Night came but we stopped only to get water for our radiator. Clouds covered the moon. I cut small fir branches and, walking ahead with the lantern, I put a branch where I could see it at the beginning of a banked curve, and going on to where my wheels would leave the ditch at the end of the curve, I deposited another branch.

I did this for what I assumed was four miles, then came back and, putting a lantern on the inner fender also, drove slowly on, safe with boughs indicating my way around the curve—where to put the wheels in the ditch and where to bring them back on the road. I did this chore twice that night, going on eight miles while walking sixteen. The next night and day were the same. In early evening we boarded the ferry to cross Yaquina Bay to the town of Newport. The tide was low and we had a difficult time getting our rig aboard. Somehow we made it and I wondered how we should get ashore. I went to the deckhands and explained that I was an old ferryboat man myself, then I pointed out my predicament. I would need a shove to get off. They spoke to some other people aboard whom they knew and when we landed there were six men besides Carl pushing as we crept up the gangway. We could never have made it under our own power. Ahead of us was a very steep street. I told Carl to run alongside of us with a brakeblock and, if I didn't make it, to block her at once. Then I charged the hill. Oh, it was a weary charge. Near the top the engine balked and Carl blocked us from rolling back and Nordi was there blocking the other wheel. I got out and saw that our engine could never pull us up to the top of that grade. Then a big logger, smelling of the pitch of firs, was at my elbow.

"What's the trouble?" he said.

"We can't pull this hill."

He looked the situation over. "I could help you with my old Packard if you got a rope."

"I've got one," I said, and from our load I drew a big strong rope. Our savior told his four passengers to get in the back seat for weight over his back wheels. Then, at his signal, we tried once more and, burning rubber, he pulled us as we struggled up and over the hill. I hurried to thank him but he had untied the rope from his axle and was gone. I sat down at the top of the hill and wept, for I was pretty well worn out. Then we drove on to Toledo.

A neighbor instructed us, and we drove up to Carl's father's house. Carl looked at it as if in terror, but finally we went to the door and knocked and went in. Carl embraced his very surprised mother. They didn't have a great deal to say to each other. After a bit he asked for his father. She said, "He's probably in the coffee shop down the street."

Carl wanted me to come with him. He was obviously agitated. They hadn't seen one another or corresponded in ten years. We entered and saw him at the counter reading a newspaper as he sipped his coffee. Carl walked over and took a seat next to him. The old man sat reading for several minutes and then turned to see who sat beside him. He recognized his son. "Hello," he said quietly. "How about a cup of coffee?"

And Carl, suddenly not our Carl, but the son of this man, said, "Yeah, I could use a cup."

After a bit he came back to me and said, "I suppose you're going to demand it, so here's a hundred and seventy-five dollars. It's all I have left. I'm going to stay here."

I took it. I had to. (It was our own money anyway.) I left, sick of him and wanting to get away.

We drove on and camped. I slept a long time and the next day Nordi was in the cab with me all the time, and there was room for Bunky. We sang a lot that day. We worked our way up the steep curvy road of Otter Crest, stopping every quarter of a mile or so, as the radiator boiled over and we had to let the engine cool a bit before we poured in more water, then on again. Now there were a great many more cars and log trucks all whizzing by us at a great rate. Nordi kept her hand on my arm as we drove, and then the road left the coast and headed inland toward Portland, eighty-five miles away. There we camped and in the morning started across the coast range. God, how that radiator leaked! Just before the first of the two crests we were to cross, we ran out of water. Bunky and I took one of the five-gallon milk cans and went down through the woods into what we assumed was a draw. We must have gone two miles before we came to a stream. We filled the can and started back. The can was unwieldy and rather heavy and we were in an area of small trees and dense brush. Eventually we came out a mile down the road from where we came in, worn out from dragging the can over big logs and through thick hazel brush. When we got to the truck we just laid down for a while before filling the radiator. Again we chugged along, climbing the steep grades and suddenly we were on top, rolling along, and made the second pass without incident and eased down to a great plain that led east between rolling hills. That night, as we camped beside the road, a cop on a motorcycle stopped by and asked us if there was anything he could do. We thanked him and asked him if there were any more steep grades between us and Portland.

"One the other side of Newberg," he said. "But you'll make it if you've come this far."

At noon we were stalled past Newberg, on the steep hill. Three times we had to stop and cool and water our engine, but we carried plenty of water and finally topped it. From then on we rolled right along. Maybe it was as sluggish travel as were all the miles behind us, but it didn't seem so. A grand sense that we were passing from one life to another was in me. Even as we ascended the hills that backed the city their steepness caused us no concern. We had a glimpse of the city below us and then the road turned going down —a wide road. Cars surrounded us. We flowed with them toward the city.

Signs informed us. We made the right turns and, avoiding the city center, rolled with many others out on the Ross Island Bridge. Oh, such joy was welling up in me. We were home where we belonged. Home to make a new start. Our rig bore us and ours down the other side of the bridge. We had crossed the Willamette and were crossing Seventh Street where my mother and I were born. Oh, God, how good it was to be alive! I looked at Nordi. She gave me a cold glance.

"I can't forgive you for the embarrassment of this trip," she said. "You left the furniture—all the things that make home."

I'd earned all this a hundred times. Not that I was mean about things or weak or stupid; but in my search for simple living—in my avoidance of the encirclement of softness—I was out of step with even those others who had the same goals as mine.

"Okay," I said, slowing the car, wondering what people would think if they knew we had no brake, that it had worn out just north of San Francisco, ten days before. I stepped on the gas, looking for a side street where I could turn off for Oregon City and Molalla and the land—the stump-littered land that seemed my only hope. "Okay," I said again, "but I needed the plow and tools, all that stuff back there, to make a go of it, Nordi."

"I know," she answered. "But I want things. Not the things in the back of the truck. I want things like other people have."

"Like polychrome floorlamps?" I asked. We had both laughed about these pretentious floorlamp monstrosities for years, but now she turned in her seat and stared at me without humor.

A feeling of brink came over me then, a feeling of great loss, not gain, as she said, "Yes, polychrome floorlamps. And all the rest of it."

EPILOGUE

And so I came home to Oregon. I cleared land and lost it. I painted again, I carved a woman in spruce, I made some miniatures and built a house of rammed earth on the Clackamas River, where I still live. Eventually, I built a sea-going boat, and then I built a small mill.

The boat was ecstasy from start to finish, for my son helped me build it. It was big, forty-six feet. I knew the pride of broadaxe work and I learned the delicate joy of adzing timbers with a superb adze. The adze is gone now, stolen long ago, and I still mourn it. It was light and lipped and its handle was curved and when you held it in your hands and bent your back as adzemen do and the thin crumbly chips spun from your hewing you were like a god and knew intimately the countless tiny planes that make an adzed surface luminous. The three-pound hammer seemed always in my hand and often the slick, that great god of chisels, was in the other. I grew to rely on the honesty of the barefoot auger and even my dreams were filled with the rough touch of oak and fir. I steamed them and bent them and wedged them in place and drove home the blunt-cut nails that still hold those planks against the pounding sea. I lost the boat in Pedro. She still fishes off Mexico.

As for the small mill, it was there that I learned the power and the priesthood of being a sawyer. It was sexual in a way, like unfolding a woman. You were dedicated to search and claim the best, and on the other side of the saw the offbearer observed your way with the log, as did the turn-down man behind you. These men loved logs—the grain and plumpness of timber—as you did, and there had to be a courtliness in your arrangement of each log's charms. You were also dedicated to the whining hunger of the saw and to the engine, and to the sweet sawdust and to the shift. Your shame was the logged-off area, the trash-ridden tear you made in the mountain's garment. About you the big logging horses, Frank and Jim, thundered their hooves in the straining, while old men who once had prowess in the woods came and watched with fierce gleams in the sadness of their eyes. While you ate your lunch they sat beside you and gave you pointers on the way it was done long ago.

I starved there before it was over, sold out and left. I walked down the road one late fall morning, walked away from it not looking back and feeling bruised and clubbed all over, the same way I'd walked away from my boat and the Bay and so many things I had aspired to hold and know but was unable to. I came home to write this story, to tell the ignominies and splendors in being a man, to try to get the sounds and colors and the shadows of at least one part of my life down on the printed page. And this too has escaped me.

COLOPHON

A Heaven in the Eye was designed by Susan Applegate of Publishers Book Works during the winter of 1984. The text is set in 14 point Cloister. Cloister Old Style was designed by Morris Benton for American Type Founders Company in 1913 and was the first successful modern revival of a Venetian type. Composition is by Irish Setter. Chapter drawings and the dust jacket cover painting are by Laurie Levich and were commissioned solely for use in *A Heaven in the Eye*. The book text is printed on 55 lb. acid-free paper and smythe sewn into signatures of 32 pages each and bound completely in Hollinston linen cloth by Bookcrafters, Inc.

No more than 100 copies of *A Heaven in the Eye* have been numbered and signed by the author. Each of these deluxe limited edition copies is bound by hand with a slipcase by Oregon Book Binding Company and bears the embossed initials of the author and the logo of Breitenbush Books.